THE LANGUAGE OF NUCLEAR WAR

Board of Advisors

This book was sponsored by the John Sloan Dickey Endowment for
International Understanding, the William Jewett Tucker Foundation,
and the Andrew W. Mellon Foundation.

THE LANGUAGE
OF NUCLEAR WAR

An Intelligent Citizen's Dictionary

ERIC SEMLER

JAMES BENJAMIN

ADAM GROSS

Sarah Rosenfield, *Senior Researcher*

PERENNIAL LIBRARY

HARPER & ROW, PUBLISHERS, New York
Cambridge, Philadelphia, San Francisco, Washington
London, Mexico City, São Paulo, Singapore, Sydney

To our parents, who are probably as shocked as we are

FIRST EDITION

Designed by Sidney Feinberg

Library of Congress Cataloging-in-Publication Data

Semler, Eric.
  The language of nuclear war.

  Bibliography: p.
  1. Nuclear warfare—Dictionaries.   2. Nuclear
weapons—Dictionaries.   I. Benjamin, James,
1965–   II. Gross, Adam.   III. Title.
U263.S44   1987   355′.0217′0321   86–45697
ISBN 0–06–055051–1
ISBN 0–06–096123–6 (pbk.)

87 88 89 90 91 MPC 10 9 8 7 6 5 4 3 2 1

Contents

Preface

The threat of nuclear war affects everyone. No other issue has such a deep significance for the entire world. Despite its fundamental importance, however, most people resist thinking about nuclear war. We believe that this disturbing lack of public interest is attributable in part to a fairly simple problem: the complexity of the language used to discuss nuclear issues. Technical terms pervade the nuclear debate; public officials, experts, and the news media alike speak of nuclear issues in a jargon that often leaves us feeling alienated and powerless.

The Language of Nuclear War attempts to correct this problem by enabling everyone to understand the obscure and sometimes incomprehensible terminology of nuclear war. We hope that, regardless of their positions on the issues, readers will learn enough to be able to reflect intelligently on the arms race and nuclear war.

The history of *The Language of Nuclear War* reflects the book's purpose. The authors are not experts; we are students who felt frustrated by our inability to penetrate nuclear jargon and concerned enough to do something about it. The idea for the book originated with Eric Semler, who realized that there was no comprehensive and clearly written dictionary of nuclear war terms. In January 1985, he began collecting the words that make up the book. Realizing the enormity of the task, he called in three friends to help. *The Language of Nuclear War* is the result of this year-long team effort.

How does one begin to put together a dictionary of nuclear war terms? First, a tremendous amount of research was carried out. There has been a wealth of material written on the subject of nuclear war and we read most of it. We incorporated information from a wide range of sources, including popular books, government documents, scientific and political journals, and articles in newspapers and magazines. In order to arrive at unbiased definitions, we used sources that represent the entire political spectrum of this highly polarized issue. The result is a book that attempts to incorporate the divergent viewpoints within the nuclear debate. In addition, we have intentionally avoided obscure technical facts and explanations. This book has been written to contain the essential facts to enable readers to think clearly on the issue and to reach their own conclusions.

As for the words chosen, we believe that they represent the most pertinent collection of nuclear war terms ever compiled. Three basic criteria were used in selecting the words. First, we have included words with a direct, strong connection to nuclear war. The term "nuclear" has many connotations and is often used rather loosely. We wanted to give the book a sharp focus and concentrate on only those terms applicable to nuclear war. Second, we have selected words that the public is likely to encounter. Most of the words in this book appear daily in newspapers, magazines, and on television. Words that at one time were used to discuss nuclear war but are now obsolete have not been included. Finally, we wanted the book to reflect the entire range of subjects that make up the nuclear war issue. Thus, *The Language of Nuclear War* encompasses words describing weapons, strategies, treaties, science, organizations, slang terms, effects, and history. In particular, we have emphasized terms that may shape the nuclear debate in coming years.

This book was written with a clear purpose: to create a dictionary of nuclear war terms that would be useful for the general public. We have lived and breathed the subject over the past year and realize now what we hope our readers will discover after reading the book: the threat of nuclear war is among the most important issues in the world today. Not thinking about nuclear war will not make it go away. Instead, we need to consider and understand the issue. Only through clear comprehension of the issues at hand can we work toward eliminating the threat of nuclear war in the future.

E. S.
J. B.
A. G.

Acknowledgments

This book was written with the generous financial support of the John Sloan Dickey Endowment for International Understanding, the William Jewett Tucker Foundation, and the Andrew W. Mellon Foundation, all administered through Dartmouth College. We wish to thank the people associated with each of these organizations for sponsoring our work on the book.

We are indebted to our faculty advisor, John Hennessey. His wisdom, counsel, and encouragement helped launch the book and guide it through to its completion. Thanks also to our advisory board: Liviu Bota, Elise Boulding, David Bradley, James Breeden, Thomas Johnson, Cathy Popkin, Thomas Powers, Leonard Rieser, and John Walsh. Their advice and encouragement were invaluable. We are especially grateful to Leonard Rieser, without whom this book would not have been written.

Also indispensable to this project were Tom McFarland, Gregory Prince, Earl Jette and the Dartmouth Ski School, and the staff at the Tucker Foundation. Special thanks to the reference librarians and government documents staff at Baker Library. Alex Huppe, Laura Dicovitsky, and the Dartmouth News Service helped spread the word and deserve our gratitude. We appreciate the advice and support offered by Chantal de Jonge Oudraat, Robert Jastrow, Andrea Robertson, Ken Novack, and Gramps Lesman. We are also grateful to Joseph Spieler, our agent, Carol Cohen, our editor, and Gerald Gross, a concerned father, for their efforts in getting this book published.

Thanks to the Blue Zoo, the Phi Palace, Brian Hurley, Beau Giannini, Shelli, Gregg, Jill, and Matt Semler, and to Elvis, for his trust.

Finally, thanks to Dartmouth, the college that we love.

ABLE TEST was the first peacetime nuclear explosion. The U.S. conducted the Able test on July 1, 1946, at Bikini Atoll in the Pacific Ocean.

A-BOMB   see ATOMIC WEAPONS

ABSOLUTE DETERRENCE is the doctrine of threatening a massive nuclear attack to prevent any type of enemy aggression. Absolute deterrence characterized U.S. policy during the Eisenhower Administration in the 1950s. Under Eisenhower, the U.S., which enjoyed considerable global superiority in nuclear weapons, vowed to respond to any type of provocation with an overwhelming nuclear strike. The U.S. policy of absolute deterrence was commonly known as MASSIVE RETALIATION.

ABSOLUTE DUD is a nuclear weapon that fails to explode.

ABSOLUTE WEAPON is a hypothetical, enormously destructive weapon. The threat posed by an absolute weapon would deter any type of enemy aggression. The term is general and used by a variety of experts including military personnel, scientists, and strategists. Such a weapon does not exist but its creation has been hypothesized. The absolute weapon is an idea similar to the DOOMSDAY MACHINE.

ABSORBED DOSE is the amount of harmful IONIZING RADIATION that enters and is absorbed by a person's body. Massive amounts of ionizing radiation are released in a nuclear explosion, and may cause RADIATION SICKNESS, cancer, genetic damage, and death. Absorbed dose is measured in units called RADS and REMS.

ACCELEROMETER is a complex, on-board instrument that helps direct a nuclear missile toward its target. The accelerometer tells a missile's GUIDANCE SYSTEM precisely where the missile is located, in what direction it is headed, and how fast it is going. The guidance system then steers the missile by changing its speed or direction. Accelerometers are an essential component of INERTIAL GUIDANCE, an important type of missile guidance system.

ACCIDENTAL ATTACK is a nuclear attack that results from faulty information or human error. An accidental attack may be prompted by malfunctioning warning systems, such as radar. If radar falsely indicated that an enemy attack was underway, authorities might launch an accidental retaliation. U.S. radar responsible for detecting enemy attacks has, in the past, mistakenly identified harmless birds or planes as incoming nuclear missiles. An accidental attack may also result from a variety of deranged or misguided human behavior. Many experts agree that the danger of accidental attack is significant, and the superpowers have established several safeguards to prevent one from being launched. The Moscow-Washington HOT LINE, for example, has been set up to enable leaders to consult with one another in a crisis and to avoid accidental attacks.

ACCIDENT MEASURES AGREEMENT (1971) is a bilateral agreement between the U.S. and the U.S.S.R. The treaty contains three main provisions. First, it contains a joint pledge to maintain and improve organizational and technical safeguards against accidental use of nuclear weapons. Second, it provides an arrangement for immediate notification in the event of an accidental or falsely perceived use of nuclear weapons. Third, the agreement calls for the advance notification of any planned missile launches that would be perceived as threatening. The U.S.S.R. has worked out similar agreements with France and Great Britain.

ACCURACY refers to a missile's ability to hit its target. The more difficult a target is to destroy, the more important accuracy becomes. Accuracy is an essential factor in determining a missile's ability to destroy a HARD TARGET, one that is reinforced,

such as a missile silo. As accuracy is increased, a missile's LE-
THALITY (ability to destroy hard targets) is greatly increased.
Accuracy is less crucial, however, for missiles targeted at unprotected areas, such as cities. In general, very accurate missiles
are thus aimed at military targets; less accurate missiles are
targeted at population and industrial centers. In recent years,
the superpowers have built small, very accurate missiles. The
MX missile, for example, is approximately three times as accurate as the older Minuteman II. According to the formula for
figuring lethality, this means that the MX is 27 times as likely
to destroy a missile silo as a Minuteman II. Accuracy is measured by a unit called CIRCULAR ERROR PROBABLE. See BIAS.

ACHESON-LILIENTHAL REPORT was a U.S. document written
by a commission led by Undersecretary of State Dean Acheson
and David Lilienthal, director of the Tennessee Valley Authority, in March 1946, which proposed that atomic energy be
placed under international control. The report was written to
provide the framework for a nuclear disarmament proposal to
be presented at a forthcoming United Nations meeting. The
Acheson-Lilienthal Report recommended that all "dangerous"
nuclear activities, such as uranium mining and reactor construction, be placed under the direct control of an international
authority associated with the U.N. Any alleged violations of this
organization's control would be dealt with by the U.N. Security
Council. Once it was written, the report was handed over to
Bernard Baruch, the U.S. representative to the disarmament
talks at the U.N., who modified the Acheson-Lilienthal Report
so that the Security Council could make decisions based on
majority vote. This change was extremely important, since it
was perceived by the Soviet Union as restricting its ability to
influence decisions in the U.S.-dominated United Nations. The
revised proposal, known as the Baruch Plan, was presented to
the U.N. in June 1946. It was rejected by the Soviet Union five
days later. See BARUCH PLAN.

ACOUSTIC DETECTION is a technique that uses sound to locate submarines and detect nuclear explosions. Acoustic detection is an important part of antisubmarine warfare, which involves locating and destroying enemy submarines armed with nuclear missiles. Acoustic detection incorporates sensors that pick up the sound made by submarines as they cruise in the world's oceans. These sensors can be deployed on ships, in aircraft, or on the ocean floor. Acoustic detection is also employed in monitoring nuclear tests to verify compliance with arms control agreements. This is accomplished by seismic stations, unmanned instruments which detect nuclear explosions by sensing the tremors they cause in the earth's crust.

ACTIVE DEFENSE is the strategy of defending targets from enemy attack by using defensive weapons. Active defense is distinct from PASSIVE DEFENSE, which aims to protect targets using measures such as civil defense and reinforcing potential targets to withstand enemy attack. Many different types of weapons may be employed in active defense, ranging from antiaircraft guns to space-based, high-technology lasers.

ACTIVE DETECTION is a general term that describes certain types of monitoring operations. Active detection involves locating an object by noticing light (or other energy) that it reflects. Active detection thus depends on energy that is external to the object. Locating an airplane by transmitting high frequency radio waves (radar) and noticing the waves that reflect off the plane is an example of active detection. Active detection is distinct from PASSIVE DETECTION, which involves locating an object by noticing light (or other energy) that it emits. Passive detection depends on energy that is internal to the object. Locating an airplane at night by noticing its wing lights is an example of passive detection. Active detection is commonly used to locate objects such as missiles, aircraft, and submarines.

ACTIVE DETERRENCE is the strategy of threatening a nuclear attack in order to restrain an opponent from launching a nuclear attack on a nation or on its allies or military forces stationed abroad. Active deterrence requires a credible commitment to use nuclear weapons in response to any enemy provocation. Active deterrence is distinct from PASSIVE DETERRENCE, which is intended more narrowly to deter only a direct enemy attack on a nation.

ACTIVE HOMING is a sophisticated technique that enables a nuclear missile to close in on its target. A missile equipped with an active homing mechanism emits a series of electronic signals similar to RADAR. As these signals bounce off the target, the missile detects and analyzes them. It uses this information to determine the target's precise location and home in on it. Active homing enhances missile ACCURACY.

ACTIVE MATERIAL   see FISSIONABLE MATERIAL

ACTIVE PENETRATION AID   see PENETRATION AID

ADVANCED CRUISE MISSILE TECHNOLOGY (ACMT) is a major U.S. military program to upgrade existing CRUISE MISSILES and to build new, more sophisticated versions. Cruise missiles are slow, low-flying, extremely accurate missiles which resemble pilotless airplanes; they are equipped to carry either nuclear or conventional warheads. Unlike BALLISTIC MISSILES, cruise missiles are powered throughout their flight by jet engines. ACMT is essentially designed to increase the range of cruise missiles; to develop more sophisticated guidance systems, which will improve accuracy; and to enhance ability to penetrate enemy defenses and evade radar. Work on advanced cruise missile technology is expected to bear fruit in the late 1980s.

ADVANCED INERTIAL REFERENCE SPHERE (AIRS) is an advanced, on-board guidance system used to direct a nuclear missile as it streaks toward its target. Unlike other guidance systems, AIRS continually adjusts a missile's direction throughout its flight. Thus, the missile is constantly kept on target. AIRS is supplemented by NAVSTAR, a group of U.S. satellites. NAVSTAR satellites inform the AIRS computer within the missile of the missile's exact position. The computer then adjusts the missile's flight based on this information. AIRS was developed by the U.S. for the MX missile.

ADVANCED MANEUVERABLE REENTRY VEHICLE   see MANEUVERABLE REENTRY VEHICLE

ADVANCED TECHNOLOGY BOMBER (ATB)   see STEALTH BOMBER

AEGIS, sometimes called Standard, is a U.S. surface-to-air missile. (See SURFACE-TO-AIR MISSILE for a complete description of this missile.)

AERODYNAMIC MISSILE is a missile designed to fly in the atmosphere, essentially like an airplane. To fly it relies on aerodynamic principles (i.e., lift, drag, and propulsion) to keep it in the air and has an engine that uses air to burn fuel. An aerodynamic missile must be distinguished from a BALLISTIC MISSILE. A ballistic missile doesn't fly; it is shot to its target like a bullet. A CRUISE MISSILE is one type of an aerodynamic missile.

AEROSOL is a theoretical method for rendering an opponent's missile defense system ineffective. Aerosols, microscopic particles, carried into space by a satellite or warhead and released in front of an opponent's space-based radar, would act as a screen for a warhead. If aerosols were released directly between a radar's line of sight and the attacking warhead's flight path, the radar would not be able to detect the warhead. The United States is conducting research on aerosols under the STRATEGIC DEFENSE INITIATIVE, commonly known as "Star Wars."

AEROSPACE DEFENSE is a general term which encompasses many systems for protecting against attacking nuclear missiles and bombers. The Antiballistic Missile Treaty of 1972 imposes restrictions on Soviet and U.S. aerospace defense systems deployed on the ground. In addition, it bans aerospace defenses at sea, in the air, and in space. The United States is conducting research on developing a high-technology aerospace defense under the STRATEGIC DEFENSE INITIATIVE, commonly known as "Star Wars."

AFSATCOM   see AIR FORCE SATELLITE COMMUNICATIONS SYSTEM

AGENCY FOR THE PROHIBITION OF NUCLEAR WEAPONS IN LATIN AMERICA   see OPANAL

AGGREGATE is a total numerical limit placed on types of nuclear weapons in arms control agreements. The SALT II Treaty established aggregate limits on nuclear missiles and bombers that the U.S. and the U.S.S.R. could deploy.

AGREED DATA BASE is the information shared between the United States and the Soviet Union about each country's nuclear arsenal. Established by the SALT II Treaty, the agreed data base is used to help verify arms-control agreements. Information given as a part of the agreed data base is matched against the information collected by a country's satellites and radar and used to ensure compliance with various arms-control agreements. The number of ballistic missiles deployed by a country is one element of the agreed data base.

AGREEMENT is a formal accord between two or more nations. Unlike a treaty, an agreement does not have to be ratified by a nation's government in order to be observed; it simply acknowledges an understanding between the negotiating nations. In order to improve their relations or achieve a common goal, nations may seek to establish an agreement between them. In 1963, the U.S. and the U.S.S.R. established the HOT LINE

AGREEMENT, which set up a direct communications link between Washington and Moscow. The HOT LINE would be used to communicate in an emergency, such as a nuclear war.

AILLERET DOCTRINE, also known as all-horizons deterrence, was conceived by General Charles Ailleret in 1967 and is a strategy for the deployment of French nuclear weapons based on France's skepticism of the U.S.'s willingness to use its nuclear weapons in defense of Europe if the U.S. itself was not threatened. The Ailleret Doctrine called for France to target its nuclear weapons to strike anywhere in the world and not just the U.S.S.R. Under the Ailleret Doctrine, French nuclear missiles would be targeted against traditional French allies, such as the United States and Great Britain. This plan revealed the great tension between the U.S. and France in the 1960s. The Ailleret Doctrine had the support of French President Charles de Gaulle but was never adopted by the government. Many of de Gaulle's ministers opposed the Ailleret Doctrine as being politically and economically unfeasible.

AIM POINT is the U.S. military term for a target in a nuclear attack.

AIRBORNE ALERT is a state of readiness in which bombers are armed and kept constantly in flight. The advantage in keeping bombers on airborne alert is that aircraft in flight are less vulnerable to a conventional or nuclear strike than those sitting on the ground. Both the U.S. and the U.S.S.R. constantly maintain a number of bombers on airborne alert. Airborne alert is distinct from GROUND ALERT, in which bombers and their crews are ready to take off on very short notice but are not yet airborne.

AIRBORNE COMMAND POST is an airplane that operates as a command center during a nuclear war. Airborne command posts are airliners modified to contain facilities that enable decision-makers to authorize the release of nuclear weapons and are equipped with airborne launch control systems, which transmit launch codes to missiles in their silos. The United States maintains several airborne command posts. The NATIONAL EMERGENCY AIRBORNE COMMAND POST serves as a flying command bunker for the National Command Authorities (the President and the Secretary of Defense). The Post-Attack Command and Control System functions as an airborne command post for the Strategic Air Command. Silk Purse, Blue Eagle, and Scope Light are code names for regional airborne command posts in Europe, the Pacific, and the Atlantic, respectively.

AIRBORNE EARLY WARNING AND CONTROL SYSTEM (AWACS) is a system that can detect an enemy nuclear strike. The purpose of airborne early warning is to notify decision-makers if an enemy attack is underway so that they can take appropriate action. Airborne early warning is provided by aircraft equipped with sensitive electronic equipment and radar. The U.S. deploys special aircraft, called Awacs, which patrol the skies between Greenland, Iceland, and Great Britain to detect possible enemy bomber attacks. Awacs are effective in this region of sky, called the radar gap, which is beyond the range of ground-based radars.

AIRBORNE LAUNCH CONTROL SYSTEM (ALCS)   see AIRBORNE COMMAND POST

AIR BREATHING refers to engines which must "inhale" air to burn their fuel. Air-breathing engines propel many types of nuclear missiles to their targets. Air-breathing missiles must travel within the atmosphere, where oxygen is abundant. CRUISE MISSILES and bombers incorporate air-breathing engines. BALLISTIC MISSILES are not propelled by air-breathing engines. Instead, they rely on BOOSTER ROCKETS, which are equipped to operate in the upper atmosphere, where the air is very thin.

AIR BURST is a nuclear explosion above the ground. When a nuclear weapon explodes above the ground, its destructive effects are spread over a wider area than if the weapon is detonated on the ground. For example, it may create a surge of radiation that could cripple computers and other sensitive electronic instruments for hundreds or thousands of miles. An air burst is distinct from a GROUND BURST, in which a nuclear weapon explodes on the surface. An air burst causes significantly less dangerous radioactive FALLOUT (radioactive debris) than a ground burst. The bombs dropped on HIROSHIMA and NAGASAKI, Japan, by the U.S. at the close of World War II were air bursts.

AIR DEFENSE is a general term that encompasses all defensive systems designed to destroy enemy aircraft and CRUISE MISSILES travelling in the lower atmosphere. Air defense is essentially a sophisticated antiaircraft weapon, designed to knock low-flying enemy aircraft and cruise missiles out of the air. Because Soviet bombers and cruise missiles are less numerous and less technologically advanced, the U.S. has not developed a major air defense system. The U.S.S.R., however, faced with a large and sophisticated force of U.S. bombers, has built a comprehensive system designed to defend against these weapons.

AIR FORCE SATELLITE COMMUNICATIONS SYSTEM (AFSAT-COM) is a part of the MINIMUM ESSENTIAL EMERGENCY COMMUNICATIONS NETWORK, the U.S. system that is designed to transmit communications during a nuclear war and particularly to enable U.S. military leaders to send undisrupted messages in a nuclear war. First set up by the Air Force in the 1970s, AFSATCOM consists of satellites that relay messages from command centers to aircraft, submarines, and underground missile silos. In the mid-1980s, AFSATCOM is being replaced by a more advanced communications system known as MILSTAR. AFSATCOM's ability to weather a nuclear attack has been disputed by some experts.

AIR-LAUNCHED BALLISTIC MISSILE (ALBM) is a missile that is launched from an aircraft and is pulled by gravity to its target in the final phase of its flight. ALBMs are distinct from AIR-

LAUNCHED CRUISE MISSILES, which are slow, low-flying, highly accurate missiles that resemble pilotless airplanes. ALBMs are normally offensive weapons, fired from attacking aircraft. The U.S. Short Range Attack Missile is an example of an ALBM. See AIR-TO-SURFACE MISSILE.

AIR-LAUNCHED CRUISE MISSILE (ALCM) is a CRUISE MISSILE transported on and launched from an airplane. Unlike ballistic missiles, which are powered by booster rockets, cruise missiles are powered by jet engines. The Soviet Union deploys two types of ALCMs:

- AS-5 Kelt is a Soviet ALCM that is deployed on the Tu-16 Badger bomber in the Soviet Naval Air Force. The AS-5 serves in tactical roles, such as attacks on enemy ships and battlefield positions. The missile is widely deployed and has a range of 160–320 km.
- AS-15 is a Soviet ALCM which is planned for deployment in the late 1980s. The AS-15 will be carried on either the Tu-95 Bear H bomber or the Blackjack RAM-P bomber. Its range is 3,000 km and it will carry a single nuclear warhead.

The United States deploys one type of ALCM:

- The U.S. ALCM, first deployed in 1982, is located at U.S. Air Force bases throughout the continental United States. It delivers a yield of 200 kilotons for its one warhead and flies about 100 feet above the ground. Its range is 2,500 km. U.S. ALCMs are delivered by B-52G, B-52H, and B-1B bombers.

AIR MOBILE MISSILE is any missile transported by and launched from aircraft. The United States' and the Soviet Union's AIR-LAUNCHED CRUISE MISSILES are examples of air mobile missiles.

AIR-TO-AIR MISSILE (AAM) is a missile launched from an aircraft at an airborne target. Air-to-air missiles are generally defensive weapons, launched against attacking aircraft or missiles. The

United States currently deploys one type of air-to-air missile capable of delivering a nuclear warhead:

- Genie, which first became operational in 1957, is an air-to-air missile launched from various types of U.S. and Canadian tactical aircraft. Genie is the only nuclear weapon used to defend North America from enemy attack. Genie has no guidance system and is thus not very accurate. Genie may be armed with either a nuclear or a conventional warhead. It has a range of about 10 km and delivers one warhead with a yield of 1.5 kilotons.

AIR-TO-GROUND MISSILE (AGM) is a missile launched from an aircraft at a target on the ground. See AIR-TO-SURFACE MISSILE.

AIR-TO-SURFACE MISSILE (ASM) is a missile launched from an aircraft at a target on the ground or on the sea. Air-to-surface missiles are generally offensive weapons, fired from attacking aircraft. The United States currently deploys one type of air-to-surface missile capable of delivering a nuclear warhead:

- Short-Range Attack Missile (SRAM) is deployed on B-52, FB-111, and B-1B bombers. Launched when the plane is relatively close to the target, SRAMs are highly maneuverable and can thus penetrate well-defended areas. The SRAM has a range of 160–220 km (high altitude) or 56–80 km (low altitude) and delivers one warhead with a yield of 170–200 kilotons.

The Soviet Union deploys five types of air-to-surface missiles:

- AS-2 Kipper is a Soviet air-to-surface missile that is deployed on the Tu-16 Badger bomber and is used primarily as an antiship missile. The missile's range is 200 km and it carries a single 1-kiloton warhead. It was first deployed in 1961.
- AS-3 Kangaroo is a large Soviet air-to-surface missile that is deployed on the Tu-95 Bear bomber. The AS-3 can carry a 800-kiloton warhead. The missile was first deployed in 1961 and has a range of 650 km.

- AS-4 Kitchen is a Soviet air-to-surface missile, first deployed in 1962, which serves as a strategic nuclear weapon or as an antiship missile when armed with a conventional warhead. The missile's range is 300–800 km and it is deployed on the Tu-95 Bear and the Tu-22m/26 Backfire bomber. The missile can be armed with a 200–350 kiloton warhead.
- AS-6 Kingfish is a Soviet air-to-surface missile with a range of 250 km that was first deployed in 1977. The missile is one of the most advanced in the Soviet arsenal and can travel at up to three times the speed of sound. The missile is in service with the Soviet Naval Air Force and is deployed on the Tu-16 Badger bomber. The AS-6 can carry a 350-kiloton nuclear warhead or a conventional warhead.
- AS-7 Kerry is a Soviet air-to-surface missile with a range of 10 km. It is deployed on Soviet tactical aircraft.

ALAMOGORDO, New Mexico, is the town near the site where the U.S. exploded the world's first nuclear device on July 16, 1945. This explosion, code named the TRINITY TEST, demonstrated that it was possible to build an effective atomic bomb. The first nuclear weapon was dropped by the United States over Hiroshima, Japan, on August 6, 1945.

ALCUM is the nickname for an AIR-LAUNCHED CRUISE MISSILE. It is derived from the initials ALCM.

ALERT STATUS   see DEFCON

ALL-HORIZONS DETERRENCE   see AILLERET DOCTRINE

ALLIANCE/REGIONALLY ORIENTED (RELATED) SYSTEMS is a U.S. term for American or Soviet nuclear weapons that are deployed to protect allies or regions beyond the homelands of the superpowers. These weapons, also known as noncentral systems, include small, tactical nuclear weapons and other nuclear weapons deployed overseas. The U.S. coined the term alliance or regionally oriented (related) systems during the

SALT negotiations as an alternative to forward based systems, a Soviet term with a slightly different nuance. The Soviet term identified these weapons as existing only to defend superpower interests. In the Soviet view, the fact that forward based systems are deployed outside a superpower's territory doesn't diminish a superpower's direct control over them. The U.S., however, wished to stress that these weapons are often deployed not to defend the U.S., but to defend allies. American and Soviet missiles in Europe are examples of alliance or regionally oriented (related) systems.

ALL-OUT WAR see GENERAL WAR

ALPHA DECAY is one type of radioactive decay, the process in which unstable elements release excess energy, or ALPHA PARTI-CLES, in order to become more stable. Elements which undergo alpha decay are created in the detonation of nuclear weapons. Alpha decay can be extremely harmful to living organisms; it can cause radiation sickness, genetic damage, cancer, or death. Alpha decay is distinct from BETA DECAY and GAMMA DECAY, in which beta particles and gamma rays are released. See RADIOAC-TIVE DECAY.

ALPHA PARTICLE is a high-energy helium nucleus which is extremely dangerous to living cells. A nuclear explosion creates many radioactive by-products that emit alpha particles. Protection from alpha particles is possible because they are comparatively large and slow-moving and do not even penetrate a piece of paper. If inhaled or ingested into the body, however, alpha particles can cause radiation sickness, genetic damage, cancer, or death. Nonetheless, alpha particles are, in general, less hazardous to humans than BETA PARTICLES or GAMMA RAYS, two other types of radiation. The existence of alpha particles was first theorized by Ernest Rutherford in 1899.

ALTERNATE LAUNCH POINT SYSTEM (ALPS) see MULTIPLE AIM POINTS SYSTEM

ALTERNATE NATIONAL MILITARY COMMAND CENTER (ANMCC) is a United States military command post which would be activated in the event of a nuclear war. Embedded in the Catoctin Mountains about 104 kilometers northwest of Washington, D.C., the ANMCC is considered invulnerable to a nuclear attack. The ANMCC serves as a backup command post to the Department of Defense, which could be more easily destroyed in a nuclear attack. The ANMCC was established in 1955.

AMERICAN BISHOPS' PASTORAL LETTER, entitled "The Challenge of Peace: God's Promise and Our Response," was overwhelmingly adopted by American Catholic bishops in May 1983. In the letter, which was drafted by a committee of five led by Joseph Cardinal Bernardin of Chicago, the bishops support a nuclear freeze and condemn the notion of limited nuclear war. They contend that engaging in nuclear war is an immoral act; therefore arming for nuclear war is also immoral. Following its approval, the letter was discussed in Roman Catholic congregations throughout the United States.

ANTARCTIC TREATY (1959) is a multilateral agreement that demilitarizes Antarctica and expressly forbids the deployment of any nuclear weapons there. The twelve countries who routinely conduct research in Antarctica, including the U.S., the U.S.S.R., France, and Britain, have signed the treaty. The Antarctic Treaty does not prohibit the use of military personnel or equipment for scientific purposes in Antarctica.

ANTIBALLISTIC MISSILE (ABM) is a missile designed to intercept and destroy attacking enemy missiles and warheads. The Soviet Union's GALOSH is an example of an antiballistic missile. The U.S. does not currently deploy any ABMs although it has done so in the past; it retired the SAFEGUARD ABM system comprised of SPARTAN and SPRINT ABMs in 1976 due to high cost and technical ineffectiveness. As a result of the Antiballistic Missile

Treaty of 1972 and its Protocol of 1974, each superpower is limited to 100 ABMs deployed at a single missile defense site.

ANTIBALLISTIC MISSILE (ABM) PROTOCOL (1974) was signed by the U.S. and the U.S.S.R. and is the protocol to the Anti-Ballistic Missile Treaty of 1972. The ABM treaty allowed each superpower to deploy two weapons systems designed to defend against attacking nuclear missiles. The ABM Protocol reduces the number of permitted defensive systems from two to one. Further, it allows both countries one opportunity to move their ABM system if sufficient advance notice is given. The Soviet ABM system, GALOSH, surrounds Moscow. The American ABM system, SAFEGUARD, was deployed to protect a missile site in Grand Forks, North Dakota. It was dismantled in 1976 because of high cost and technical ineffectiveness.

ANTIBALLISTIC MISSILE (ABM) SYSTEM   see BALLISTIC MISSILE DEFENSE SYSTEM

ANTIBALLISTIC MISSILE (ABM) TREATY (1972)   see SALT I

ANTIMATTER WEAPON is a theoretical type of nuclear weapon which would be many times more powerful than current nuclear weapons. Antimatter weapons would derive their tremendous destructive power from the collision of atoms and extremely rare antimatter particles. When these two objects collide, they mutually annihilate each other and release a great amount of energy. The reaction caused by such a collision would create an extremely powerful explosion. Antimatter weapons could, in theory, be used as part of a defensive shield designed to destroy attacking nuclear missiles.

ANTIMISSILE MISSILE is a general term for any missile designed to intercept and destroy incoming enemy missiles. The United States' GENIE and the Soviet Union's GALOSH missiles are examples. Antimissile missiles used specifically against attacking nuclear warheads are known as ANTIBALLISTIC MISSILES.

ANTISATELLITE (ASAT) WEAPON is a weapons system designed to destroy enemy military satellites vital to communications, surveillance, and early warning of a nuclear attack. Negotiations to ban ASAT weapons were suspended in 1979; the Soviet Union has urged a resumption of these talks. The U.S. has been reluctant to negotiate an ASAT treaty because it claims that a ban on ASATs would be impossible to verify. Contrary to popular opinion, the development of ASAT technology is not included in the U.S. STRATEGIC DEFENSE INITIATIVE, commonly known as "Star Wars." Antisatellite weapons are often referred to as killer satellites.

- U.S.S.R. ASAT: The Soviet Union began testing the world's first ASAT system in 1968. The Soviet ASAT is a ground-based, nonnuclear weapon that is launched toward its target on top of an SS-9 missile. The Soviet ASAT is considered primitive, because it can only destroy enemy satellites in very low orbits. The Soviet ASAT cannot strike the most important enemy satellites (those responsible for military communications and early warning of an attack), which reside in higher orbits. Another drawback is that the Soviet ASAT must sit on the ground until enemy satellites pass overhead. It may take days or weeks before satellites orbit within its range.

- U.S. ASAT: The United States began to work on ASAT weapons in the early 1960s, but it has yet to put one into operation. During the 1980s, the U.S. has been developing an advanced ASAT called a Miniature Homing Vehicle (MHV). The MHV is carried into space by a rocket which is fired from an F-15 fighter plane. It is considered to be more sophisticated than the Soviet ASAT, because it is very accurate and can strike satellites orbiting at a variety of altitudes.

ANTISATELLITE (ASAT) WEAPONS TALKS were a series of negotiations between the U.S. and the U.S.S.R. that were suspended in 1979 after a general deterioration in U.S.-Soviet relations. The goal of the talks was the elimination of weapons deployed to destroy satellites. The Soviet Union has urged a resumption of the ASAT talks; the U.S. has been reluctant because it claims that a ban on antisatellite weapons would be impossible to verify.

ANTISUBMARINE MISSILE is a missile launched from the ground, ships, or submarines that is targeted at enemy submarines. The United States currently deploys two types of nuclear-armed antisubmarine missiles:

- ASROC is a ship-launched antisubmarine missile. First operational in 1961, ASROC missiles are deployed on frigates, destroyers, and cruisers. They fly through the air and then enter the water in the immediate vicinity of their target. ASROC missiles, which can deliver either a conventional or a nuclear warhead, have a range of 1.8–11 km and deliver a single 1-kiloton warhead.
- SUBROC is a submarine-launched antisubmarine missile. First operational in 1965, SUBROC missiles are equipped for nuclear warheads only. They break through the surface, fly through the air, and then reenter the water in the immediate vicinity of their target. SUBROC missiles have a range of 40–56 km and deliver a single 1- to 5-kiloton warhead.

ANTISUBMARINE WARFARE (ASW) includes all military operations intended to destroy enemy submarines. Effective ASW could play an important role in defending against a nuclear attack; it is especially important in destroying enemy submarines that carry nuclear missiles. ASW is extremely difficult to conduct effectively, however. The vastness of the ocean and the difficulty of pinpointing objects hundreds or thousands of feet underwater combine to make the detection and destruction of enemy submarines extremely difficult. Another major drawback of ASW is that a nation would have to destroy all of its enemy's submarines simultaneously, since if even one slipped by it could still launch a highly destructive nuclear attack. ASW encompasses three distinct steps: detection, confirming that an enemy sub is patrolling; localization, fixing the submarine's position; and destruction. Nuclear-armed antisubmarine missiles and nuclear depth charges are among the weapons used to destroy subs once they have been localized. The U.S.'s ASW program is much more advanced than the Soviet Union's, but is nonetheless not completely reliable.

ANZUS PACT (1951) is a treaty that binds Australia, New Zealand, and the United States, calling for mutual defense if any of the signatories is attacked. The treaty's name is derived from the initials of the three signatories. The treaty's future was called into question in 1986 as a result of a dispute that began when New Zealand prohibited nuclear-armed or nuclear-powered U.S. ships from docking at its ports. In the past, these types of ships called at New Zealand's ports, and the U.S. has contended that the visits are an essential part of the ANZUS alliance. New Zealand's Prime Minister David Lange has steadfastly refused to admit the ships, however, and U.S. Secretary of State George Schultz announced in June 1986 that the U.S. was suspending its security guarantee for New Zealand. Australia and the U.S. have retained the alliance.

APOGEE is the highest altitude reached by an object circling the earth. Before reaching its apogee, a BALLISTIC MISSILE is powered by BOOSTER ROCKETS; after the apogee, it is pulled by gravity to its target.

AREA DEFENSE protects a broad geographical area, such as a city, from enemy nuclear attack. The Soviet Union's GALOSH system, which is designed to defend Moscow from incoming nuclear missiles, is an example of an area defense. Area defense is distinct from POINT DEFENSE, which protects a small area, such as a military installation.

AREA TARGET is a target that encompasses a large region, such as a city. An area target is distinct from a POINT TARGET, which is a specific site, such as an underground missile silo.

ARMED FORCES SPECIAL WEAPONS PROJECT   see DEFENSE
NUCLEAR AGENCY

ARMS CONTROL   see NUCLEAR ARMS CONTROL

ARMS CONTROL AGREEMENT VERIFICATION   see VERIFICA-
TION

ARMS CONTROL AND DISARMAMENT AGENCY (ACDA)   see
UNITED STATES ARMS CONTROL AND DISARMAMENT AGENCY

ARMS CONTROL ASSOCIATION is a private organization which
promotes understanding of arms control and its relationship to
U.S. national security. Established in 1971 and located in
Washington, D.C., the Arms Control Association has 2,000
members. The Arms Control Association is partially funded by
the Carnegie Endowment for International Peace and operates
a telephone "hot line" which provides information on nuclear
weapons issues to the public. It publishes a variety of materials,
including the monthly periodical *Arms Control Today.*

ARMS CONTROL IMPACT STATEMENT (ACIS)   see UNITED
STATES ARMS CONTROL AND DISARMAMENT AGENCY

ARMS CONTROL THROUGH DEFENSE (ACD) is the theory of
enhancing national security by simultaneously reducing the
number of nuclear weapons and deploying defense systems designed to strike down attacking nuclear missiles. Under a policy
of ACD, a nation would seek to negotiate deep arms reductions,
while also deploying systems for defending against a nuclear
attack. Conceived in the early 1960s, ACD has never been the
official policy of a nuclear weapons state. In the 1980s, U.S.
President Ronald Reagan has promoted arms control through
defense in conjunction with his STRATEGIC DEFENSE INITIATIVE,
commonly known as "Star Wars."

ARMS LIMITATION   see NUCLEAR ARMS CONTROL

ARMS RACE   see NUCLEAR ARMS RACE

ARMS RACE STABILITY is a condition which exists when neither superpower perceives itself to be at a disadvantage in the nuclear arms race. Neither side feels compelled to develop major new weapons programs and neither side feels it has to compete with the other in building or improving its nuclear arsenal.

ARMS REDUCTION   see NUCLEAR ARMS CONTROL

ARRIVAL TIME is the total time which elapses between the launch of a nuclear weapon and its detonation at its target. Modern nuclear missiles have a very short arrival time. Land-based missiles launched from the homeland of one of the superpowers, for example, can strike their targets in about a half hour. Many experts have expressed concern over shrinking arrival time. As arrival time diminishes, they contend, a nation's time to interpret indications of enemy attack decreases. This, in turn, may create enormous pressure on decision-makers and may increase the chances of misperception leading to accidental nuclear war. Arrival time is distinct from REACTION TIME, which is the time between an initial warning of enemy attack and the arrival of enemy missiles. Arrival time is also called travel time.

ARTILLERY-FIRED ATOMIC PROJECTILE (AFAP) is a type of nuclear warhead fired from artillery guns. AFAPs are tactical nuclear weapons, intended for battlefield use. See NUCLEAR ARTILLERY.

AS-MISSILE is the NATO code which designates Soviet air-to-surface nuclear missiles. The AS-2 Kipper, AS-3 Kangaroo, AS-4 Kitchen, AS-6 Kingfish, and AS-7 Kerry are air-to-surface missiles. (See AIR-TO-SURFACE MISSILE for a complete description of these missiles.) The AS-5 Kelt and AS-15 are air-launched cruise missiles. (See AIR-LAUNCHED CRUISE MISSILE for a complete description of these missiles.)

ASROC (ANTISUBMARINE ROCKET) is a U.S. antisubmarine missile. See ANTISUBMARINE MISSILE for a complete description.

ASSURED DESTRUCTION   see MUTUAL ASSURED DESTRUCTION

ASTRODOME DEFENSE is a nickname for a hypothetical defense system that could destroy all incoming warheads fired by an attacker. An astrodome defense would be leakproof and cover vast distances of space in order to wipe out all attacking missiles. It is analogous to a roof that prevents any raindrops from leaking into a sports arena during a storm. Throughout the nuclear era, defense experts have debated whether it is technologically and economically feasible to build an astrodome defense.

ATMOSPHERIC NUCLEAR TEST is any nuclear test at or above ground level. Atmospheric nuclear tests release a significant amount of dangerous radioactive material into the environment. They are prohibited by the LIMITED TEST BAN TREATY of 1963. Since that agreement was signed, only France and China, which have never signed the treaty, have conducted atmospheric nuclear tests.

ATOM is the basic building block of matter. An atom is the smallest amount of an element that still contains all the properties of that element. According to current theories of atomic structure, an atom contains a tiny, compact, positively charged nucleus and less dense, negatively charged electrons, which orbit the nucleus. The nucleus, which is composed of protons and neutrons, is the key to nuclear and atomic weapons. In fission reactions, which are the essential mechanism of nuclear reactors and traditional atomic weapons, one heavy nucleus is split. In fusion reactions, which are the key to more powerful thermonuclear weapons, two light nuclei are combined. Both types of reactions release tremendous energy. The discovery of how to split the atom led directly to the development of the first nuclear weapons. See ATOMIC WEAPONS, NUCLEAR WEAPONS.

ATOMIC BLACKMAIL   see NUCLEAR BLACKMAIL

ATOMIC BLITZ is an all-out nuclear attack. Atomic blitz was a well-known expression in the late 1940s. The term has its origins in the series of devastating conventional bombing attacks launched by Nazi Germany against Great Britain in World War II. Atomic blitz is synonymous with MASSIVE RETALIATION, the U.S. policy in the 1950s of responding to communist aggression anywhere in the world with an allout nuclear strike.

ATOMIC BOMB   see ATOMIC WEAPONS

ATOMIC BOMB CASUALTY COMMISSION (ABCC) was a U.S. government commission which studied the effects of the atomic bombs dropped on the Japanese cities of Hiroshima and Nagasaki in August 1945. Established in 1947, the ABCC conducted tests on victims and others who lived in the area where the bombs were dropped. The ABCC sought to correlate long-term medical effects such as leukemia and birth defects with the radiation release when the bombs were dropped. In 1975, the ABCC became the Radiation Effects Research Foundation, which is financed by both the United States and Japan.

ATOMIC BOMB DOME is one of the few structures not leveled when the U.S. dropped the first atomic bomb on Hiroshima, Japan, in August 1945. Originally Hiroshima Prefecture's Industrial Promotion Hall, the Dome is now a gutted skeleton, left standing as a permanent reminder of the destruction that resulted from the first aggressive use of nuclear weapons.

ATOMIC DEMOLITION MUNITION (ADM) is a nuclear mine. Exploded on the ground or underwater, ADMs are tactical nuclear weapons designed for battlefield use to blow up bridges and dams and otherwise hinder the movement of enemy troops. ADMs are much more destructive than ordinary mines. The U.S. currently deploys two types of ADMs, with varying destructive power. Some ADMs are small enough to be carried in a soldier's backpack.

ATOMIC DIPLOMACY is a foreign policy strategy that involves using the threat of nuclear aggression to achieve foreign policy goals. As discussed in *Atomic Diplomacy* by Gar Alperovitz, the term describes U.S. foreign policy at the close of World War II and in the immediate postwar period. During that time, the United States was the only nation in the world with nuclear weapons. Commentators suggest that, because of this monopoly, the Truman Administration pursued a very assertive foreign policy, leading to confrontations with the Soviet Union in Eastern Europe and the Far East. Atomic diplomacy, experts have implied, led to the Cold War and the nuclear arms race. The effectiveness of atomic diplomacy diminished as the U.S.S.R. established and expanded its nuclear arsenal and gradually achieved parity with the U.S.

ATOMIC ENERGY ACT OF 1946, also known as the McMahon Act, is a U.S. law that mandated complete government monopoly over nearly all aspects of nuclear technology. The McMahon Act required that a five-member civilian board (called the ATOMIC ENERGY COMMISSION) assume ownership of U.S. nuclear material and the facilities that produce and use it. It thus dissolved the Army's wartime MANHATTAN PROJECT and placed control over the entire U.S. nuclear weapons program in the hands of civilians. In addition, the McMahon Act placed tight controls on the export of U.S. nuclear technology. In this way, it forced U.S. allies such as Great Britain and France to develop their nuclear weapons independently. It was signed into law by U.S. President Harry Truman on August 1, 1946.

ATOMIC ENERGY ACT OF 1954 allowed, for the first time, private ownership of facilities which produce and use nuclear material, such as nuclear power plants. This act completely revised the ATOMIC ENERGY ACT OF 1946, which mandated government monopoly over nearly all aspects of U.S. nuclear technology.

ATOMIC ENERGY COMMISSION (AEC) was a U.S. government
organization, composed of five civilian members, which completely controlled nearly all peaceful and military aspects of U.S.
nuclear technology from 1946 to 1954. Established by the
ATOMIC ENERGY ACT OF 1946, the AEC assumed ownership of
U.S. nuclear material and the facilities that produced and used
it, and thus held control over the entire U.S. nuclear weapons
program. The AEC held physical possession of U.S. nuclear
weapons, and would only turn them over to the military with
Presidential authorization. Its first chairman was David Lilienthal. In 1954, the AEC's power was severely restricted by the
second Atomic Energy Act. After that law was passed, the AEC
no longer controlled either U.S. nuclear weapons or reactors.
The AEC was abolished by the Energy Reorganization Act of
1974, and its duties were split into two new agencies, the Energy Research Development Administration and the Nuclear
Regulatory Commission.

ATOMIC ENERGY DETECTION SYSTEM (AEDS) is a U.S. network for monitoring Soviet nuclear testing. AEDS, constructed
after World War II, incorporates instruments which detect nuclear explosions by sensing the tremors they cause in the earth's
crust. AEDS is comprised of sensors placed in Norway, South
Korea, and other countries around the borders of the U.S.S.R.

ATOMIC MATERIAL see FISSIONABLE MATERIAL

ATOMIC WEAPON is a nuclear weapon whose destructive power
comes from fission, the splitting of large, unstable atoms.
Atomic weapons can create very powerful explosions, capable of
devastating entire cities. Sometimes called fission weapons, they
were the first nuclear weapons built, and were dropped on
Hiroshima and Nagasaki in August 1945. Atomic weapons are
much less powerful than thermonuclear weapons, which were
first developed by the U.S. in the early 1950s and now dominate
the world's nuclear arsenal. See GUN-ASSEMBLY, IMPLOSION.

ATOMS-FOR-PEACE PLAN was a proposal which called for cooperation among nations in the use of atomic energy for peaceful
purposes. Introduced by U.S. President Dwight Eisenhower in
a speech before the United Nations General Assembly in December 1953, the plan urged nations that deployed nuclear
weapons to commit themselves to peaceful uses of nuclear technology. This would be accomplished by placing nuclear material
under the authority of an INTERNATIONAL ATOMIC ENERGY
AGENCY (IAEA), to be established by the U.N. The Atoms-for-
Peace plan would have initiated sweeping changes in the way
that atomic energy was controlled. It would have eventually
entrusted the IAEA with the responsibility of controlling all of
the world's atomic energy, with the goal of ensuring that nuclear weapons would eventually be abolished. Two years after
the first Atoms-for-Peace conference assembled in 1955, the
U.N. set up the International Atomic Energy Agency. The
IAEA has not, however, assumed the broad authority envisioned in the Atoms-for-Peace Plan.

ATOMS-FOR-PEACE PROGRAM was a United States program of
offering nuclear technology and materials to less developed
countries. In return, these nations promised to use U.S. assistance only for peaceful purposes. The program, inaugurated by
U.S. President Dwight Eisenhower in December 1953, established policy for the export of U.S. nuclear technology for two
decades. The Atoms-for-Peace Program was severely restricted
in 1974, after India used Atoms-for-Peace assistance from Canada and the U.S. to build the "peaceful" nuclear device it
exploded in May 1974. India found a loophole in the Atoms-for-
Peace agreement by interpreting a provision for "peaceful" uses
to include "peaceful" explosions. As a result of India's nuclear
test, the Nuclear Suppliers Group was established in 1975 to set
strict guidelines for the transfer of nuclear technology.

AWACS see AIRBORNE EARLY WARNING AND CONTROL SYSTEM

B

B-1 BOMBER is a U.S. strategic bomber program, canceled in 1977 by President Jimmy Carter because of its high cost. The B-1 would have replaced the U.S.'s aging fleet of B-52D bombers. The B-1 was reintroduced as the B-1B by President Ronald Reagan in 1981. See LONG-RANGE BOMBER.

B-1B BOMBER is a U.S. long-range bomber. See LONG-RANGE BOMBER for a complete description of the B-1B.

B-52 BOMBER is a U.S. long-range bomber. See LONG-RANGE BOMBER for a complete description of the B-52.

BABY TOOTH SURVEY, released in 1962, determined that unbridled nuclear testing in the 1950s had greatly increased the amount of deadly strontium-90 in the environment. Strontium-90 is a radioactive substance released in nuclear explosions. It is extremely dangerous, particularly to the bones and teeth of young children. The researchers who conducted the Baby Tooth Survey, the Committee for Nuclear Information (CNI), collected over 80,000 baby teeth and determined that the level of strontium-90 in them had increased 14-fold between 1949 and 1957. The Baby Tooth Survey helped to stimulate the public outrage that led to the signing of the LIMITED TEST BAN TREATY of 1963.

BACK-CHANNEL NEGOTIATIONS are informal arms control negotiations. Instead of negotiating in official forums established by governments, negotiators may choose to use personal and private discussions to talk about arms control. Back-channel negotiations have often been used as a more effective means of reaching an agreement, especially in tension-filled situations in which deadlocks have stifled negotiations. The well-known

WALK IN THE WOODS during the START negotiations, in which Soviet and American representatives abandoned official meetings and agreed to an arms control proposal during a walk in a forest near Geneva, is an example of back-channel negotiations. Back-channel negotiations are also called sidebar negotiations.

BACKFIRE is the NATO code for the Soviet Tu-22m/26 intermediate-range bomber. See INTERMEDIATE-RANGE BOMBER for a complete description of the Backfire.

BACKGROUND RADIATION is radiation which occurs naturally in the environment. Sources of background radiation include cosmic rays from outer space, radioactive minerals in the earth, and radioactive tissue within the human body. Background radiation, though it is being constantly emitted, is extremely slight. One would need to be exposed to at least one thousand times the average background dose to suffer serious physical effects. Even low levels of background radiation, however, can cause genetic damage and defects. A nuclear explosion creates levels of radiation much greater than background radiation.

BACK-UP MISSILE   see RELOAD MISSILE

BADGER is the NATO code for the Soviet Tu-16 medium-range bomber. See MEDIUM-RANGE BOMBER for a complete description of the Badger.

BALANCE OF TERROR describes the post-World War II balance of power between the superpowers. It characterizes MUTUAL ASSURED DESTRUCTION, a condition in which the superpowers are restrained from aggression by their ability to inflict unacceptable damage upon each other. The balance of terror is based on each superpower's capacity to absorb a nuclear strike and then counter with an unacceptable destructive retaliation. In this way, the superpowers have relied on the threat of destruction in order to avoid war.

BALASHIKA MILITARY DEFENSE COLLEGE   see CIVIL DEFENSE

BALLISTIC MISSILE is one type of nuclear missile. A ballistic missile is propelled by booster rockets into the upper atmosphere. After several minutes, the booster rockets burn out and the missile falls down through the atmosphere, pulled by gravity to its target. Ballistic missiles derive their name from the BALLISTIC TRAJECTORY that they follow. In a ballistic trajectory, the final phase of an object's flight is determined solely by gravity and wind resistance. Ballistic missiles are distinct from CRUISE MISSILES, which are slow, low-flying missiles that resemble pilotless airplanes. Unlike ballistic missiles, cruise missiles are powered throughout their flight by jet engines. Ballistic missiles form a central component of a nation's nuclear arsenal. Thousands of ballistic missiles are currently deployed, based in submarines and underground missile silos and on bombers. Ballistic missiles are extremely versatile: They can be used over battlefield or intercontinental distances. In addition, they can carry extremely powerful or relatively small nuclear warheads. See INTERCONTINENTAL BALLISTIC MISSILE, INTERMEDIATE-RANGE BALLISTIC MISSILE, MEDIUM-RANGE BALLISTIC MISSILE, SHORT-RANGE BALLISTIC MISSILE, SUBMARINE-LAUNCHED BALLISTIC MISSILE.

BALLISTIC MISSILE DEFENSE (BMD) SYSTEM is a system that defends against incoming missiles and warheads. It consists of radars to identify and track attacking nuclear weapons as well as missiles to intercept and destroy them. As a result of the Antiballistic Missile Treaty of 1972 and its 1974 protocol, both superpowers are limited to one BMD system. The Soviet Union has deployed its GALOSH BMD system around its capital, Moscow. In 1974, the United States deployed a BMD system, called SAFEGUARD, to protect a missile site at Grand Forks, North Dakota. Safeguard was deactivated in 1976, because of its high cost and technical ineffectiveness. The U.S. is conducting research on high-technology BMD systems under the STRATEGIC DEFENSE INITIATIVE, commonly known as "Star Wars." BMD systems are also known as antiballistic missile systems and nuclear defense.

BALLISTIC MISSILE EARLY WARNING SYSTEM (BMEWS) is a U.S. radar system which detects attacking nuclear missiles. BMEWS is designed to notify decision-makers if an enemy attack is underway so they can take appropriate action. First deployed in 1960, BMEWS stations are located in Alaska, Greenland, and Great Britain. The BMEWS station in Britain serves the additional function of monitoring enemy attacks on Europe. Three additional stations will be deployed in the late 1980s.

BALLISTIC MISSILE SUBMARINE (SSB) is a submarine that can carry and launch ballistic missiles. Nuclear-powered SSBs are an effective way to deliver ballistic missiles. They are very difficult to detect and can hide in the earth's oceans for months without having to surface or return to port. Most ballistic missile submarines serve a strategic role—their missiles are intended for use against the territory of one of the superpowers. These submarines are the least vulnerable part of the strategic TRIAD, which also includes land-based INTERCONTINENTAL BALLISTIC MISSILES (ICBMs) and LONG-RANGE BOMBERS. In general, submarine-launched ballistic missiles are not as accurate as ICBMs, but technological improvements in the future could eliminate this shortcoming. Both the U.S. and the Soviet Union began deploying ballistic missile submarines in the late 1950s and early 1960s. The Soviet Union currently deploys ten types of SSBs:

- DELTA II carries 16 SS-N-8 submarine-launched ballistic missiles (SLBMs) and has been deployed since 1975.
- Delta III carries 16 SS-N-18 SLBMs, which are currently being replaced by the more accurate SS-N-23s. The Delta III class was first deployed in 1976.
- Delta IV is a more advanced version of the Delta III and will be deployed in the late 1980s. Delta IVs will carry sixteen SS-N-23 SLBMs.

- GOLF II has been deployed since the early 1960s and carries three SS-N-5 SLBMs. Golf submarines are among the oldest submarines in service with the Soviet navy. Unlike most ballistic missile submarines, Golfs are diesel- rather than nuclear-powered. Although Golf submarines are now considered outdated, the Soviets still deploy several of them with missiles intended for targets in Western Europe.
- Golf III has been deployed since the early 1960s and carries six SS-N-8 SLBMs.
- HOTEL II has been deployed since the mid-1960s and carries three SS-N-5 SLBMs. Hotel submarines are the smallest ballistic missile submarines in the Soviet navy and are being replaced by the more modern Delta and Typhoon submarines. By the mid-1980s, only three Hotel submarines were still in service.
- Hotel II has been deployed since the mid-1960s. It carries six SS-N-8 SLBMs.
- TYPHOON, first launched in 1980, is the newest and largest Soviet nuclear-powered submarine. It carries 20 SS-N-20 submarine-launched ballistic missiles; each missile has a range of over 8,000 km. The long range of the SS-N-20 allows the Typhoon to hit targets in the continental U.S. while patrolling in Soviet territorial waters. Eight Typhoon submarines are planned to be operational by the early 1990s.
- YANKEE I submarines, first deployed in 1967, are nuclear-powered and carry 16 SS-N-6 SLBMs. They are gradually being replaced by more advanced Delta submarines.
- Yankee II submarines carry 12 SS-N-17 SLBMs.

The United States deploys two types of ballistic missile submarines:

- POSEIDON (*Lafayette* class) is a nuclear-powered submarine that carries Poseidon submarine-launched ballistic missiles. Since 1979, some Poseidon submarines have also been equipped with newer Trident missiles. The Poseidon submarine can carry 16 missiles. First deployed in 1962, the Poseidon submarine will be replaced in the early 1990s by the Trident submarine.

- TRIDENT (*Ohio* class) is the most modern type of submarine deployed by the U.S. The Trident is nuclear-powered and carries 24 Trident missiles. First deployed in 1979, the Trident is gradually replacing the older Poseidon submarine. Trident submarines carry more missiles, stay at sea longer, and operate faster and more quietly than Poseidon submarines.

Great Britain deploys one type of ballistic missile submarine:

- POLARIS was first deployed in 1959 by the United States and can carry 16 Polaris missiles. In 1978 the U.S. finished converting all of its Polaris submarines into Poseidon submarines. British Polaris submarines are being modified under the CHEVALINE program. Great Britain will replace its modified Polaris submarines with Trident submarines during the 1990s.

France deploys one type of ballistic missile submarine:

- RÉDOUTABLE is a class of French nuclear-powered submarines that carries submarine-launched ballistic missiles. The French name for such a missile is MER-SOL BALLISTIQUE STRATÉGIQUE (MSBS). The first Rédoutable submarine was launched in 1967; by the mid-1980s six were operational. One of the newest French submarines, *L'Inflexible*, was launched in 1985 and carries 16 M-4 MSBSs. The older French submarines are equipped with 16 M-20 MSBSs, but these missiles will be replaced by the M-4 in the early 1990s.

Finally, China deploys one type of ballistic missile submarine:

- XIA, first deployed in 1981, carries either 12 or 16 CSS-N-3 SLBMs. Two Xia submarines were in service by the mid-1980s; China plans to deploy four more by the 1990s.

BALLISTIC TRAJECTORY is the path a BALLISTIC MISSILE follows after its BOOSTER ROCKETS burn up and fall back to earth. A ballistic missile is propelled by booster rockets into the atmosphere. After its rockets burn out, its follows a ballistic trajectory, determined purely by gravity and wind resistance. A stone thrown outward follows a ballistic trajectory as soon as it leaves the hand of the person throwing it.

BALLOON is a light, hollow sphere of metal released from an attacking nuclear missile in order to deceive enemy defense systems. Some balloons contain warheads, while others do not. Balloons thus force defense systems to squander time and ammunition to destroy all balloons in sight, whether or not they contain warheads.

BARGAINING CHIPS are existing or planned weapons systems that one nation agrees to discard or limit in return for concessions from its partner in arms control negotiations. In 1972, for example, the United States used its development of a superior antiballistic missile system as a bargaining chip to induce the Soviet Union to sign the treaty limiting such systems.

BARUCH PLAN was a U.S. plan which proposed that atomic energy be placed under international control. The Baruch Plan was presented to the United Nations in June 1946. It recommended that all "dangerous" nuclear activities, such as uranium mining and reactor construction, be placed under the direct control of an international authority associated with the U.N. Any alleged violations of this organization's control would be dealt with by the U.N. Security Council. The Baruch Plan, however, mandated that the Security Council could only make decisions based on majority vote. This provision was extremely important, since it was perceived by the Soviet Union as restricting its ability to influence decisions in the U.S.-dominated United Nations. The Soviet Union, represented by Andrei Gromyko, rejected the proposal five days after it was announced. It countered with a proposal to abolish all existing atomic arsenals *before* any discussion could be held on an international authority and safeguard procedures. The United States turned down the Soviet Union's counterproposal, because it would have required the U.S. to voluntarily sacrifice its monopoly on nuclear weapons.

BASE HARDENING   see HARDENING

BASELINE TERMINAL DEFENSE SYSTEM   see LOW ALTITUDE DEFENSE SYSTEM

BASIC DETERRENCE is the fundamental condition in which two rival nations are restrained from fighting a nuclear war. Basic deterrence results from a condition in which nations are capable of absorbing a nuclear attack and then inflicting an unacceptably destructive RETALIATION. With limited means for defending against a nuclear attack, both superpowers have relied on basic deterrence to avoid nuclear war.

BASIC PRINCIPLES AGREEMENT (1972) is an agreement between the U.S. and the U.S.S.R. which states that the superpowers share similar objectives for peace. The Basic Principles Agreement states common goals rather than specific arms-control measures. In the agreement, both nations agree to coexist peacefully. They vow to make special efforts to limit nuclear weapons and to conclude concrete agreements toward achieving this goal. The ultimate objective of their efforts is the achievement of complete nuclear disarmament. The Basic Principles Agreement is not a binding treaty. It simply states the superpowers' shared hopes for world peace.

BASING MODE refers to the way in which a nuclear weapons system is deployed. Nuclear weapons may be deployed in a variety of basing modes. The superpowers deploy nuclear missiles on the ground, in the air, and at sea. In addition, there are several basing modes within these general categories. Land-based missiles, for example, can be deployed in fixed underground MISSILE SILOS or on trucklike vehicles.

BATTLEFIELD NUCLEAR WEAPON see TACTICAL NUCLEAR WEAPON

BATTLE MANAGEMENT is a theoretical network that would coordinate all aspects of a defense system designed to protect against attacking nuclear missiles, gathering all the information necessary for a defensive system to locate and intercept an incoming missile. It would, for example, identify incoming warheads and fire laser beams to destroy them. The United States is conducting research on battle management systems under the STRATEGIC DEFENSE INITIATIVE, commonly known as "Star Wars."

BATTLE MIRROR is a hypothetical mirror that would reflect a powerful laser beam toward an attacking nuclear missile. A battle mirror would be used in a high-technology system designed to defend against incoming nuclear warheads. In a system that uses battle mirrors, a ground-based laser weapon would fire a powerful beam of highly concentrated light into the sky. This beam would be aimed at a mirror in orbit high above the earth. This mirror, called a relay mirror, would then reflect the beam at the battle mirror, positioned in orbit much closer to the earth. The battle mirror would, in turn, reflect the beam of light toward an attacking missile. The light beam would burn a hole in the skin of the attacking missile and deactivate the sensitive electronic equipment responsible for guiding it to its target. Battle mirrors would have to be huge (as big as 90 feet in diameter) and nearly flawless. The slightest imperfection could cause the light beam to scatter and thus lose its effectiveness. The United States is conducting research on battle mirrors under the STRATEGIC DEFENSIVE INITIATIVE, commonly known as "Star Wars."

BEAM WEAPON is a hypothetical weapon designed as part of a system for protecting against attacking nuclear missiles. It is a general term, encompassing various types of high-technology weapons, including lasers and particle beams. Beam weapons would generate a concentrated, high-speed stream of light or particles that could burn a hole in the skin of an attacking missile and deactivate the sensitive electronic equipment responsible for guiding it to its target. The United States is conducting research on beam weapons under the STRATEGIC DEFENSE INITIATIVE, commonly known as "Star Wars."

BEAR is the NATO code for the Soviet Tu-95 long-range bomber. See LONG-RANGE BOMBER for a complete description of the Bear.

BENT SPEAR   see NUCLEAR INCIDENT

BETA DECAY is one type of radioactive decay, the process in which unstable elements release excess energy in order to become more stable. Elements which undergo beta decay are created in the detonation of nuclear weapons. In beta decay, unstable by-products of a nuclear reaction release beta particles. Beta decay can be extremely harmful to living organisms; it can cause radiation sickness, genetic damage, cancer, or death. Beta decay is distinct from alpha decay and gamma decay, in which alpha particles and gamma rays are released.

BETA PARTICLE is a high-energy electron which is extremely dangerous to living cells. A nuclear explosion creates many radioactive by-products which emit beta particles. Protection from beta particles is possible because they cannot penetrate even a thin sheet of metal. Beta particles can burn skin, however, and if inhaled or ingested into the body, they can cause radiation sickness, genetic damage, cancer, or death. Beta particles are, in general, more hazardous than alpha particles but less dangerous than gamma rays, two other types of radiation. The existence of beta particles was first theorized by Ernest Rutherford in 1899.

BIAS is a measure of how far a missile misses its target. Bias is a very important factor in determining how missiles are targeted. Very accurate missiles, which have a low bias, are usually targeted at well-defended military installations. Less accurate missiles, which have a high bias, are targeted primarily at unprotected cities and industrial centers. In recent years, the superpowers have developed smaller weapons with extremely low bias. See CIRCULAR ERROR PROBABLE.

BIG BIRD is a hypothetical method for deploying nuclear missiles. Big Bird would involve deploying missiles on cargo planes which would be in the air twenty-four hours a day. In this way, missiles would be moving targets and their vulnerability to enemy attack would thus be reduced. Big Bird was first conceived as a method of deploying the U.S.'s MX missile. The plan was abandoned, however, and the U.S. eventually decided to deploy the MX in existing underground missile silos. Big Bird is also the generic name for a series of U.S. satellites.

BIKINI ATOLL is a small volcanic atoll in the Marshall Islands in the South Pacific. It was a major U.S. nuclear test site in the 1940s and 1950s; the U.S. conducted the famous BRAVO TEST there on March 1, 1954. The U.S. now conducts its nuclear tests at the NEVADA TEST SITE in the western United States.

BILATERALISM is the theory that arms control agreements must be negotiated and agreed to by two nations acting together. Bilateralism stresses reciprocity in order to prevent one nation from gaining a potentially destabilizing advantage over a rival. SALT I and SALT II are examples of successful bilateralism—they are reciprocal arrangements between the United States and the Soviet Union. Bilateralism is distinct from unilateralism, which advocates independent action by a single nation, and from multilateralism, which involves agreements reached between many nations.

BIRTH-TO-DEATH TRACKING is the monitoring of an attacking nuclear warhead throughout its entire flight. Birth-to-death tracking keeps a constant watch on a warhead, from the time it is released in outer space (birth) until it is destroyed or reaches its target (death). With birth-to-death tracking providing constant information on a warhead's position, speed, and direction, a defensive system would have a better chance of destroying the warhead.

BISON is the NATO code for the Soviet Mya-4 long-range bomber. See LONG-RANGE BOMBER for a complete description of the Bison.

BLACK BOOK is the nickname of the book which outlines the U.S. President's options in the event of a nuclear war. It also provides instructions on how to execute the central U.S. nuclear war plan, known as the SINGLE INTEGRATED OPERATIONAL PLAN. The black book is carried in the FOOTBALL, the top secret briefcase, which is within the President's reach at all times.

BLACK BOXES   see SEISMIC STATION

BLACKJACK is the NATO code for the Soviet RAM-P long-range bomber. See LONG-RANGE BOMBER for a complete description of the Blackjack.

BLACK MARIAH is a slang term for a theoretical Soviet missile that would be invulnerable to a modern space-based system designed to strike down attacking nuclear missiles. A Black Mariah would be able to slip through enemy defenses and devastate its target.

BLACKOUT is a theoretical method for rendering an opponent's missile defense system ineffective. Blackout would be used specifically to prevent ground-based radar from detecting attacking nuclear warheads. Blackout would involve detonating a nuclear warhead in the sky directly between a radar's line of sight and a second attacking warhead's flight path. Radar signals would not be able to pass through the part of the sky where the explosion took place. Thus, the radar would be temporarily "blinded," unable to see through this part of the sky. The second warhead could then sneak through the radar's blind spot and proceed toward its target undetected. A similar process which involves "blinding" heat sensors rather than radar is called REDOUT. The United States is conducting research on blackout under the STRATEGIC DEFENSE INITIATIVE, commonly known as "Star Wars."

BLACK RAIN is rain colored black by debris and laced with deadly radioactive fallout. Black rain was first observed at HIROSHIMA, Japan, after the first atomic bomb was dropped there on August 6, 1945. Black rain may cause radiation sickness, genetic damage, cancer, or death, and may follow any nuclear explosion.

BLANKET   see TAMPER

BLAST SHELTER is a natural or man-made structure which provides protection during a nuclear attack. A blast shelter is essentially a barrier between a person and the immediate destructive effects of a nuclear explosion. It is thus distinct from a FALLOUT SHELTER, which is a sophisticated installation equipped to provide protection for weeks or months after a nuclear attack. Construction of blast and fallout shelters is a CIVIL DEFENSE measure, intended to minimize the destruction caused in a nuclear war. The United States, which has not pursued an extensive civil defense program, has not built blast shelters for the public. The Soviet Union, however, has constructed a network of blast shelters, including Moscow's subway system. Like other civil defense measures, construction of shelters may signal a willingness to fight a nuclear war and may thus be destabilizing.

BLAST SHOCK   see SHOCK WAVE

BLAST WAVE   see SHOCK WAVE

BLINDER is the NATO code for the Soviet Tu-22 medium-range bomber. See MEDIUM-RANGE BOMBER for a complete description of the Blinder.

BLUE BOOK is the nickname for the guidelines that have been established by the International Atomic Energy Agency (IAEA) to prevent the spread of nuclear weapons. The IAEA enforces the rules outlined in the Blue Book in order to prevent nations from using nuclear technology and material to develop nuclear weapons. The Blue Book is a product of the NONPROLIF-ERATION TREATY of 1968, which set up a variety of safeguards intended to prevent the spread of nuclear weapons. The official title of the Blue Book is "The Structure and Content of Agreements between the Agency and States Required in Connection with the Treaty on the Nonproliferation of Nuclear Weapons."

BLUE EAGLE   see AIRBORNE COMMAND POST

BOCK'S CAR was the U.S. B-29 bomber that dropped the second atomic bomb on Nagasaki, Japan, on August 9, 1945. The plane was piloted by Major Charles Sweeney.

BOLT FROM THE BLUE   see SURPRISE ATTACK

BOOSTER ROCKET propels a ballistic missile into space and directs it toward its target. Booster rockets consist of one or several stages, which drop back to earth after they burn up. Booster rockets are only ignited for a small part (about 15%) of a ballistic missile's total flight time. After they burn out, gravity takes over and pulls the ballistic missile to its target. Two types of booster rockets are used to propel ballistic missiles: SOLID-FUELED ENGINES and LIQUID-FUELED ENGINES. Booster rockets are also used to propel spacecraft, such as the rockets that travelled to the moon in the 1960s and '70s.

BOOST PHASE is the initial part of a ballistic missile's flight. During the boost phase, which lasts from two to five minutes, a missile is propelled upward through the atmosphere by its booster rockets. The boost phase begins with the lift-off and is followed by the POST-BOOST, MIDCOURSE, and TERMINAL PHASES of a missile's flight. A ballistic missile can be easily identified by enemy satellite systems during a boost phase, because its booster rockets leave a signature trail of exhaust and hot gas.

BOOST PHASE DEFENSE   see BOOST PHASE INTERCEPTION

BOOST PHASE INTERCEPTION is the destruction of attacking ballistic missiles during the first two- to five-minute period (called the boost phase) after they are launched. In boost phase interception, satellites equipped with sensors would detect heat emitted from a missile's booster rockets. Interception during the boost phase is desirable because a defense system would face fewer targets than in later phases of a missile's flight. Following the boost phase, the number of targets increases; a ballistic missile can release many warheads and decoys if it survives the boost phase. An attacker, however, can lessen the effectiveness of boost phase interception by shortening a missile's boost phase with booster rockets that burn out faster.

BRAVO TEST was the first explosion of a true thermonuclear weapon. Conducted by the United States on March 1, 1954, at Bikini Atoll, the Bravo test released a destructive energy of about 15 MEGATONS. The Bravo explosion was also one of the worst nuclear accidents ever: 289 local natives, 28 U.S. servicemen, and 23 Japanese fishermen sailing in the *Lucky Dragon* in nearby waters were seriously contaminated by the blast. Dangerous radioactive fallout blanketed a total area of over 7,000 square miles.

BREAKOUT is a phenomenon that enables one superpower to gain a decisive advantage in the nuclear arms race. Breakout occurs when one superpower exploits loopholes in arms-control agreements to suddenly undertake a significant expansion of its nuclear arsenal. Breakout could lead to a decisive shift in the balance of power and could thus be highly destabilizing.

BRINKSMANSHIP was a U.S. foreign policy strategy during the Eisenhower Administration. Brinksmanship, first articulated by Secretary of State John Foster Dulles, was a corollary to the famed MASSIVE RETALIATION strategy. Massive retaliation held that the U.S. could respond to communist aggression anywhere in the world with a devastating, all-out nuclear attack against the Soviet Union. Brinksmanship essentially involved exploiting the threat of massive retaliation in a crisis in order to force an opponent to back down. The U.S. was willing to go to the brink of war, and if the opponent did not back down, the U.S. would launch a full-scale nuclear attack. This strategy began to lose its effectiveness as the U.S.S.R.'s nuclear arsenal grew comparable to that of the U.S. Brinksmanship was phased out by the early 1960s.

BROKEN ARROW   see NUCLEAR ACCIDENT

BROKEN-BACK WAR is a nuclear war that continues unabated even after each side has been totally devastated.

BUILD-DOWN was a U.S. proposal for reducing the number of nuclear warheads deployed by the U.S. and the Soviet Union by dismantling two old nuclear warheads for each new warhead deployed. In this way, the superpowers could modernize their nuclear arsenals while reducing their size. President Ronald Reagan adopted the build-down principle in October 1983 as a basic element in the U.S. position at the STRATEGIC ARMS REDUCTION TALKS (START) held in Geneva, Switzerland. Reagan also established complex, specific guidelines for the build-down proposal. Build-down encouraged deploying single-warhead missiles rather than multiple-warhead missiles. In addition, it emphasized deploying warheads on missiles launched from submarines rather than underground missile silos. The Soviets rejected build-down because it would have reduced the number of warheads on the types of weapons that form the bulk of their nuclear arsenal. The original build-down of a two-for-one reduction (without specific guidelines) was proposed by U.S. Senators Sam Nunn, William Cohen, and Charles Percy in September 1983.

BUS see POST-BOOST VEHICLE

C

CADIN PINETREE RADAR see PINETREE

CAMPAIGN FOR NUCLEAR DISARMAMENT (CND) is the largest antinuclear movement in Great Britain. The CND was created in 1957 in response to the first British test of thermonuclear weapons with the goal of forcing Great Britain to abolish all its nuclear weapons. Among its founders in 1958 was philosopher and mathematician Bertrand Russell. After CND demonstrations failed to influence the British government, protests died down and CND membership drastically declined. During the 1960s, the CND went into a state of dormancy. It was revived, however, in 1977 in response to U.S. President Jimmy Carter's controversial proposal to deploy NEUTRON BOMBS in Europe. The CND remobilized and gathered a petition with 250,000 signatures in protest of the neutron bomb's deployment. Carter later canceled the program. In October 1983, the CND organized an antinuclear rally in which 300,000 protesters marched through Hyde Park, London. This demonstration was one of the largest antinuclear rallies in history.

CAMP DAVID, Maryland, is the location of an underground installation that would serve as a United States military command post in a nuclear war. Originally known as "Shangri-La" when it was established by President Franklin Roosevelt, the private wooded grounds have become famous as a weekend retreat for U.S. Presidents and their colleagues and guests. Named after President Dwight Eisenhower's grandson, Camp David is linked by an underground cable to the ALTERNATE NATIONAL MILITARY COMMAND CENTER, another emergency command post located eight miles away.

CARTE BLANCHE was a well-known U.S. WAR GAME held in West Germany in 1955. Carte Blanche simulated the use of small, battlefield nuclear weapons by NATO forces in response to a Russian invasion of West Germany. Carte Blanche was not merely a computer simulation; it involved actual troop maneuvers. Predicted casualties in Carte Blanche were 1.7 million dead and 3.5 million wounded, including millions of German civilians. Carte Blanche prompted concern and protest in West Germany.

CATALYTIC WAR is a type of nuclear war in which a third country deliberately triggers war between the superpowers.

CAT HOUSE is the U.S. name for a Soviet radar system that detects attacking nuclear missiles. First deployed in the 1970s, the Cat House is a highly sophisticated radar that can track many objects simultaneously. Cat House is part of the Soviet GALOSH defense system, which protects Moscow from a nuclear missile attack.

CENTER FOR DEFENSE INFORMATION (CDI) is a nonpartisan research organization that analyzes U.S. military programs. Founded in 1972 and located in Washington, D.C., it is considered to be an authoritative source on the U.S. military budget and nuclear weapons programs. It is staffed by former members of the military, elected public officials, and educators. The center provides a series of internships; sponsors lectures, seminars, and campaigns; and publishes *The Defense Monitor* ten times per year.

CENTRAL NUCLEAR WAR refers to an all-out nuclear war between the U.S. and the U.S.S.R. A central nuclear war would involve massive, devastating nuclear attacks on the homelands of the superpowers. Central nuclear war is distinct from LIMITED NUCLEAR WAR, in which the use of nuclear weapons is carefully and deliberately restricted. In most scenarios of limited nuclear war, nuclear weapons would be used in a specific geographic region, such as the Middle East, and the homelands of superpowers would not be attacked.

CENTRAL SYSTEMS are nuclear weapons considered fundamental in a nation's military force. Central systems are usually thought of as highly destructive nuclear missiles that can cover large distances and strike deep into enemy territory. The U.S. has regarded its nuclear missiles based in underground missile silos, on submarines, and on long-range bombers as central systems.

CHAFF is a theoretical method for rendering an opponent's defense system ineffective. Chaff, thin metal strips resembling confetti, would be carried into space in a satellite or warhead and released in front of an opponent's space-based radar. The radar would see chaff as an attacking warhead rather than harmless strips of metal. Thus, the defense system would waste time and ammunition to destroy this phony warhead while real warheads continued unhindered toward their targets. Chaff could also act as a screen for a warhead. If it was released directly between the radar's line of sight and the attacking warhead's flight path, the radar would not be able to detect the warhead. The United States is conducting research on chaff under the STRATEGIC DEFENSE INITIATIVE, commonly known as "Star Wars."

CHAIN REACTION   see NUCLEAR CHAIN REACTION

CHALLENGE INSPECTION is one type of visit to another nation's nuclear facilities in order to verify nuclear arms-control agreements. Challenge inspections would be held in response to a contention by one nation that another may be violating an arms-control agreement. Information gathered by radar or satellites could lead to a challenge inspection. Challenge inspections have never been used to verify a nuclear arms-control agreement, because they have been perceived as a threat to national security.

CHEMICAL LASER WEAPON (CLW) is a hypothetical weapon designed as part of a high-technology system for protecting against attacking nuclear missiles. Chemical laser weapons would, by means of a complex chemical reaction, generate a concentrated, high-speed stream of light that could burn a hole in the skin of an attacking missile and deactivate the sensitive electronic equipment responsible for guiding it to its target. Chemical laser weapons would function like super-concentrated spotlights; they would focus enormous energy on targets in order to destroy them. CLWs could be deployed in space or on the ground. The United States is conducting research on chemical laser weapons under the STRATEGIC DEFENSE INITIATIVE, commonly known as "Star Wars."

CHEMICAL ROCKET is a theoretical weapon which would be part of a high-technology system for protecting against attacking nuclear missiles. Chemical rockets would be based in space and fired at incoming nuclear warheads. As it approached its target, a chemical rocket would release nonnuclear projectiles, called SMART ROCKS, which would destroy the target by impact. The United States is conducting research on chemical rockets under the auspices of the STRATEGIC DEFENSE INITIATIVE, commonly known as "Star Wars."

CHEVALINE is a British program to improve the U.K.'s fleet of Polaris submarines and missiles. It was begun in the late 1960s and will be completed by the late 1980s. Essentially, the Chevaline program involves modifications of the front ends of British Polaris submarines, increasing the range, accuracy, and number of warheads on Polaris missiles and decreasing the destructive power of each warhead.

CIRCULAR ERROR PROBABLE (CEP) is a unit used to measure the accuracy of missiles. CEP is an important factor in determining how missiles are targeted. Very accurate missiles, which have a low CEP, are usually targeted at well-defended military installations. Less accurate missiles, which have a high CEP, are targeted primarily at unprotected cities and industrial centers. In recent years, the superpowers have developed smaller weapons with extremely low CEPs. CEP is the radius of the circle within which there is 50% probability that a missile will land. See BIAS.

CIVIL DEFENSE refers to a variety of measures designed to minimize the destruction that would be caused by a nuclear war. Civil defense plans are laid out specifically to protect people, natural resources, and the structure of society. Civil defense includes maintenance of BLAST and FALLOUT SHELTERS and plans for evacuation of cities and emergency functioning of the government. The role of civil defense is very controversial. Proponents argue that civil defense measures would save many lives in a nuclear war and that it is thus irresponsible to ignore civil defense. Critics of civil defense counter with two arguments. First, they contend that civil defense would not, in fact, be able to mitigate the effects of a nuclear war. Second, they assert that a country which pursues civil defense is signaling its readiness to fight a nuclear war. In recent years, the United States has almost completely abandoned its civil defense program. The U.S.S.R., on the other hand, maintains an extensive civil defense network, including a civil defense college at Balashika and numerous public blast and radiation shelters.

CIVIL NUCLEAR POWER is a nation that has the capacity to build nuclear weapons, but has intentionally decided not to develop them. India, which exploded a "peaceful" nuclear device in 1974, is an example of a civil nuclear power.

CLEAN NUCLEAR WEAPON is a nuclear weapon that produces only a few radioactive by-products. A clean nuclear weapon incorporates a specific design called fission-fusion, which is intended to produce a powerful explosion, but to disperse only a marginal amount of deadly radiation. In this way, a clean nuclear weapon is designed to destroy buildings and other structures, but not necessarily to kill people. A clean nuclear weapon is distinct from a DIRTY NUCLEAR WEAPON, which creates many radioactive by-products. Dirty nuclear weapons are designed to be able to kill people while leaving buildings and other structures intact. A clean nuclear weapon is also called a minimum residual radioactivity weapon.

CLIP-IN WARHEAD is a proposed type of nuclear warhead that could be easily "clipped" onto the tip of a missile. In this way, a clip-in warhead could be transferred onto a conventional weapon, such as a torpedo. Proponents argue that clip-in warheads would be more economical than separate conventional and nuclear systems; one weapon could serve both roles. Further, they would be easier to protect than existing systems, since they could be moved around quite easily. Critics, however, contend that clip-in warheads would greatly complicate arms control because they would further blur the distinction between nuclear and conventional weapons. Clip-in warheads are also known as insertable warheads.

CLOSE IN FALLOUT   see EARLY RADIOACTIVE FALLOUT

CLOSELY SPACED BASING (CSB) is a hypothetical method for deploying nuclear missiles. Closely spaced basing would involve placing a group of nuclear missiles in a tightly spaced cluster of underground missile silos. In this way, they could be protected from attacking nuclear missiles. This seemingly incongruous concept is made possible by the idea of FRATRICIDE. When a nuclear weapon explodes, it produces a tremendous amount of lingering debris, which would, in fratricide, disable or destroy subsequent incoming warheads. Closely spaced basing would increase the chances of fratricide by concentrating targets (missile silos) in a specific location. Closely spaced basing was first conceived as a method of deploying the U.S.'s MX missile. The plan was abandoned, however, and the U.S. eventually decided to deploy the MX in existing underground missile silos. Closely spaced basing is nicknamed "dense pack."

CLUSTER RELEASE is a method for protecting attacking nuclear missiles from enemy defenses. As a nuclear missile streaks toward its target, it may release hundreds of different objects, including warheads, decoys, and other debris. Cluster release is a technique for unleashing all of these objects simultaneously. Cluster release would thus overwhelm enemy defenses by providing hundreds of targets at the same time.

COBRA DANE is a U.S. radar station that detects attacking nuclear missiles and monitors Soviet missile tests. Cobra Dane is designed to notify decision-makers if an enemy attack is underway so that they can take appropriate action and is used to verify compliance with arms control agreements. First deployed in 1977, Cobra Dane is located in Alaska. It uses phased array radar, a technologically advanced type of radar that can monitor many different objects simultaneously.

COLD LAUNCH is a technique used to fire a nuclear missile so that it does not destroy the underground silo in which it is housed. In a cold launch, also known as a pop-up launch, a missile is ejected from the silo before the rockets used to propel it into space are fully ignited. The rockets, which would damage the silo with their heat and force, ignite after the missile has been ejected from the silo. A cold launch has two basic advantages. First, it provides more room to accommodate larger, more powerful missiles in the silo because it does not need to be equipped with excessive protective shielding. Second, since the silo is not destroyed, it may be used to launch another missile within a few hours. Cold launch is distinct from a hot launch, in which the silo is severely damaged. See HOT LAUNCH, RAPID RELOAD.

COLLATERAL DAMAGE is unintended destruction that affects the area surrounding the target of a nuclear attack.

COMBAT ALERT STATUS   see QUICK REACTION ALERT

COMBAT RADIUS refers to the maximum distance a fully loaded aircraft can fly and still have enough fuel to return to its departure point. Combat radius is distinct from range. Range refers more generally to the maximum possible distance an aircraft or missile can cover. Combat radius is also called tactical operating radius.

COMMAND, CONTROL, AND COMMUNICATIONS (C³)   see COMMAND, CONTROL, COMMUNICATIONS, AND INTELLIGENCE (C³I)

COMMAND, CONTROL, COMMUNICATIONS, AND INTELLI-GENCE (C³I) is a central network for regulating military operations. It encompasses the facilities, personnel, and procedures used by a nation's decision-makers to coordinate nuclear forces. C³I serves two basic functions. First, it provides intelligence by evaluating enemy weapons systems, monitoring them for an attack, and assessing damage after a nuclear war. Second, C³I oversees a nation's entire military force. The United States' C³I, officially known as the NATIONAL MILITARY COMMAND SYSTEM, and more commonly referred to as the "nerves" of the military operations, is led by the National Command Authorities (the President and the Secretary of Defense). Similarly, the Soviet Union's C³I functions under the command of the Politburo, the ruling body in the U.S.S.R.

COMMAND DISABLE SYSTEM (CDS) is a safety device that is intended to deactivate a nuclear missile before it is launched. A CDS is implanted in some nuclear warheads. When the proper code is inserted into it, the CDS disarms a warhead by destroying important components of it.

COMMAND GUIDANCE is a technique for steering a ballistic missile to its target by transmitting commands to the missile from earth. Command guidance is a type of remote control. Essentially, a missile guided by command guidance is driven to its target in the same manner that a child drives a radio-controlled toy car. Electronic signals with the missile's flight instructions are sent through space. Command guidance must be distinguished from INERTIAL GUIDANCE, in which a missile's flight directions are programmed into instruments located within the missile itself.

COMMISSION ON STRATEGIC FORCES   see SCOWCROFT COMMISSION

COMMITTEE FOR NUCLEAR INFORMATION (CNI)   see BABY TOOTH SURVEY

COMMITTEE ON DISARMAMENT (CD)   see CONFERENCE ON DISARMAMENT

COMMITTEE ON THE PRESENT DANGER (CPD) is a private research and educational organization that monitors arms control negotiations and the military balance between the superpowers. Founded in 1976 by arms-control experts Paul Nitze and Eugene Rostow, the CPD seeks to raise public awareness of the dangers of signing arms-control agreements that give the Soviet Union an advantage over the United States. Headquartered in Washington, D.C., CPD also supports new weapons programs to enhance national security. CPD, which includes members such as Secretary of State George Schultz and former Secretary of Defense James Schlesinger, strongly opposes SALT II, the treaty signed in 1979 between the Soviet Union and the United States. CPD members claim that the treaty is "fatally flawed," because it gives the Soviet Union an unfair advantage over the U.S. CPD was created in opposition to President Jimmy Carter's arms-control policies. Many of its members, including Schultz, Rostow, and Nitze, served under President Ronald Reagan. The CPD has a membership of about 14,000.

COMMONALITY refers to characteristics shared by two different weapons systems. Commonality is usually used to describe features that make two weapons systems *look* very similar, so that satellites, radar, and other detection devices cannot tell the weapons systems apart. For example, it is often very difficult to distinguish between bombers, which can deliver nuclear weapons, and tankers, which refuel bombers in flight. Commonality can make verification of nuclear arms-control agreements very difficult. Negotiators have designated specific distinguishing features, called OBSERVABLE DIFFERENCES, to counteract commonality and enable verification.

COMPELLENCE   see INTRAWAR DETERRENCE

COMPLETELY PREFERENTIAL DEFENSE is a strategy for defending against attacking nuclear warheads. In completely preferential defense, specific incoming warheads in flight are targeted for destruction while others are allowed to continue unchallenged toward their targets. The theory behind such a strategy is to ensure the survival of particularly important targets, while conceding that other targets must be sacrificed. In this way, the survival of certain important targets is guaranteed. A completely preferential defense is distinct from a semi-preferential defense, which is a strategy for selecting which enemy missiles to destroy before they are launched.

COMPLIANCE is the act of observing the terms of nuclear arms control agreements. Satellites and radar are among the instruments used to ensure compliance. See COOPERATIVE MEANS OF VERIFICATION, NATIONAL TECHNICAL MEANS OF VERIFICATION.

COMPREHENSIVE TEST BAN (CTB) refers to a complete cessation of all nuclear weapons testing. A comprehensive test ban would significantly impede development of new nuclear weapons—testing is an essential part of the process of building new weapons. The U.S. and the U.S.S.R. pledged in the LIMITED TEST BAN TREATY of 1963 to work actively toward a comprehensive test ban, and trilateral discussions on this topic (involving the United States, Great Britain, and the Soviet Union) were held in the late 1970s. However, no comprehensive test ban agreement has been reached. Verification and "the role of testing in maintaining an effective nuclear deterrent" are stumbling blocks that have been cited by the U.S.; the Soviets attribute the failure to achieve a comprehensive test ban treaty to an American desire to build new weapons systems.

COMPREHENSIVE TEST BAN (CTB) TREATY has never been achieved. The goal of negotiations on a CTB treaty has been to prohibit nuclear testing in all environments, including underwater, underground, in the atmosphere, and in outer space. A comprehensive test ban would make it almost impossible to develop new nuclear weapons and improve old ones. Negotiations between the U.S., the U.S.S.R., and Great Britain were held intermittently between 1962 and 1979 and were suspended in 1980 after a general deterioration in U.S.-Soviet relations. Verification of nuclear tests has been a major stumbling block in negotiating this treaty.

CONDITIONAL RESTRAINT is an action in which one nation limits or forgoes development of a particular military program on the condition that another nation follows suit. Conditional restraint is often discussed as a possible means of achieving nuclear arms control. Conditional restraint is sometimes called mutual example force restraint/reduction.

CONFERENCE OF THE COMMITTEE ON DISARMAMENT (CCD)   see CONFERENCE ON DISARMAMENT

CONFERENCE ON DISARMAMENT (CD) is one of the central international forums for negotiating disarmament issues. Closely but unofficially tied to the United Nations, the CD is made up of 40 nations representing all geographical regions and political groupings in the world. Membership includes all five nations that deploy nuclear weapons (China, France, Great Britain, the Soviet Union, and the United States). In 1962 the

CD was established by a U.S.-U.S.S.R. agreement, which stipulates that all other nations be invited to join. From 1978 to 1984, the CD was known as the Committee on Disarmament; before that, it was called the Conference of the Committee on Disarmament (CCD). The CCD, in turn, was an expanded version of the original Eighteen-Nation Disarmament Committee founded in 1962. The CD is held periodically in Geneva, Switzerland.

CONFIDENCE BUILDING MEASURES (CBMs) are agreements that promote better communication between the superpowers. First conceived in the early 1970s as a part of the Helsinki Accords, examples of CBMs include advance notification of nuclear tests and the Moscow-Washington HOT LINE. CBMs establish a climate of trust and openness favorable to negotiating nuclear arms-control agreements. CBMs also reduce the risks of misperception and accidental nuclear war. During the SALT negotiations, CBMs periodically arose as an issue closely related to the actual limitation of nuclear weapons. CBMs are also known as Confidence and Security Building Measures (CSBMs).

CONFLICT ESCALATION   see ESCALATION, CONTROLLED ESCALATION

CONFLICT MANAGEMENT   see CRISIS MANAGEMENT

CONSTELLATION SIZE is the number of satellites needed to constantly monitor an adversary's missile launch sites. Constellation size is a critical factor in establishing an effective missile defense. U.S. experts have often disagreed on the number of satellites that are necessary to monitor Soviet missile launch areas. Estimates of constellation size range from 100 to 1600 satellites.

CONTAMINATION is the absorption of harmful radiation, such as that released when a nuclear weapon explodes. People, places, and things can be contaminated. Contamination in humans can cause radiation sickness, cancer, and death. Widespread contamination would follow a nuclear war.

CONTROLLABILITY is the capacity of a nuclear weapons system to receive and respond to orders from command centers. STRATEGIC BOMBERS, for example, maintain a high level of controllability, because their crews can follow directions after launch. Unlike computer-guided missiles, U.S. and Soviet aircraft can be recalled or retargeted while in the air. Controllability of submarines, on the other hand, is more difficult, because decision-makers must communicate with rapidly traveling submarines in remote areas of the ocean.

CONTROLLED CHAIN REACTION   see NUCLEAR CHAIN REACTION

CONTROLLED COUNTERFORCE WAR is a nuclear war in which one or both sides attempts to defeat its enemy by striking military targets only. In this way, the enemy's ability to fight back would be neutralized. Controlled counterforce also involves avoiding damage to cities and industrial centers. Some experts have criticized the concept of controlled counterforce war. They contend that it would be impossible, once nuclear weapons have been introduced into a conflict, to limit their use.

CONTROLLED ESCALATION is a strategy for deliberately and carefully limiting the use of nuclear weapons in a conflict. According to proponents of controlled escalation, an all-out nuclear holocaust is not necessarily inevitable if nuclear weapons are introduced into a conflict. Instead, they contend, it is possible to restrict the use of nuclear weapons to specific military targets. In this way, the scope of a nuclear war could be truly limited. Nuclear weapons would thus have a legitimate policy role. Controlled escalation has been widely criticized as unrealistic and misleading. Many experts argue that once nuclear weapons are introduced into a conflict, leaders would quickly escalate the conflict into an all-out nuclear war. Controlled escalation forms the cornerstone of the doctrine of LIMITED NUCLEAR WAR, which became official U.S. strategy in 1974. Two strategies, ESCALATION DOMINANCE and ESCALATION MATCHING, would ensure that escalation remains controlled in a nuclear war.

CONTROLLED FUSION   see NUCLEAR CHAIN REACTION

CONTROLLED NUCLEAR WAR   see LIMITED NUCLEAR WAR

CONTROLLED RESPONSE is a strategy intended to manage armed conflict in order to avoid escalation and all-out nuclear war. Controlled response incorporates the policy of reacting to enemy aggression with an equal or only slightly higher level of force. Secretary of Defense Robert McNamara introduced the concept of controlled response in 1961 and it subsequently became official U.S. policy. Controlled response was conceived as a part of the doctrine of FLEXIBLE RESPONSE, an alternative to MASSIVE RETALIATION, which was U.S. strategy during the 1950s. Under a policy of massive retaliation, the U.S. reserved the right to respond to communist aggression anywhere in the world with a devastating, all-out nuclear attack.

CONVENTIONAL WEAPON is a nonnuclear, nonchemical weapon. It is an extremely broad term, encompassing many different types of weapons. Guns, hand grenades, and land mines are examples of conventional weapons.

COOPERATIVE MEANS OF VERIFICATION include a variety of measures to ensure compliance with nuclear arms-control agreements. Cooperative means of verification encompass measures which rely on active collaboration between nations, such as on-site inspections of military installations. Cooperative means of verification are distinct from NATIONAL TECHNICAL MEANS OF VERIFICATION, the technological network used to ensure compliance with arms-control agreements. National technical means incorporate a variety of technical instruments, including satellites and radar. Since they are difficult to negotiate, cooperative means of verification have been utilized only to a very limited extent.

COOPERATIVE MEASURES   see COOPERATIVE MEANS OF VERIFICATION

CORRTEX is a system under development by the U.S. in the mid-1980s for monitoring nuclear testing. Corrtex will incorporate underground cables and be able to detect and measure underground nuclear tests very accurately. In 1986, President Ronald Reagan proposed using Corrtex as a state-of-the-art tool for monitoring nuclear tests.

COSMOS is a Soviet satellite system that performs a wide variety of functions. Cosmos satellites have been deployed since the 1960s, and serve a number of roles, including monitoring enemy nuclear attacks and gathering weather information.

COUNCIL FOR A LIVABLE WORLD (CLW) is a nonpartisan organization devoted to the prevention of nuclear war. The CLW was founded in 1962 by eminent nuclear physicist Leo Szilard, who was closely associated with the development of the first atomic bomb. The CLW primarily concentrates its efforts on lobbying the United States Senate, which must ratify any U.S. arms-control agreement. With a membership of about 20,000, CLW raises money in support of Senate candidates who favor nuclear arms control. Headquartered in Boston with a legislative office in Washington, D.C., CLW also operates a nuclear arms-control telephone hotline, which is a taped message that provides an up-to-date account on arms-control matters currently being addressed in Congress.

COUNTERCITY STRATEGY   see COUNTERVALUE

COUNTERCITY STRIKE   see COUNTERVALUE

COUNTERDETERRENCE is a condition in which nations are restrained from fighting a nuclear war. In counterdeterrence, no nation can pursue aggressive policies without inviting a devastating nuclear attack. In this way, counterdeterrence may lead to international stability, since no nation can profit from any sort of aggressive behavior. Counterdeterrence is also known as self-deterrence.

COUNTERFORCE refers to a nuclear attack specifically intended to destroy enemy military installations. If the superpowers could restrict themselves to counterforce attacks, cities and industrial centers would not necessarily be annihilated in a nuclear war. This fundamental idea has served as the basis for modern theories of LIMITED NUCLEAR WAR. A counterforce attack has also been proposed as an effective way to defeat an enemy in a single nuclear attack. If an effective counterforce strike were launched, an enemy's ability to retaliate would be completely neutralized. Under the name of "no-cities," counterforce was announced as U.S. policy in 1962. Counterforce is distinct from COUNTERVALUE, which refers to a nuclear attack specifically intended to destroy enemy cities and industrial centers.

COUNTERFORCE DETERRENCE is a condition in which nations are restrained from fighting a nuclear war. In counterforce deterrence, no nation can pursue aggressive policies without inviting a devastating nuclear attack on its military installations. Counterforce deterrence is distinct from COUNTERVALUE DETERRENCE, in which nations are restrained by the threat of a destructive nuclear strike on their cities and industrial centers.

COUNTERFORCE-PLUS AVOIDANCE is a nuclear attack on enemy military targets specifically intended to avoid the destruction of population and industrial centers. A counterforce-plus avoidance strike could be motivated by moral, economic, or political concerns. The term was popularized by American defense analyst Herman Kahn. Counterforce-plus avoidance is distinct from COUNTERFORCE-PLUS BONUS, which is a nuclear attack on enemy military targets with the added intention of destroying population and industrial centers.

COUNTERFORCE-PLUS BONUS is a nuclear attack on enemy military targets with the added intention of destroying as much of the enemy's population and property as possible. In counterforce-plus bonus, an attacker obtains a "bonus" by attempting to deny the enemy an opportunity to gain revenge. The term was popularized by American defense analyst Herman Kahn. Counterforce-plus bonus is distinct from COUNTERFORCE-PLUS AVOIDANCE, which is a nuclear strike on enemy military targets with the specific intention of avoiding the destruction of population and industrial centers.

COUNTERFORCE STRATEGY see COUNTERFORCE

COUNTERFORCE STRIKE see COUNTERFORCE

COUNTERMILITARY POTENTIAL (CMP) see LETHALITY

COUNTERRECOVERY ATTACK is a second nuclear strike that hinders an opponent's ability to recover from the damage inflicted by a preceding nuclear attack. A counterrecovery attack is not launched against military targets. Instead, the targets of a counterrecovery attack are those that would be used by the enemy to rebuild military forces after they have been destroyed. Targets in a counterrecovery attack would include weapons factories, oil refineries, steel plants, and coal mines.

COUNTERVAILING STRATEGY was official U.S. nuclear strategy under the Carter Administration. Heralded as a strategic innovation, countervailing strategy was essentially only a refinement of the LIMITED NUCLEAR WAR strategy that was established as the SCHLESINGER DOCTRINE of 1973. The countervailing strategy specifically emphasized flexibility in the use of U.S. nuclear weapons, so that the President would have many options if he chose to use them. According to the doctrine of limited nuclear war, the use of nuclear weapons can be restricted in a conflict, and an all-out nuclear holocaust is not inevitable if they are used. Countervailing strategy was established in President Carter's Presidential Directive 59.

COUNTERVALUE refers to a nuclear attack specifically intended to destroy enemy cities and industrial centers. If an effective countervalue attack was launched, millions of people would die and priceless cultural and economic centers would be destroyed. The psychological impact of such a strike could, in theory, coerce an enemy into giving up. The U.S. nuclear attacks on the Japanese cities of Hiroshima and Nagasaki near the close of World War II were examples of effective countervalue attacks. A countervalue strike has also been proposed as an effective way of preventing an enemy from recovering from a nuclear war and rebuilding itself so that it could seek revenge. Countervalue is distinct from COUNTERFORCE, which refers to a nuclear attack specifically intended to destroy enemy military installations.

COUNTERVALUE DETERRENCE is a condition in which nations are restrained from fighting a nuclear war. In countervalue deterrence, no nation can pursue aggressive policies without inviting a devastating nuclear attack on its cities and industrial centers. Countervalue deterrence is distinct from counterforce deterrence, in which nations are restrained by the threat of a destructive nuclear strike on their military installations.

COUNTERVALUE STRATEGY   see COUNTERVALUE

COUNTERVALUE STRIKE   see COUNTERVALUE

COUNTERWEAPONS is a general term that describes weapons which are used to defend against attacking nuclear missiles.

COUNTING RULES are a criterion for determining whether a missile is classified as a single-warhead missile or one capable of carrying many warheads. Missiles capable of carrying several warheads are known as MIRV (multiple independently targetable reentry vehicles) missiles. Counting rules were established specifically for the SALT II accord, which limited the total number of nuclear weapons the U.S. and the U.S.S.R. could deploy, and set a sublimit on the number of MIRVs. Counting rules clarified a major point of contention during the treaty negotiations: Should a missile be classified as a MIRV if it is capable of carrying more than one warhead but is deployed with only a single warhead? Counting rules established that any missile that had been tested with MIRVs should be counted as a MIRV missile regardless of whether it was deployed as such.

COUPLING   see STRATEGIC COUPLING

COVER ALL   see POST-ATTACK COMMAND AND CONTROL SYSTEM

CREDIBILITY is a condition in which a nation's threats are believable. Credibility restrains nations from launching a nuclear attack. In order to maintain credibility, a nation must convince an opponent that it is both willing and able to carry out its threats. Credibility is backed up by military power. Credibility played a major role in the CUBAN MISSILE CRISIS of 1962. The crisis occurred when the U.S. discovered Soviet nuclear missiles were going to be introduced into Cuba. President John Kennedy decided that the missiles had to be removed at all costs and hinted he would use a nuclear strike as a last resort. Faced with a U.S. naval blockade of Cuba and the President's credible resolve to launch a nuclear attack against the Soviet Union, the Soviets removed their missiles from Cuba.

CREDIBLE FIRST-STRIKE CAPABILITY is a condition in which a nation is perceived to be able to destroy an enemy in a single nuclear attack. Both superpowers strive to maintain a capability to absorb a nuclear strike and retaliate with an equally or more devastating attack. In this way, they may be deterred from launching a nuclear attack out of the fear that it will invite an unacceptably destructive retaliation. With a credible first-strike capability, however, a superpower could launch a nuclear attack powerful enough to wipe out an enemy's capacity to retaliate. A credible first strike could be very destabilizing—it could prompt either side to launch a nuclear attack. The term credible first-strike capability was popularized by American defense analyst Herman Kahn.

CRISIS MANAGEMENT is the process in which leaders confront a crisis in order to achieve a favorable outcome. The Cuban Missile Crisis of 1962 is a classic example of crisis management. In October 1962 President John Kennedy set up a naval blockade around Cuba in order to prevent the Soviet Union from installing nuclear missiles there. Soviet ships heading for Cuba came within a few miles of the U.S. blockade before eventually turning back. Following these anxious moments, tension gradually dissipated, and a few days later the U.S.S.R. agreed to remove its missiles from Cuba. The confrontation nearly led to war between the superpowers, but was avoided because of effective crisis management. In the aftermath of the Cuban Missile Crisis, several nuclear arms-control agreements were signed between the United States and the Soviet Union in order to bolster crisis management. In particular, the HOT LINE AGREEMENT of 1964 set up a direct communications link between Moscow and Washington to be used in a crisis.

CRISIS RELOCATION is a plan for evacuating cities and areas around missile sites in a nuclear war. Crisis relocation is a vital component of CIVIL DEFENSE, the broad program designed to limit the damage caused by a nuclear war. The United States has relied almost exclusively on crisis relocation in its civil defense policy; the U.S.S.R. has combined plans for crisis relocation with numerous BLAST and FALLOUT SHELTERS. Crisis relocation is very controversial: Proponents claim that it could save millions of lives in a nuclear war and that it must therefore be pursued. Critics, however, contend that crisis relocation is impractical and would not, in fact, be able to mitigate the effects of a nuclear war. Further, some experts argue that extensive crisis relocation planning signals a readiness to fight a nuclear war and is thus destabilizing.

CRISIS STABILITY is a condition in which neither superpower feels compelled to use nuclear weapons in a conflict. In crisis stability, both superpowers reason that if a nuclear attack were launched, the enemy would be able to inflict an unacceptably destructive retaliation. In this way, each side would lose more than it would gain by launching a nuclear attack.

CRITICALITY is the condition that exists when a CRITICAL MASS is present. A critical mass is the minimum amount of URANIUM or PLUTONIUM necessary to fuel a nuclear reactor or weapon. At criticality, a self-sustaining reaction occurs which can lead to a nuclear explosion.

CRITICAL MASS is the minimum amount of URANIUM or PLUTONIUM necessary to fuel a nuclear reactor or weapon. As soon as a critical mass exists, a self-sustaining reaction occurs which can lead to a nuclear explosion. Uranium and plutonium are highly radioactive substances used to fuel all nuclear weapons.

CROSS-TARGETING is the practice of aiming two warheads from separate missiles at the same target. Theoretically, the use of two warheads could increase the chance that a target will be destroyed. Critics, however, contend that cross-targeting is an ineffective and expensive method of destroying a target. When a nuclear warhead explodes, it can destroy many things nearby, including other incoming nuclear warheads. In this way, the effects from the first warhead's explosion might damage or destroy the second warhead before it could reach the target.

CRUISE MISSILE is a slow, low-flying, highly accurate missile that resembles a pilotless airplane. Cruise missiles are powered by jet engines throughout their flight and are designed to be very maneuverable, in order to sneak around enemy defenses. Cruise missiles are distinct from BALLISTIC MISSILES, which are propelled into the upper atmosphere by BOOSTER ROCKETS. After the rockets burn out, ballistic missiles fall down through the atmosphere, pulled by gravity to their targets. Cruise missiles can be launched from aircraft, submarines, ships, or land-based launchers. Because cruise missiles are easily concealed and can carry conventional or nuclear warheads, they complicate arms-control negotiations. An early and crude prototype of the cruise missile was the German V-1 "buzz" bomb, used by Nazi Germany against England during World War II. Both the U.S. and the U.S.S.R. are currently improving their cruise missile technology. See AIR-LAUNCHED CRUISE MISSILE, SEA-LAUNCHED CRUISE MISSILE, GROUND-LAUNCHED CRUISE MISSILE, TOMAHAWK CRUISE MISSILE.

CRUISE MISSILE CARRIER (CMC) is a term created during the SALT negotiations. It refers to any aircraft which has a range of over 600 km and can deliver CRUISE MISSILES. Cruise missiles are slow, low-flying, extremely accurate missiles that resemble pilotless airplanes; they are equipped to carry either nuclear or conventional warheads. Under SALT II's complex system of classifying nuclear weapons, CMCs are classed as heavy bombers and are limited by the treaty. The U.S. B-52G and the Soviet Tu-95 Bear are examples of CMCs.

CRUISE MISSILE SUBMARINE (SSG) is a submarine that is capable of carrying and launching CRUISE MISSILES. Cruise missiles are slow, low-flying missiles designed to be very accurate and maneuverable. Most cruise missiles have a short range; cruise missiles fired from Soviet submarines are thus not intended for use against the continental United States. Cruise missile submarines can target their missiles against naval vessels as well as land-based targets. Cruise missile submarines must be distinguished from BALLISTIC MISSILE SUBMARINES, which carry more powerful ballistic missiles intended for use against the homelands of the superpowers. Currently, only the Soviet Union maintains a fleet of cruise missile submarines. The U.S. discontinued its cruise missile submarine program in 1965.

CSS-MISSILE is the U.S. code designating Chinese surface-to-surface nuclear missiles. The CSS-1 is a medium-range ballistic missile. See MEDIUM-RANGE BALLISTIC MISSILE for a complete description of the CSS-1. The CSS-2 is an intermediate-range ballistic missile. See INTERMEDIATE-RANGE BALLISTIC MISSILE for a complete description of the CSS-2. The CSS-3 and CSS-4 are intercontinental ballistic missiles. See INTERCONTINENTAL BALLISTIC MISSILE for a complete description of these missiles.

CSS-N-MISSILE is the U.S. code designating Chinese submarine-launched ballistic missiles (SLBMs). In the mid-1980s, the CSS-N-3 was the only SLBM deployed by China. See SUBMARINE-LAUNCHED BALLISTIC MISSILE for a complete description of the CSS-N-3.

CUBAN MISSILE CRISIS was a U.S.-U.S.S.R. confrontation that very nearly led to war between the superpowers. The Cuban Missile Crisis was indeed a very serious incident; in the words of President John Kennedy, the chances of nuclear war were "between one in three and even." The crisis began on October 16, 1962, when U.S. intelligence reports confirmed that the U.S.S.R. was installing nuclear missiles in Cuba. President Kennedy and his advisors quickly determined that the missiles posed a threat to U.S. security and had to be removed. Kennedy's advisors (the Excom, or Executive Committee of the National Security Council) considered a variety of possible actions, including an air strike against the missile sites, an invasion of Cuba, and a naval blockade around Cuba. Kennedy opted for the blockade, and on October 24 he quarantined Cuba. Soviet ships heading for Cuba came within a few miles of the blockade, but eventually turned back. Following these anxious moments, tension gradually dissipated until, on October 28, the U.S.S.R.

agreed to remove its missiles from Cuba. A myriad of other issues was involved in the Cuban Missile Crisis, including the precarious state of West Berlin, the Bay of Pigs invasion of 1961, the U.S. deployment of Jupiter missiles in Turkey, and traditional American policy of closing the Western Hemisphere to hostile outside powers. The resolution of the Cuban Missile Crisis led to a series of important nuclear arms-control agreements, including the HOT LINE AGREEMENT and the LIMITED TEST BAN TREATY.

D

DAMAGE LIMITATION is any measure intended to reduce the destruction caused during a nuclear war. Damage limitation may include a variety of measures to limit damage to either side in a nuclear war. CIVIL DEFENSE is an important means of limiting damage inflicted by an enemy; attacking only enemy military installations is a way to restrict destruction of enemy territory.

THE DAY AFTER is a television film that depicts a devastating, all-out nuclear war. The film concentrates on the absolute tragedy and destruction inflicted on the area around Lawrence, Kansas, rather than addressing who is responsible for starting the war. *The Day After* was aired by ABC on November 29, 1983, and was seen by about 95 million Americans. The film was extremely controversial when shown on American television. Some critics claimed that it was too grisly for young children to watch; others asserted that it sensationalized and trivialized nuclear war. Still others contended that nuclear war could never occur in the way the film suggests. The film stars Jason Robards as a doctor at the University of Kansas hospital in Lawrence.

D-CUBED is the nickname for a "drop-dead decision," the judgment to abandon plans to build a particular type of weapon.

DECAPITATION ATTACK is a nuclear strike targeted at a nation's leaders and primary command posts. It is intended to wipe out an enemy's ability to coordinate decisions and relay orders for a counterattack. Thus, the purpose of a decapitation attack is to paralyze an enemy in a single nuclear strike.

DECEPTIVE BASING is a theoretical technique to protect radar installations from enemy attack. In deceptive basing, each radar would be moved periodically among a number of protective shelters reinforced against the effects of a nuclear attack. The radar would be carried in the back of trucks or along train tracks. Since an opponent would never be sure of the radar's location, the radar would be very hard to pinpoint and destroy. Deceptive basing has also been considered to protect the various long-range nuclear missiles. Deceptive basing would probably be a violation of the Antiballistic Missile Treaty of 1972, which stipulates that any radar sites built by the U.S. or U.S.S.R. must be immobile.

DECLARED FACILITIES are areas approved in arms-control agreements for testing or manufacturing nuclear weapons.

DECOUPLING has two completely different meanings. First, it refers to a scenario in which the United States, faced with a Soviet attack on Western Europe, abandons its allies. Presumably, the U.S. would "decouple" its forces from those of NATO out of fear of a devastating Soviet nuclear attack on the continental U.S. Decoupling also refers to a complex method of muffling underground nuclear tests in order to hide them from other nations. This type of decoupling would impede verification of arms-control and test-ban agreements.

DECOY is a device that misleads an opponent's defense system. Decoys accompany attacking nuclear warheads, and are released in order to divert an opponent's forces and improve the chances that attacking nuclear warheads will penetrate defenses. Decoys deceive by appearing more important than they actually are. They force a missile defense system to waste time and ammunition by turning attention away from attacking warheads. Several types of decoys are currently under development. CHAFF and AEROSOLS confuse a defense system by making warheads difficult to detect, but they do not physically resemble warheads. Dummy warheads, however, look like actual warheads but carry no nuclear explosive. Some modern intercontinental ballistic missiles can carry up to 100 decoys.

DEEP UNDERGROUND MISSILE BASING (DUMB) is a hypothetical method for deploying nuclear missiles. DUMB would involve placing nuclear missiles in underground missile silos located deep below the earth's surface. In this way, they would be effectively insulated from enemy attack. DUMB was first conceived as a method of deploying the U.S.'s MX MISSILE. The plan was abandoned, however, and the U.S. eventually decided to deploy the MX in existing underground missile silos.

DEFCON   see DEFENSE READINESS CONDITIONS

DEFENSE ATOMIC SUPPORT AGENCY   see DEFENSE NUCLEAR ' AGENCY

DEFENSE NUCLEAR AGENCY (DNA) is the central U.S. government agency that coordinates research, development, and testing of U.S. nuclear weapons. DNA manages the Department of Defense's nuclear weapons stockpile and provides assistance to the Joint Chiefs of Staff and the military services on all matters concerning nuclear weapons. The DNA is the oldest agency in the Department of Defense. Its roots can be traced back to 1942 to the MANHATTAN PROJECT, which was the U.S. World War II program to build the first atomic bomb. The Manhattan Project was dissolved by the ATOMIC ENERGY ACT OF 1946 and replaced by the Armed Forces Special Weapons Project, which became the Defense Atomic Support Agency in 1959. The Defense Atomic Support Agency was renamed the Defense Nuclear Agency in 1971.

DEFENSE READINESS CONDITION (DEFCON) is the scale that reflects the level of preparedness of U.S. military forces. DEFCONs are measured on a scale from 5 to 1. DEFCON 5 describes a state in which forces are at normal readiness, while DEFCON 1, referred to as the "cocked pistol," indicates a state of extreme emergency, when forces are poised for attack. Not all U.S. military forces are simultaneously at the same DEF-CON. The DEFCON varies depending upon the type of weapon with which troops are equipped and the region in which they are deployed. For example, U.S. troops in South Korea are always at DEFCON 4 but soldiers tending nuclear missiles deployed in the continental U.S. are normally kept at DEF-CON 5. During the Cuban Missile Crisis, President John F. Kennedy raised the DEFCON of U.S. forces to DEFCON 2 (a status just below wartime conditions).

DEFENSE SUPPORT PROGRAM (DSP) SATELLITE is an advanced U.S. intelligence satellite. DSP satellites incorporate various types of sensors and perform a variety of extremely important functions, including early warning of enemy attack and detection of nuclear tests. The most modern DSP satellites were first launched into the atmosphere in 1981.

DEFENSE TECHNOLOGIES STUDY   SEE FLETCHER COMMISSION

DELAYED RADIOACTIVE FALLOUT is radioactive debris created in a nuclear explosion that rises into the atmosphere and remains there for weeks or months before falling to the ground. When a nuclear weapon explodes, it destroys anything in the area. The resulting debris is drawn up into the atmosphere. As it rises, FALLOUT is bathed in radiation from the explosion. Delayed radioactive fallout is then picked up by winds and is carried around the earth, spreading harmful effects of delayed radioactive fallout over a wide area. This type of fallout may be intensely radioactive and can be very dangerous. It can cause nausea, hair loss, internal bleeding, genetic damage, and cancer. Delayed radioacative fallout must be distinguished from EARLY RADIOACTIVE FALLOUT, which falls to the earth within 24 hours of a nuclear explosion and is more radioactive. Delayed radioactive fallout is also called global radioactive fallout and worldwide radioactive fallout.

DELIBERATE CONCEALMENT is the practice of intentionally hiding nuclear weapons in order that an opponent cannot verify their existence so that they would be more difficult to locate and destroy in a nuclear war. Further, by deliberately concealing weapons, a nation could avoid having them included in arms-control agreements. Deliberate concealment is often outlawed in arms-control agreements because it creates an atmosphere of distrust and is considered destabilizing. The SALT accords, which establish numerical limits on the number of nuclear weapons that both the U.S. and the U.S.S.R. can deploy, prohibit deliberate concealment. An example of deliberate concealment is camouflaging nuclear missile silos.

DELIBERATE ESCALATION is an official NATO strategy of raising the intensity of combat in order to force an enemy to surrender. The purpose of deliberate escalation is to use the threat of nuclear agression to force the enemy to back down in a conflict. Deliberate escalation is a primary component of NATO's top-secret plan for fighting a nuclear war. It also forms part of NATO's policy of flexible response, which enables NATO to match enemy aggression with a variety of responses.

DELIVERY SYSTEM   see NUCLEAR DELIVERY SYSTEM

DELIVERY VEHICLE   see NUCLEAR DELIVERY VEHICLE

DELTA SUBMARINE is a class of Soviet nuclear-powered submarines. See BALLISTIC MISSILE SUBMARINE for a complete description of the Delta.

DEMIRVING requires that missiles currently equipped with more than one warhead be modified so they can carry only one warhead. MIRV missiles, which were developed by the superpowers in the early 1970s, can deliver more than one warhead. In this way, a single MIRV missile is capable of destroying more than one target. MIRVs have complicated arms-control negotiations because it is almost impossible to tell whether a missile is a MIRV. Thus, it is extremely difficult to verify negotiated limits on nuclear warheads. DeMIRVing was proposed by the United States during the START negotiations as a means of resolving this arms-control dilemma.

DENSE PACK   see CLOSELY SPACED BASING

DENUCLEARIZATION is a disarmament measure that prohibits the deployment of nuclear weapons in a given territorial region. It may entail two separate actions: prohibiting nuclear weapons from being introduced into an area in which they are not currently deployed, or removing nuclear weapons from a territory where they are already deployed. Several arms-control agreements, including the ANTARCTIC TREATY of 1959 and the TREATY OF TLATELOLCO of 1967, have denuclearized wide areas of the world. See NUCLEAR-FREE ZONE.

DENUCLEARIZED ZONE   see NUCLEAR-FREE ZONE

DEPLOYMENT is the positioning of a weapon so that it is ready to be used. Many land-based missiles, for example, are deployed when they are placed into underground missile silos. Deployment is the final stage in the establishment of a weapons system. If follows development, testing, flight testing, and production.

DEPRESSED TRAJECTORY describes the path that a BALLISTIC MISSILE could follow as it streaks toward its target. Ballistic missiles are propelled into the upper atmosphere by BOOSTER ROCKETS. After the rockets burn out, the missile falls down through the atmosphere, pulled by gravity to its target. Unlike the normal trajectory (called a MINIMUM ENERGY TRAJECTORY), a depressed trajectory involves flying close to the earth in order to avoid radar and other enemy defenses and to reach the target faster.

DETECTION is a very general term with two basic meanings. First, it refers to monitoring other nations' nuclear tests. Several types of instruments, including satellites and seismic stations, are used to detect these explosions. Detection also refers to locating enemy aircraft, submarines, and missiles. Two types of detection are used in this sense: ACTIVE DETECTION and PASSIVE DETECTION.

DÉTENTE describes a policy of lessening tensions in relations between two or more countries. The term is usually applied to relations between the United States and the Soviet Union in the 1960s and early 1970s, when the two superpowers backed away from the hostility of the Cold War and established relations based on peaceful coexistence. Many experts contend that détente began with the LIMITED TEST BAN and HOT LINE AGREEMENTS signed during the Kennedy Administration, and reached its pinnacle in the early 1970s with several important arms-control agreements, including the SALT accords. Détente was jeopardized in the late 1970s by the Soviet Union's invasion of Afghanistan and resulting U.S. policies such as the boycott of the 1980 Summer Olympics.

DETERRENCE   see NUCLEAR DETERRENCE

DETERRENCE BY DENIAL is the strategy of threatening a limited nuclear attack in order to restrain an enemy from invading a specific territorial region. In deterrence by denial, a country would threaten to use battlefield nuclear weapons to convince an enemy that any invasion would be met by a limited, though very destructive, nuclear attack. Deterrence by denial is distinct from DETERRENCE BY PUNISHMENT, which involves using the threat of an all-out nuclear attack in order to deter any type of enemy aggression.

DETERRENCE BY PUNISHMENT is the strategy of threatening an all-out nuclear attack in order to deter any type of enemy aggression. In deterrence by punishment, nations are restrained from aggressive behavior by the knowledge that they will be punished by a devastating, all-out nuclear strike. Formulated by the United States in the early 1950s, deterrence by punishment theory has been the foundation for later policies of MASSIVE RETALIATION and MUTUAL ASSURED DESTRUCTION. Deterrence by punishment is distinct from DETERRENCE BY DENIAL, which involves using the threat of a limited nuclear attack in order to restrain an enemy from invading a specific territorial region.

DETERRENCE-ONLY is a strategy of relying on the threat of MU- TUAL ASSURED DESTRUCTION (MAD) as the only factor in avoiding nuclear war between the superpowers. MAD is a condition in which both superpowers are capable of absorbing a nuclear attack and then inflicting an unacceptably destructive retalia- tion. Supporters of deterrence-only believe that the threat of mutual assured destruction can, by itself, deter a nuclear ex- change between the superpowers. Critics, however, contend that MAD is immoral because it requires the superpowers to rely on the threat of terror to restrain each side from engaging in a nuclear war. The term deterrence-only was popularized by American defense analyst Herman Kahn.

DETERRENCE-PLUS   see EXTENDED DETERRENCE

DETERRENCE-PLUS INSURANCE is a strategy of recognizing that nuclear war could occur and that a nation must be prepared to deal with its consequences. Deterrence-plus insurance requires that a nation take steps to limit potential damage in the event of a nuclear war. Deterrence-plus insurance strategy is based on the assumption that it may be possible to survive a nuclear war. It suggests that a nation must be willing to buy insurance—to spend money on preparations to limit damage, to facilitate recovery, and to obtain the most positive outcome. The term deterrence-plus insurance was popularized by American defense analyst Herman Kahn.

DETERRENT   see NUCLEAR DETERRENT

DEUTERIUM is a type of hydrogen that contains one extra neutron. Deuterium is used to fuel THERMONUCLEAR WEAPONS. In these weapons, deuterium is commonly fused with TRITIUM, another variety of hydrogen. This process releases tremendous amounts of energy. Deuterium is not radioactive and exists in nature in small amounts.

DEVELOPMENT is the process of conducting research on, designing, and building prototypes of new nuclear weapons. Development is the initial stage in the establishment of a weapons system. It precedes NUCLEAR TESTING, PRODUCTION, and DEPLOYMENT.

DF-1 is a Chinese short-range ballistic missile. See SHORT-RANGE BALLISTIC MISSILE for a complete description of the DF-1.

DIRECT APPROACH is a negotiating strategy of addressing only arms-control issues in arms-control negotiations. In a direct approach, major political disputes are subordinated and negotiators focus on arms control. A direct approach is distinct from an INDIRECT APPROACH, which gives other political disputes priority over nuclear arms control. The U.S.S.R. has traditionally followed a direct approach in arms-control negotiations, while the U.S. has sought to link arms control to other issues, such as human rights.

DIRECT COMMUNICATIONS LINK   see HOT LINE

DIRECT DEFENSE is an official NATO strategy of countering an enemy at any level at which it chooses to fight. Direct defense is a primary component of NATO's top-secret plan for fighting a nuclear war. It also forms part of NATO's policy of FLEXIBLE RESPONSE, which enables NATO to match enemy aggression with a variety of responses.

DIRECTED-ENERGY WEAPON (DEW) is a theoretical weapon designed as part of a high-technology shield against nuclear warheads. The primary advantage of a DEW is its ability to destroy a target very quickly. DEWs destroy their targets by focusing intense beams of energy on a warhead's surface; their beams can travel at or near the speed of light. This "directed energy" can destroy a warhead or disable its sensitive electronics inside. DEWs include a wide variety of weapons, depending on the exact type of energy that is employed. Light or subatomic particles are two kinds of energy that can be incorporated into directed-energy weapons. DEWs can either be based on the ground or in space. The United States is conducting research into directed-energy weapons under the STRATEGIC DEFENSE INITIATIVE, commonly known as "Star Wars."

DIRECT RADIATION   see PROMPT RADIATION

DIRTY HARRY   see HARRY SHOT

DIRTY NUCLEAR WEAPON is a nuclear weapon that produces many radioactive by-products. A dirty nuclear weapon incorporates a specific design called FISSION-FUSION-FISSION, which is intended to produce a powerful explosion and to disperse a lot of deadly radiation. In this way, a dirty nuclear weapon is intended to kill people while leaving buildings and other structures intact. The well-known NEUTRON BOMB, which was proposed for deployment in Europe by U.S. President Jimmy Carter in the 1970s, is an example of a dirty nuclear weapon. A dirty nuclear weapon is distinct from a CLEAN NUCLEAR WEAPON, which creates only marginal radioactive by-products. A clean nuclear weapon is designed to destroy buildings and other structures, but not necessarily to kill people. A dirty nuclear weapon is also called a salted weapon.

DISARMAMENT   see NUCLEAR DISARMAMENT

DISARMAMENT COMMISSION (DC) is the United Nations forum for discussing nuclear disarmament issues. Established in 1952, the DC includes every member of the United Nations. It mainly functions as an arena for world opinion in order to influence the policies of the five nations that deploy nuclear weapons (China, France, Great Britain, the Soviet Union, and the United States). Despite its attempts to focus world attention on the need for disarmament, it has received very little attention from governments. The DC was inactive from 1965 to 1978. It was revived following the U.N. Special Session on Disarmament in 1978. The DC is called into full session on rare occasions; limited membership meets several weeks each year.

DISARMAMENT DIVIDEND is a United Nations term that refers to the economic benefits of reducing armaments. A disarmament dividend involves rechanneling labor and money spent to build weapons in order to bring about greater satisfaction of civilian economic needs in a nation.

DISARMING FIRST STRIKE is a nuclear attack that destroys an enemy's nuclear weapons before they can be launched in response. If a nation launched an effective disarming first strike, it would nullify an enemy's ability to retaliate. In this way, many experts contend, it would be able to win a nuclear war. Both superpowers construct nuclear arsenals and take other measures intended to prevent the other side from launching a disarming first strike. See FIRST STRIKE.

DISCRIMINATION is the process of distinguishing between targets and nontargets. Incoming nuclear warheads can be deployed with many DECOYS in order to deceive enemy defenses. If a defensive system cannot discriminate between threatening nuclear warheads and harmless decoys, it will waste time and ammunition.

DISENGAGEMENT   see NUCLEAR DISENGAGEMENT

DISPERSAL is the relocating and spreading out of civilian and military forces in order to increase their chances of survival in a nuclear attack. Dispersal includes moving both people and weapons. Submarines armed with nuclear missiles are dispersed throughout the world's oceans to make them less vulnerable to attack. Dispersal is also an element of CIVIL DEFENSE and could involve evacuating important military leaders or the inhabitants of cities to safer areas.

DISTANT EARLY WARNING (DEW) LINE is a U.S. radar system that detects attacking enemy bombers and is being upgraded to monitor incoming CRUISE MISSILES. Cruise missiles are slow, low-flying, highly accurate missiles that resemble pilotless airplanes. The DEW Line is designed to notify decision-makers if an enemy attack is underway so that they can take appropriate action. The DEW Line is formed by a chain of over 30 radar stations that stretch within the Arctic Circle from Alaska to Iceland. The DEW Line was created in 1958.

DOG HOUSE is the U.S. name for a Soviet radar system that detects attacking nuclear missiles. First deployed in the late 1960s, the Dog House is a highly sophisticated radar that can track many objects simultaneously. Dog House is part of the GALOSH defense system, which protects Moscow from a nuclear missile attack.

DOOMSDAY CLOCK is a metaphorical timepiece that counts down the amount of time left before civilization is destroyed. When the clock reaches midnight, civilization will end. The doomsday clock appears monthly on the cover of the *Bulletin of the Atomic Scientists.* In the January 1984 issue of the *Bulletin of the Atomic Scientists,* the doomsday clock moved to three minutes before midnight.

DOOMSDAY MACHINE is a hypothetical weapon that could destroy the earth. American defense analyst Herman Kahn introduced (but did not recommend) the idea of a doomsday machine. Kahn envisioned a doomsday machine in the form of a large computer wired to a huge stockpile of nuclear weapons. When the computer sensed that an enemy had committed an act that it was programmed to consider intolerable, it would automatically trigger doomsday bombs. Without any means for human control or intervention, a doomsday machine would automatically blow up the entire world in response to enemy provocation. Kahn claimed that if it could ever be built, a doomsday machine would be the ultimate deterrent. He reasoned that no nation would place its own and the world's existence in jeopardy by engaging in aggression that would threaten to activate a doomsday machine. Kahn estimated in 1960 that a doomsday machine could be built with existing technology at a cost of about ten billion dollars.

DOOMSDAY PLANE   see NATIONAL EMERGENCY AIRBORNE COMMAND POST

DOSE   see ABSORBED DOSE

DOUBLE FLASH refers to the two bursts of light that are emitted as a nuclear weapon explodes. The double flash is unique to nuclear explosions—it is thus an identifying trademark for nuclear tests and other nuclear detonations. Satellites that monitor the detonation of nuclear weapons use the double flash to identify such explosions.

DR. STRANGELOVE is a 1964 English film about the destruction of the earth in a nuclear war. A comedy, this film was critically acclaimed and sparked controversy. It was considered anti-American because of its mocking representation of the politicians and generals in charge of the U.S. nuclear arsenal. The story begins with a deranged U.S. general launching a nuclear attack against the Soviet Union. The general justifies the attack because he believes that the Soviets are planning to poison the U.S. water supply with fluoride. The U.S. President is able to recall all but one of the bombers launched in the attack. When he learns that the Soviets will detonate a "doomsday device" if their territory is attacked, he turns to his physicist advisor Dr. Strangelove. The crazed Dr. Strangelove, an ex-Nazi, trys to console the President by telling him that humanity can survive if a select few live in deep underground shelters for 100 years. All efforts to stop the plane fail and the plane's pilot, played by

Slim Pickens, personally rides the nuclear missile down to the ground like a cowboy riding a horse. The bomb's detonation triggers the doomsday device (see DOOMSDAY MACHINE) and the entire earth is destroyed. The film was directed by Stanley Kubrick and stars Peter Sellers as the U.S. President and as Dr. Strangelove. The film's complete title is Dr. *Strangelove or How I Learned To Stop Worrying and Love the Bomb.*

DUAL CAPABLE SYSTEMS are weapons that can be equipped with either nuclear or conventional explosives. Dual capable systems have complicated arms-control negotiations, because it is impossible to be certain whether or not they are armed with nuclear warheads. In this way, it becomes extremely difficult to verify negotiated limits on nuclear weapons.

DUAL KEY has two meanings. First, it refers to a safety measure that requires two different keys to launch a U.S. nuclear missile. In order for a nuclear missile to be launched, two crew officers must each insert a key into the release mechanism. The two keys must be inserted at the same time, so that one officer cannot by himself launch a nuclear missile. Dual key also refers to a political arrangement in which one nation's nuclear weapons are based in another country. The U.S., for example, deploys nuclear missiles in many other countries, including West Germany, Italy, and Turkey. The dual key is intended to ensure that both nations share responsibility for launching these missiles. About half of NATO's nuclear weapons are under dual-key control.

DUAL PHENOMENOLOGY is a requirement that any indication of enemy nuclear attack be confirmed independently by both satellites and radar. Dual phenomenology is a safeguard against accidental nuclear war.

DUAL-TRACK DECISION linked the deployment of new U.S. nuclear weapons in Western Europe with simultaneous negotiations on limiting or eliminating altogether nuclear weapons in

Europe. The dual-track decision was proposed by French President Valéry Giscard d'Estaing in January 1979 and adopted by NATO a few months later. Presidents Jimmy Carter and Ronald Reagan both supported the dual-track decision. Dual track was an attempt to appeal to Western Europeans divided over nuclear issues. The deployment of U.S. TOMAHAWK CRUISE and PERSHING II MISSILES in Western Europe represented one component of the dual-track decision. The second element was the INTERMEDIATE-RANGE NUCLEAR FORCES (INF) TALKS between the U.S. and the U.S.S.R., which aimed at reducing the number of nuclear weapons deployed in Europe. Only one element of the dual-track decision remains in place. The U.S. began deploying its missiles in Western Europe in December 1983. As a result, the Soviet Union immediately walked out of the INF talks.

DULL SWORD   see NUCLEAR INCIDENT

DUST DEFENSE is a theoretical technique for protecting land-based nuclear missiles against enemy attack. In a dust defense, several nuclear warheads would be planted underground near a missile site. If the missile site were attacked, the underground warheads would be detonated several minutes before the attacking warheads arrived. This underground explosion would throw an enormous cloud of dust into the air, directly in the path of the attacking warheads. As the incoming warheads passed through the cloud, the dust particles in the cloud would scrape off the warheads' protective heatshields like sandpaper scraping varnish off wood. Without their heat shields, the warheads would burn up before they could reach their targets. Dust defense is also known as environmental defense.

DWARF DUD is a nuclear weapon that is less destructive than expected.

DYAD is a nuclear arsenal that is composed of missiles based on submarines and bombers. A dyad must be distinguished from a TRIAD, which includes missiles deployed on submarines and aircraft as well as in underground silos.

DYNAMIC OVERPRESSURE is essentially a strong, destructive wind created in the aftermath of a nuclear explosion. Dynamic overpressure pushes objects outward in the same way that a hurricane knocks things over. Overpressure can collapse buildings, uproot trees, and crush people. It is distinct from STATIC OVERPRESSURE, which is also created in a nuclear explosion. Dynamic overpressure is a horizontal force moving out from the center of explosion while static overpressure is a vertical force pushing down from above.

E

EARLY RADIOACTIVE FALLOUT is radioactive debris that rises into the atmosphere and falls to the earth shortly after a nuclear explosion. When a nuclear weapon explodes, it destroys anything in the area. The resulting debris is drawn up into the atmosphere. As it rises, FALLOUT is bathed in radiation from the explosion. Early radioactive fallout remains in the atmosphere for less than 24 hours and then falls to earth. Because it stays in the atmosphere for such a short time, it remains highly radioactive. It may thus be extremely dangerous when it does fall to earth. Early radioactive fallout can cause nausea, hair loss, internal bleeding, genetic damage, and cancer. It is distinct from DELAYED RADIOACTIVE FALLOUT, which may take months or years to fall back to the earth and is generally less harmful. Early radioactive fallout is also called local radioactive fallout and close-in fallout.

EARLY WARNING encompasses a variety of satellite and radar systems designed to detect an enemy nuclear attack soon after it has been launched. Early warning is an extremely broad term, which includes many different types of sophisticated installations. Both the U.S. and the U.S.S.R. maintain advanced early-warning systems. The purpose of early warning is to notify decision-makers if an enemy attack is underway so that they can take appropriate action.

EARTH PENETRATOR (EP) is a device that would enable a nuclear weapon to penetrate the ground before it explodes. The purpose of an earth penetrator is to create maximum damage and minimum radioactive fallout. Earth penetrators, which would be attached to nuclear weapons, would enhance an incoming missile's accuracy and enable it to destroy enemy targets (such as missile silos) buried deep underground. Just prior to impact, an attacking nuclear warhead would release an earth penetrator into the ground. Earth penetrators could limit the harmful effects of a nuclear explosion. The U.S. considered using earth penetrators on PERSHING II MISSILES, but rejected the idea because of budget restraints and planning changes. The United States has been conducting research on earth penetrators since the 1970s, but they have not yet been deployed.

ECONOMIC FEASIBILITY addresses the issue of whether a nuclear weapon can be built at an acceptable cost. Economic feasibility is a major issue in the construction of any nuclear weapons system. The United States, for example, dismantled its SAFEGUARD antiballistic missile system in 1976, partly because its high cost did not make it economically feasible. It is considered in conjunction with SCIENTIFIC FEASIBILITY, TECHNICAL FEASIBILITY, and OPERATIONAL FEASIBILITY.

EIGHTEEN-NATION DISARMAMENT COMMITTEE (ENDC) see CONFERENCE ON DISARMAMENT

ELECTROMAGNETIC LAUNCHER   see ELECTROMAGNETIC RAIL GUN

ELECTROMAGNETIC PULSE (EMP) is a burst of radiation released immediately after a nuclear explosion. The EMP is essentially an electric field and a magnetic field moving away from the blast. The electromagnetic pulse burns out electronic circuitry, destroying communications systems, computers, and other sophisticated electronic instruments. The implications of the EMP are uncertain, but some experts assert that the EMP released by one large nuclear explosion over the central United States could cause an electrical blackout affecting the entire country. Further, it is possible that the EMP would damage the circuitry in missiles so that they would be unable to reach their targets. The EMP was first detected during a nuclear test at Johnston Island in 1962.

ELECTROMAGNETIC RADIATION   see RADIATION

ELECTROMAGNETIC RAIL GUN is a theoretical weapon that could be used to destroy attacking nuclear warheads and enemy satellites. The gun would fire small, computer-guided, nonnuclear projectiles at speeds approaching the speed of light. These projectiles, called SMART ROCKS, would not carry an explosive, but would destroy a target by impact. The U.S. is conducting research on electromagnetic rail guns under the STRATEGIC DEFENSE INITIATIVE, commonly known as "Star Wars." An electromagnetic rail gun, which would be deployed in space, is also known as a hypervelocity gun, rail gun, or electromagnetic launcher.

ELECTRON BEAM WEAPON is a hypothetical weapon that would disable incoming nuclear warheads. It would shoot a powerful stream of electrons that could focus enormous energy on incoming warheads and disable their inner electronics. An electron beam travels in a straight line toward its target. Under normal circumstances, its path is obstructed by the earth's magnetic field. However, an electron beam weapon would use a LASER (a highly concentrated beam of light) to clear a channel through the earth's magnetic field and enable the electron beam to strike its target. The laser beam would function like a snowplow that clears a path for automobiles on a snow-covered highway. The United States, which has been working intermittently since 1958 to develop an electron beam weapon, is conducting research on it under the STRATEGIC DEFENSE INITIATIVE.

ELECTRONIC COUNTER-COUNTERMEASURE (ECCM) is an action taken by one side to ensure the effective operation of its electronic equipment in response to an adversary's attempts to tamper with that equipment. ECCM is a general term that describes a variety of actions taken in response to an electronic countermeasure (ECM). For example, an attacker might try to disable an opponent's radar by broadcasting competing radar signals at the same frequency as the original signals. This type of action is an ECM. An appropriate electronic counter-countermeasure would involve broadcasting the original radar signals at an even higher frequency to cancel out the effects of the competing radar waves.

ELECTRONIC COUNTERMEASURE (ECM) is an action taken by an attacker to render ineffective the sensitive electronic equipment used by a defender against attacking missiles. An ECM attempts to confuse or temporarily disable an opponent's satellites, sensors, or missiles; it does not involve blowing them up. An example of an ECM is jamming an opponent's RADAR. Radar detects attacking missiles by analyzing radio waves reflected off an airborne missile. An ECM would involve broadcasting competing radio waves that could cover up the radio waves reflected off the missile. The radar would thus be ineffective, unable to detect the missile.

EMERGENCY ACTION MESSAGE (EAM) is the the means by which an order to release nuclear weapons is transmitted from the National Command Authorities (the United States President and Secretary of Defense) to the crew who launch the weapons. The specially coded EAM is received by two launch controllers, who must decode and validate it. The EAM must meet rigid specifications before command posts and launch crew members will accept its authenticity. As coding and decoding takes place, the process can be halted if an EAM fails to satisfy proper codes. The EAM contains the Nuclear Control Order (NCO), which actually directs the crew whether or not to launch nuclear weapons. The NCO can order the crew to launch all their missiles, some of their missiles, or only to prepare them for launching. Emergency Action Messages are transmitted over the PRIMARY ALERTING SYSTEM, also known as the Red Phone.

EMERGENCY ROCKET COMMUNICATION SYSTEM (ERCS) is a specially equipped "robot" missile that transmits emergency messages from Washington to sites where nuclear weapons are deployed. ERCS missiles are not armed with any kind of explosive; instead, their nosecones are packed with sophisticated radio transmitters. In a nuclear war, ERCS missiles could be launched as a backup means of beaming messages to U.S. missile installations and bomber bases. A small fleet of eight ERCS missiles is deployed in Missouri. ERCS has been described as "gimmicky," and some experts have expressed doubt that it could ever work. ERCS was first deployed in 1961.

ENCRYPTION is the process of placing a message into code. Encryption of TELEMETRY, the stream of technical data transmitted by missiles in flight, interferes with verification of arms-control agreements. Encryption of telemetry is prohibited by SALT I.

ENDOATMOSPHERIC DEFENSE refers to defense systems that intercept and destroy attacking nuclear warheads within the earth's atmosphere. They operate at altitudes of less than 300,000 feet. An example of an endoatmospheric defense is the Soviet Union's GALOSH system, which is deployed around Moscow.

ENHANCED RADIATION WEAPON (ERW)   see NEUTRON BOMB

ENIWETOK ATOLL is a small volcanic atoll in the Marshall Islands in the South Pacific. It was a major U.S. nuclear test site in the 1940s and 1950s. The U.S. now conducts its nuclear tests at the NEVADA TEST SITE in the western United States.

ENOLA GAY was the U.S. B-29 bomber that dropped the first atomic bomb on Hiroshima, Japan, on August 6, 1945. The plane was named for the mother of its pilot, Colonel Paul Tibbets.

ENRICHED NUCLEAR FUEL is uranium that has been refined so that it can be used in nuclear weapons and reactors. Uranium exists in nature in two varieties: uranium-238 (U-238) and uranium-235 (U-235). Almost all naturally occurring uranium is U-238, which cannot sustain a nuclear reaction. The percentage of U-235 (which can fuel a nuclear reaction) in the uranium mixture used in nuclear weapons and reactors must therefore be increased. This process, similar to strengthening a gin-and-tonic cocktail by adding more gin, is known as enrichment. Enrichment, a complex and expensive process, yields enriched nuclear fuel. Uranium enriched to about 90% U-235 is considered suitable for nuclear weapons.

ENRICHED URANIUM see ENRICHED NUCLEAR FUEL

ENRICHMENT is the technique for obtaining uranium to fuel nuclear weapons and reactors. Uranium exists in nature in two varieties: uranium-238 (U-238) and uranium-235 (U-235). Almost all naturally occurring uranium is U-238, which cannot sustain a nuclear reaction. The percentage of U-235 (which can fuel a nuclear reaction) must therefore be increased. This process is known as enrichment. Enrichment must be distinguished from REPROCESSING, the technique for obtaining PLUTONIUM from the mixture of waste products produced by a nuclear reactor. Enrichment is an extremely complex and expensive process, first developed in the United States during World War II. Enrichment technology has been closely monitored in an effort to prevent the proliferation of nuclear weapons. Enrichment was first developed by the U.S. during World War II.

ENVIRONMENTAL DEFENSE see DUST DEFENSE

EQUIVALENT MEGATONNAGE (EMT) is a complex unit often used to measure the total destructive power of two or more nuclear weapons exploded together over the same target. The principle behind EMT is that a combination of several small nuclear weapons will cause more damage than a single large weapon. For example, two 500-kiloton weapons would be more destructive than a single 1-megaton weapon. EMT is usually applied only to weapons targeted at unprotected areas, such as cities or industrial centers.

ESCALATION is any increase in the level of a conflict. Escalation essentially involves crossing a threshold. If desired results are not achieved at one level of force, one or both sides raises the ante. A classic example of escalation is the move from using conventional to nuclear weapons. In the nuclear sense, escalation is an important concept for two reasons. First, runaway escalation is a central element in most scenarios of all-out nuclear war. Second, controlled escalation is the cornerstone of the doctrine of LIMITED NUCLEAR WAR. According to this notion, which became official U.S. strategy in 1974, escalation can be limited so that only a small number of nuclear weapons are used in a conflict. See CONTROLLED ESCALATION.

ESCALATION CONTROLS are strategies intended to limit the use of nuclear weapons after they have been introduced into a conflict. Escalation controls would prevent an all-out nuclear holocaust and are the mechanism that would enable a limited nuclear war to be fought. Two types of escalation controls are commonly discussed: ESCALATION DOMINANCE and ESCALATION MATCHING. See CONTROLLED ESCALATION, LIMITED NUCLEAR WAR.

ESCALATION DOMINANCE is a strategy of maintaining an ability to remain superior to an enemy at every possible stage of a conflict. Escalation dominance would limit the escalation of a crisis by allowing a stronger nation to coerce a weaker nation into backing down during a conflict. The weaker nation would realize that launching an attack would invite undesirable consequences and it would thus seek conciliation rather than conflict.

ESCALATION MATCHING is a strategy of maintaining an ability to effectively counter an enemy at every possible stage of a conflict. Escalation matching relies on a willingness to match another nation blow for blow in a crisis. It is a strategy to limit the escalation of a crisis by allowing a nation to coerce another nation into backing down during a conflict and convincing the enemy of a nation's resolve. The second nation would realize that launching an attack would invite an equally destructive retaliation and it would thus seek conciliation rather than conflict.

ESSENTIAL EQUIVALENCE is a condition in which two nations' nuclear arsenals are roughly equivalent in capabilities and effectiveness, but do not contain numerically equal numbers of weapons. SALT I was based on essential equivalence: It allowed the Soviet Union to deploy greater numbers of weapons as compensation for U.S. technological superiority.

EUROMISSILES are nuclear missiles deployed in Europe and intended to strike deep behind enemy lines and into an opponent's homeland. The U.S., the U.S.S.R., Great Britain, and France currently deploy Euromissiles. Euromissiles have been very controversial and have complicated arms-control negotiations between the superpowers. Essentially, the problem is that American and Soviet Euromissiles serve different purposes. American nuclear missiles deployed in Western Europe pose a direct threat to the Soviet homeland, while Soviet Euromissiles do not threaten the continental United States. The U.S. contends that it is justified in deploying Euromissiles because it has a commitment to protect its NATO allies in Europe. The Soviet Union, however, has objected to U.S. missiles in Europe because they claim that the U.S. is not part of Europe and has no right to introduce its nuclear missiles there. The U.S.S.R., part of which is geographically in Europe, believes it is justified in deploying Euromissiles to protect itself from NATO forces. The American PERSHING II and the Soviet SS-20 are examples of Euromissiles.

EURO-STRATEGIC WEAPONS   see EUROMISSILES

EVASIVE REENTRY VEHICLE   see MARV

EXCALIBUR   see X-RAY LASER WEAPON

EXCIMER LASER WEAPON is a hypothetical weapon that would disable incoming nuclear warheads. Excimer laser weapons would have to be ground-based, because they are too bulky to be lifted into orbit. Excimer lasers generate highly concentrated beams of light that can quickly focus their energy on and disable a missile. The beam of an excimer laser weapon would be aimed at mirrors suspended in space. These mirrors would reflect the excimer laser beam onto an incoming warhead. Excimer is short for excited dimer (dimer refers to two linked atoms). Excimer lasers are formed by molecules made of two atoms tied together. When the linked atoms become unattached, they give off light. The United States is conducting research on excimer laser weapons under the auspices of the STRATEGIC DEFENSE INITIATIVE, commonly known as "Star Wars."

EXEMPLARY ATTACK   see NUCLEAR SHOW OF FORCE

EXISTENTIAL DETERRENCE is the concept that the uncertainty of the destructive power of modern nuclear weapons will deter a nation from launching a nuclear attack. Essentially, the idea is that a nuclear attack would have unknown consequences and could possibly destroy both an attacker and an enemy. Thus, a nation will voluntarily refrain from launching a nuclear attack out of the fear that it could backfire. Existential deterrence might result out of the fear of NUCLEAR WINTER. Nuclear winter is a hypothetical situation in which the earth would undergo severe and perilous climatic changes immediately following a nuclear war. Nuclear winter has raised speculation as to whether a nation would be endangering itself by launching a nuclear attack.

EXOATMOSPHERIC BURST see NUCLEAR EXOATMOSPHERIC BURST

EXOATMOSPHERIC DEFENSE refers to theoretical defense systems that intercept and destroy attacking nuclear warheads outside the earth's atmosphere. They operate at altitudes above 300,000 feet. The U.S. is conducting research on exoatmospheric defense under the STRATEGIC DEFENSE INITIATIVE, commonly known as "Star Wars."

EXTENDED DETERRENCE is a condition in which nations are restrained from attacking a superpower's allies or troops stationed abroad. In extended deterrence, no nation can threaten allies or overseas forces without inviting a devastating nuclear attack. The U.S. has followed a policy of extended deterrence in order to deter aggression against its NATO allies. In the post–World War II era, the United States has vowed to launch a nuclear attack in response to a Soviet invasion of Western Europe. Extended deterrence is also known as deterrence plus.

F

FAIL-DEADLY refers to a system that fires nuclear weapons without orders from authorities. A nuclear attack may prevent headquarters from sending orders to launch nuclear weapons. Crew officers could attribute this lack of communication to an enemy strike on command centers and decide to launch nuclear weapons on their own. In this way, crew officers would launch nuclear weapons independently, without instructions from authorities. Fail-deadly applies mainly to submarines. Fail-deadly is distinct from fail-safe, which applies to land-based missile crews. In fail-safe, crew officers maintain mechanisms that prevent the launching of missiles without proper orders and release codes.

FAIL-SAFE   see POSITIVE CONTROL

FALLOUT is composed of the debris from a nuclear explosion. When a nuclear weapon explodes, it destroys buildings, trees, people, and anything else in the area. Pulverized in the blast, this debris is drawn up into the earth's atmosphere. As it rises, fallout is bathed in radiation from the explosion. It is then picked up by air currents and carried around the earth. Fallout can remain in the atmosphere for months or years. It returns to the earth either under its own weight or in rain or snow. Fallout may be intensely radioactive, and can cause nausea, hair loss, internal bleeding, genetic damage, and cancer. Fallout is a particularly devastating effect of a nuclear explosion. Fallout created in an all-out nuclear war could cause millions of deaths and contaminate the earth's food and water supply. Fallout is also called radioactive fallout.

FALLOUT CITY   see SAINT GEORGE

FALLOUT PATTERN is the area that would be covered by dangerous radioactive FALLOUT following a nuclear explosion. Fallout
is radioactive debris created in a nuclear explosion. Fallout can
be extremely dangerous; exposure to it can cause genetic damage, radiation sickness, and cancer. A fallout pattern is usually
depicted as a cigar-shaped area downwind of the explosion.
However, predicting a fallout pattern is difficult. When trying
to project the fallout pattern that would follow a nuclear war,
stategists must take into account variables such as wind and
weather conditions, which might dramatically change in the
regions affected, making it difficult to predict a fallout pattern
accurately.

FALLOUT RADIATION consists of deadly radiation emitted from
FALLOUT, the debris created by a nuclear explosion. When a
nuclear weapon explodes, it pulverizes any objects in the area
and contaminates this debris with radioactive by-products. Contaminated debris, called fallout, is sucked up into the atmosphere and eventually falls back to earth. Fallout radiation
affects a wide area and may take weeks, months, or even years
to return to earth. Fallout radiation, released from by-products
of a nuclear explosion, is distinct from PROMPT RADIATION,
emitted during the detonation itself, which is released within
the first minute after a nuclear explosion. See RADIATION, IONIZ-
ING RADIATION, NUCLEAR RADIATION.

FALLOUT SHELTER is a sophisticated installation equipped to protect people for weeks or months from deadly radioactive fallout,
fires, and many other destructive effects of a nuclear attack. It
is thus distinct from a BLAST SHELTER, which is intended only
as a barrier between a person and the immediate destructive
effects of a nuclear explosion. In order to provide effective
protection, fallout shelters would have to be fitted with air filters
to keep out dangerous radioactive particles; an adequate self-
contained heating system; a device to detect radiation; and
enough medicine, food, and water for several months. Con-

struction of blast and fallout shelters is a CIVIL DEFENSE measure, intended to minimize the destruction caused in a nuclear war. No nation has constructed effective fallout shelters for the general public, but some fallout shelters have been built to protect important government authorities. Like other civil defense measures, construction of shelters may signal a willingness to fight a nuclear war and may thus be destabilizing.

FAST-BURN BOOSTER is a rocket that propels a BALLISTIC MISSILE into space and directs it toward its target. After it burns out, gravity takes over and pulls the missile to its target. Fast-burn boosters are specially designed to burn out rapidly, so that they can propel a missile into the upper atmosphere within 100 seconds or less. Because a missile is most vulnerable to enemy defenses during the portion of its flight in which booster rockets are ignited, fast-burn boosters could help missiles evade enemy defenses. Some experts claim that fast-burn boosters can be developed with available technology at a reasonable cost.

FAST FLYER is a nickname for a BALLISTIC MISSILE. A ballistic missile is propelled into the upper atmosphere by BOOSTER ROCKETS. After its rockets burn out, gravity takes over and pulls a ballistic missile to its target. Ballistic missiles characteristically travel very fast and carry powerful nuclear warheads. Author Strobe Talbott claims that U.S. President Ronald Reagan coined this term.

FAT MAN was the second atomic weapon used in World War II. It was dropped by the U.S. on NAGASAKI, Japan, on August 9, 1945. Fat Man, which was over ten feet long and weighed about 9,000 pounds, was also the second nuclear device to be fueled by PLUTONIUM. The first plutonium device was exploded in the Trinity Test at Alamogordo, New Mexico, in July 1945. Plutonium is a highly radioactive substance that today fuels most nuclear weapons. Fat Man was designed at Los Alamos, New Mexico, by a team of scientists led by J. Robert Oppenheimer. Along with Little Boy, the bomb dropped on Hiro-shima, Fat Man was the product of the MANHATTAN PROJECT, the U.S.'s wartime drive to build the first nuclear weapons.

FB-111 is a U.S. intermediate-range bomber. See INTERMEDIATE-RANGE BOMBER for a complete description of the FB-111.

FEDERAL EMERGENCY MANAGEMENT ADMINISTRATION (FEMA) is the U.S. government agency responsible for prepar-ing the nation for nuclear war. FEMA is authorized to plan for the recovery of the U.S. after a nuclear war; it is the govern-ment's primary organ for planning and carrying out civil de-fense. FEMA must also prepare and facilitate the recovery of the U.S. population in a wide range of emergencies.

FEDERATION OF AMERICAN SCIENTISTS (FAS) is an organiza-tion that educates the public on arms-control topics and has advocated various arms-control proposals in the years since World War II. It was founded in 1945 as the Federation of Atomic Scientists by veterans of the MANHATTAN PROJECT, the U.S.'s World War II drive to build the first nuclear weapons. The FAS is based in Washington, D.C., and has 5,000 mem-bers, including many prominent American scientists and engi-neers. The FAS has supported the LIMITED TEST BAN TREATY of 1963 and a NUCLEAR FREEZE, and has opposed the STRATEGIC DEFENSE INITIATIVE, commonly known as "Star Wars."

FERTILE MATERIAL   see FISSIONABLE MATERIAL

FIGHTER-BOMBER   see TACTICAL AIRCRAFT

FINITE DETERRENCE   see MINIMUM DETERRENCE

FIREBALL is the sphere of superheated, burning gas that forms immediately after a nuclear weapon is detonated. The fireball is a mini-sun—a blinding, intensely hot ball of energy, which hangs in the sky for as long as ten seconds after a nuclear explosion. The fireball emits thermal radiation, a concentrated wave of heat and light which can cause blindness, burns, and mass fires. The intensity of the fireball depends on the size of the nuclear weapon that is exploded.

FIREBREAK is the barrier that separates the use of conventional weapons from the use of nuclear weapons in a conflict. The firebreak is the psychological resistance to introducing nuclear weapons into a conflict. Since the close of World War II, nuclear weapons have never been used in battle. Many experts agree that this total restraint has been instrumental in preventing an all-out nuclear war. Once nuclear weapons (even small, battlefield nuclear weapons) are used, they argue, it becomes very difficult to prevent a conflict from escalating into a devastating nuclear holocaust. The firebreak is thus a barrier that aims to prevent a conflict from spreading into the nuclear realm. It is a concept borrowed from fire fighting, in which a firebreak is a temporary barrier constructed to prevent a blaze from spreading. Another name for firebreak is "the pause."

FIRESTORM, a massive conflagration which engulfs a wide area, such as a city, is one possible effect of conventional or nuclear explosions over a populated area. The tremendous heat released in a nuclear explosion can trigger a firestorm; once started, it is fed by gas mains, trees, gasoline tanks, and other flammable items. Firestorms are very destructive: They can burn for days and reach temperatures of 2,000 to 3,000°C. A firestorm occurred in Hiroshima, Japan, after the U.S. dropped the first atomic bomb in August 1945. Dresden, Germany, was also a victim of a firestorm after intense Allied conventional bombing during World War II.

FIRST-GENERATION WEAPONS   see GENERATION WEAPONS

FIRST STRIKE is a massive nuclear attack launched before an enemy has used nuclear weapons. The doctrine of deterrence has been developed in order to prevent the superpowers from launching a first strike. According to this concept, each superpower is able to absorb a first strike and then inflict an unacceptably destructive retaliation. In this way, any first strike would be suicidal. In accordance with deterrence theory, the superpowers have undertaken a variety of measures in order to prevent each other from being able to launch a first strike. Nonetheless, most scenarios of nuclear war depict a first strike as the "trigger" which would set off a devastating, all-out nuclear war.

FIRST-STRIKE CAPABILITY   see CREDIBLE FIRST-STRIKE CAPABILITY

FIRST USE is the introduction by one side of nuclear weapons into a conflict. The Soviet Union has made a NO FIRST USE pledge, in which it has vowed never to introduce nuclear weapons into a conflict. NATO, however, has reserved the right to first use, because it perceives the Soviet Union to have a decisive advantage in conventional forces in Europe. According to NATO policy, a Soviet conventional invasion of Western Europe could be countered with nuclear weapons.

FISSILE MATERIAL   see FISSIONABLE MATERIAL

FISSION   see NUCLEAR FISSION

FISSIONABLE MATERIAL is used to fuel nuclear reactors and weapons. When fissionable material is fissioned, or split, a tremendous amount of energy is released. URANIUM and PLUTONIUM are fissionable materials commonly used to fuel nuclear weapons. Fissionable material is sometimes called fissile material, nuclear material, or fertile material. Fissionable material that has been processed to fuel nuclear weapons is known as weapons-grade nuclear fuel or weapons-grade material.

FISSION-FUSION WEAPON is one type of THERMONUCLEAR WEAPON. Thermonuclear weapons are the most powerful type of nuclear weapons. In a fission-fusion weapon, an atom-splitting (fission) reaction generates very high temperatures, which trigger the combining of atoms (fusion). This fusion reaction, the same type of reaction that occurs in the center of the sun, releases tremendous energy. Fission-fusion weapons release highly dangerous PROMPT RADIATION; they are not, however, as destructive as FISSION-FUSION-FISSION WEAPONS. The NEUTRON BOMB is a fission-fusion weapon.

FISSION-FUSION-FISSION WEAPON is one type of THERMONUCLEAR WEAPON. Thermonuclear weapons are the most powerful type of nuclear weapons. In a fission-fusion-fission weapon, three basic steps take place. First, an atom-splitting (fission) reaction generates very high temperatures. This heat triggers the second step, the combining of atoms (fusion). Fusion, which releases tremendous energy, is the process that takes place in the center of the sun. The fusion reaction then triggers the final step, the fission of the TAMPER, the URANIUM shell that surrounds the core of the weapon. This third step can double the destructive power of the weapon, thus making fission-fusion-fission weapons the most powerful nuclear weapons currently in existence.

FISSION WEAPON   see ATOMIC WEAPON

FIXED LAUNCHER is an immobile structure that holds a nuclear missile in position ready for launch. Most fixed launchers are housed in underground missile silos, but a few are maintained aboveground. Because it is immobile, a fixed launcher is a "sitting duck" and could easily be destroyed in a nuclear attack. To make them less vulnerable, many underground fixed launchers are specially reinforced with concrete and earth. Most of the missiles deployed in the U.S. and the Soviet Union are positioned on underground fixed launchers. Fixed launchers are distinct from MOBILE LAUNCHERS, which are carried by trucklike vehicles or aircraft.

FLARE DUD is a nuclear weapon that explodes at a greater altitude than anticipated. Because it explodes higher than expected, its destructive power is not as great.

FLASH BURN is caused by exposure to a burst of THERMAL RADIA-
TION, the intense light and heat released by a nuclear explosion.
Flash burns result from a split-second exposure to radiation, and
can cause blindness or severe burns.

FLASH NUDET is U.S. military code for the detonation of a nuclear
weapon.

FLETCHER COMMISSION conducted an official study in 1983 to
assess the feasibility of a high-technology defensive shield against
attacking nuclear missiles. The Fletcher Commission evaluated
available technology and concluded that such a system could be
built. The commission recommended to President Ronald Reagan that the U.S. should pursue research leading to the establishment of a modern, innovative system to defend the United
States and its allies from nuclear attack and that the U.S. pursue
a comprehensive, "leakproof" defense. The Fletcher Commission was carried out in conjunction with the Hoffman Study,
which addressed the policy implications of building a defense
system to strike down attacking missiles. The Fletcher Commission, officially named the Defense Technologies Study, was led
by NASA administrator James Fletcher and conducted under
the auspices of the U.S. STRATEGIC DEFENSE INITIATIVE, commonly known as "Star Wars."

FLEXIBILITY has two different meanings. First, flexibility reflects a
nation's capacity to choose from a number of military options
during a conflict. For example, military leaders could decide
between fighting a war with nuclear or conventional weapons.
Second, flexibility is an approach in arms-control negotiations
in which one or both sides is willing to make concessions and
change its bargaining position.

FLEXIBLE RESPONSE is the strategy of countering enemy aggression with a variety of possible responses depending on the nature and seriousness of enemy aggression. Flexible response
could range from limited defense with conventional military

forces to all-out nuclear war. Flexible response replaced MASSIVE RETALIATION as official U.S. policy in the early 1960s. Massive retaliation was the policy of responding to communist aggression anywhere in the world with an all-out nuclear attack. Flexible response, however, usually involves using nuclear weapons as a last resort. Flexible response was adopted in 1967 as the official NATO strategy for responding to Soviet aggression against Western Europe. Flexible response is sometimes called controlled response or graduated response.

FOOTBALL is the nickname of the briefcase whose contents allow the U.S. President to launch a nuclear attack. The Football contains top-secret release codes and the BLACK BOOK, which outlines the President's options in the event of a nuclear war. The Football is usually carried by a military aide to the President and is always within the President's reach.

FORCE AÉRIENNE STRATÉGIQUE (FAS) is the branch of the French air force that is responsible for nuclear air strikes deep into enemy territory. Two types of aircraft serve in the FAS: the Mirage IVA and the Mirage 2000N. See MEDIUM-RANGE BOMBER for a complete description of these aircraft.

FORCE AÉRIENNE TACTIQUE (FAT) is the branch of the French air force that is responsible for nuclear air strikes over battlefield distances. France deploys three types of aircraft for such missions, the Jaguar A, the Mirage IIIE, and the Super Étendard.

FORCE DE FRAPPE is the nickname of the independent French nuclear arsenal. The force de frappe was conceived by French President Charles de Gaulle in 1963. Like its U.S. and Soviet counterparts, the force de frappe includes nuclear missiles based in underground missile silos and on submarines and bombers, and is intended to strike deep into the homeland of an enemy. France also deploys a considerable number of small nuclear weapons, intended for battlefield use. The existence of the force de frappe has complicated arms-control negotiations between the superpowers. The Soviets often include the force de frappe with U.S. and British nuclear weapons in determining the number of missiles deployed by NATO countries in Europe. But the U.S. contends that the force de frappe is truly independent from the U.S. In fact, France is not involved in the military branch of NATO and has developed independent strategies for the use of its nuclear weapons. The AILLERET DOCTRINE, the FOURQUET PLAN, and the MÉRY PLAN are examples of such strategies. Force de frappe translates roughly into English as "strike force."

FORCE EXCHANGES are mathematical predictions of how U.S. and Soviet nuclear arsenals would interact in the event of a nuclear war. Force exchanges allow military planners to predict the outcome of a nuclear attack and are important in formulating effective war-fighting strategy. Pen-and-paper mathematical predictions are one method for determining force exchanges. A second method involves computer-simulated war games that create mock nuclear war situations and results.

FORCE MANAGEMENT is the process of determining the effectiveness of a nuclear attack after it has been launched. Force management provides information necessary for reassembling military forces and selecting new targets during a nuclear war. Both the U.S. and the U.S.S.R. use advanced systems for conducting force management.

FORCE MULTIPLIER is the nickname for a basic discovery that leads to a dynamic innovation and major technical breakthrough. The discovery of how to split the atom during World War II was a force multiplier that ultimately led to the development of nuclear weapons.

FORCE STRUCTURE describes the composition of a nation's military forces. Many factors comprise a nation's force structure, including the size of its military, the types of weapons it deploys, and its personnel. The diversified manner in which the U.S.

deploys nuclear weapons is part of its overall force structure. The U.S. nuclear arsenal is built upon a foundation of nuclear weapons deployed in underground silos and on submarines and bombers.

FOREST GREEN   see NUCLEAR DETONATION DETECTION SYSTEM

FORWARD-BASED SYSTEMS (FBS) is a Soviet term for U.S. and Soviet nuclear weapons that are deployed beyond the homelands of the superpowers in order to protect allies. These weapons, also known as noncentral systems, include small, TACTICAL NUCLEAR WEAPONS and other nuclear weapons deployed overseas. U.S. and Soviet missiles in Europe are examples of forward-based systems. The Soviets coined the term forward-based systems during the SALT negotiations as an alternative to alliance or regionally oriented (related) systems, a U.S. term with a slightly different nuance. The Soviet term identified these weapons as existing only to defend superpower interests. In the Soviet view, the fact that forward-based systems are deployed outside a superpower's territory doesn't diminish a superpower's direct control over them. The U.S., however, wished to stress that these weapons are often deployed not to defend the U.S., but to defend allies.

FOURQUET PLAN, formulated by French Chief of Staff Michel Fourquet in 1968, was a strategy for the use of French nuclear weapons. The plan was based on a scenario in which the Soviet army had defeated NATO forces and was in a position to invade France. To judge whether the Soviets intended to attack France, a small nuclear warhead would be fired behind Soviet lines as a warning shot. This would be a "test of intentions," with the purpose of warning the Soviets of France's intention to launch a nuclear attack if invaded. The Fourquet Plan replaced the AILLERET DOCTRINE as France's nuclear strategy and was in turn replaced by the MÉRY PLAN in 1974.

FRACTIONAL ORBITAL BOMBARDMENT SYSTEM (FOBS) was a Soviet method for deploying a nuclear weapon in orbit above the earth. In the late 1960s, the U.S.S.R. began testing FOBS. The system involved launching an SS-9 missile armed with a nuclear warhead into space. Once in space, the missile would release its warhead in orbit above the earth. Suspended in orbit, the warhead would travel around the earth just like the moon. Unlike the moon, however, the warhead would not remain in orbit indefinitely. When the warhead reached a certain predetermined position above the earth it would reenter the atmosphere and drop toward its target. An ORBITAL BOMBARDMENT SYSTEM (OBS) was developed before FOBS, but it never went beyond the testing stage. OBS was similar to FOBS, but the warhead would have remained in orbit longer. A Soviet FOBS might have been operational in the early 1970s. Such systems were later specifically banned by SALT II.

FRACTIONATION is the practice of deploying several warheads on a single missile. Each warhead thus carries a fraction of the missile's total destructive power and allows a single missile to deploy warheads against many targets. This technology, known as MIRV (multiple independently targetable reentry vehicles), has been very controversial. Proponents argue that fractionation is a cheaper and more effective way of deploying nuclear missiles. Critics believe, however, that fractionation complicates arms-control negotiations because it is difficult to verify the number of warheads carried by a single missile. The SALT II accord of 1979 set numerical limits on the number of multiple-warhead missiles that the U.S. and the U.S.S.R. could deploy. Great Britain, France, and China also deploy missiles equipped with fractionation.

FRANCK REPORT, written near the close of World War II, recommended that U.S. atomic weapons be demonstrated over a deserted area and not used in an attack against Japanese cities. The Franck Report predicted that an atomic attack on Japan would create an unhealthy environment for the postwar control of nuclear arms; it also contains one of the first predictions of an unbridled postwar arms race. The INTERIM COMMITTEE, which was responsible for recommending to President Harry Truman how U.S. atomic weapons should be used, rejected the Franck Report and recommended that American atomic bombs be dropped on Japanese cities. The Franck Report, drawn up by a six-member committee of scientists chaired by James Franck, was dated June 11, 1945, a little less than two months before the atomic attack on Hiroshima.

FRATRICIDE is a phenomenon in which an attacking nuclear missile may reduce the effectiveness of subsequent missiles. When a nuclear weapon explodes, it produces a tremendous amount of lingering debris. If fratricide occurred, this debris would disable or destroy subsequent incoming warheads. Fratricide has been considered as a factor in protecting nuclear missiles against an enemy attack. Although the concept is widely disputed, it is believed that the if missiles are deployed in a closely based cluster of underground missile silos, fratricide will prevent an enemy attack from being effective.

FREE-ELECTRON LASER (FEL) WEAPON is a hypothetical weapon designed as part of a high-technology system for protecting against attacking nuclear missiles. Free-electron laser weapons would generate a concentrated, high-speed stream of light. This light beam could burn a hole in the skin of an attacking missile and deactivate the sensitive electronic equipment responsible for guiding it to its target. Free-electron laser weapons would function like super-concentrated spotlights; they would focus enormous energy on targets in order to destroy them. They could be deployed in space or on the ground. The

United States is conducting research on free-electron laser weapons under the STRATEGIC DEFENSE INITIATIVE, commonly known as "Star Wars."

FREE-FALL WEAPON is a nuclear weapon directed entirely by gravity. Free-fall weapons are not equipped with guidance systems to help them home in on their targets. The atomic bombs dropped on Hiroshima and Nagasaki, Japan, in August 1945 were free-fall weapons.

FREEZE   see NUCLEAR FREEZE

FROG-7 is a Soviet short-range ballistic missile. See SHORT-RANGE BALLISTIC MISSILE for a complete description of the Frog-7.

FUNCTIONAL KILL involves disabling, rather than blowing up, attacking warheads or enemy satellites. In a functional kill the outer surface of a target is penetrated and sensitive electronics inside are destroyed, causing a target to malfunction rather than explode. Since no explosion occurs in a functional kill, it is more difficult to verify. DIRECTED-ENERGY WEAPONS (DEW) are theoretical weapons that could be used in a functional kill. DEWs destroy their targets by focusing intense beams of energy on a warhead's surface. This directed energy can destroy a warhead or disable its sensitive electronics inside. A functional kill is also called a soft kill.

FUNCTIONALLY RELATED OBSERVABLE DIFFERENCES (FRODs) are structural, easily observed differences between aircraft that determine how an aircraft delivers its weapons and are directly related to the function of the aircraft. Bomb bay doors and wing pods are examples of FRODs. An aircraft with bomb bay doors drops bombs, while an aircraft with wing pods delivers CRUISE MISSILES. FRODs are particularly important in order to classify aircraft according to the guidelines of SALT II. FRODs are also able to be distinguished by satellites. In this way, FRODs allow both the U.S. and the U.S.S.R. to make sure each other is abiding by arms-control agreements.

FUSION   see NUCLEAR FUSION

FUSION WEAPON   see THERMONUCLEAR WEAPON

FUTURE SECURITY STRATEGY   see HOFFMAN STUDY

G

GAITHER COMMITTEE recommended in 1957 that the U.S. drastically increase military spending and embark upon a multibillion-dollar CIVIL DEFENSE program. Appointed by President Dwight Eisenhower and composed of prominent experts, the Gaither Committee direly predicted an increase in the arms race and continued escalation of the Cold War. President Eisenhower rejected the Gaither Report in favor of more moderate increases in U.S. military spending and attempts to negotiate arms-control agreements with the Soviets. California attorney Rowen Gaither chaired the Gaither Committee; its final report was written by arms-control expert Paul Nitze.

GALOSH is a Soviet ANTIBALLISTIC MISSILE (ABM) system that protects Moscow, the Soviet capital, from enemy nuclear attack. The Galosh system is designed to intercept and destroy incoming nuclear warheads. It is composed of RADAR tracking installations and Galosh missiles. Galosh is the only system of its kind in the world. The U.S. used to deploy a similar system, called SAFEGUARD, designed to defend a missile site in North Dakota. Safeguard was dismantled in 1976, however, because of high cost and technical ineffectiveness. The Soviets are modernizing and expanding the Galosh system during the mid-1980s. See BALLISTIC MISSILE DEFENSE SYSTEM.

GAMMA DECAY is one type of RADIOACTIVE DECAY, the process in which unstable elements release excess energy in order to become more stable. Elements that undergo gamma decay are created in the detonation of nuclear weapons. In gamma decay, unstable by-products of a nuclear reaction release gamma rays. Gamma decay can be extremely harmful to living organisms; it can cause radiation sickness, genetic damage, cancer, or death.

Gamma decay is distinct from ALPHA DECAY and BETA DECAY, in which alpha and beta particles are released. See RADIOACTIVE DECAY.

GAMMA RAY is a high-energy burst of radiation that is extremely dangerous to living cells. Gamma rays are released in two ways. First, a wave of gamma rays (called PROMPT RADIATION) is released immediately after a nuclear explosion. Second, a nuclear explosion creates by-products which are drawn into the atmosphere and disperse gamma rays (called FALLOUT RADIATION) over a wide area. Gamma rays cause severe cell mutations and are thus exceedingly harmful to living organisms. Protection from gamma rays is very difficult because they penetrate even thick concrete. Gamma rays were discovered by P. Villard in 1900.

GAPOSIS describes the American public's historical sensitivity to claims of U.S. nuclear inferiority. Since the 1950s, American public figures have raised alarming images of a missile gap, a bomber gap, an ABM gap, and a window of vulnerability, among others. These alleged deficiencies in the U.S. nuclear arsenal have been, for the most part, created for political purposes.

GENERAL AND COMPLETE DISARMAMENT (GCD) is a United Nations term for completely eliminating nuclear weapons. The United Nations General Assembly has established GCD as its goal in the field of disarmament. GCD involves abolishing nuclear weapons under a system of international control and aims to have nations defend themselves with nonnuclear arms. Nikita Khrushchev, General Secretary of the Soviet Union, introduced discussion of GCD at the United Nations General Assembly in 1959. During the last two decades, both the Soviet Union and the United States have submitted plans for General and Complete Disarmament to the United Nations. In most of these proposals, nations would agree to hand over inspection and control responsibilities to an international disarmament organization. The United Nations reaffirmed its commitment to GCD at its Special Session on Disarmament in New York in 1978.

GENERAL NUCLEAR RESPONSE is an all-out nuclear strike on an enemy. General nuclear response also forms part of NATO's policy of FLEXIBLE RESPONSE, which enables NATO to match enemy aggression with a variety of responses. NATO doctrine would authorize a general nuclear response if an enemy refused to back down during a conflict.

GENERAL WAR is an enormously destructive nuclear war, in which the superpowers exhaust their nuclear arsenals. Widespread death and devastation would result from a general war. Many scenarios portray general war as the result of uncontrolled escalation once nuclear weapons have been introduced into a conflict. General war is also called all-out war.

GENERATED ALERT is a situation in which a nation takes steps to prepare for war. In a generated alert, a nation increases the readiness of its forces from regular peacetime status to full war-fighting capacity, involving actions such as sending submarines out of port, spreading bombers out on a runway, and releasing nuclear weapons from storage facilities.

GENERATION WEAPONS establish categories for three types of nuclear weapons and characterize the technological advances made in the development of nuclear weapons.

- First-generation weapons are atomic weapons, which draw their destructive power from fission (atom-splitting). First-generation weapons were first developed by the United States during World War II, as part of the MANHATTAN PROJECT. They are the least powerful and the least sophisticated nuclear weapons.

- Second-generation weapons are thermonuclear weapons, which draw their destructive power from fusion (the forced combination of atoms). Second-generation weapons were first developed by the U.S. in the 1950s, and presently dominate the world's nuclear arsenal. They are the most powerful nuclear weapons.
- Third-generation weapons are specially modified thermonuclear weapons, which are designed to produce specific effects. They involve no new basic technology, but involve refinements on existing weapons. The NEUTRON BOMB, which creates a great deal of deadly radiation and a relatively small explosion, is an example of a third-generation weapon. Third-generation weapons are very controversial. Proponents claim that third-generation weapons must be developed, because they could be used effectively in a nuclear war and because they are the key to maintaining PARITY in the arms race. Critics, however, contend that third-generation weapons do not differ substantively from second-generation weapons and are thus merely a drain on national resources.

GENIE is a U.S. air-to-air missile. See AIR-TO-AIR MISSILE for a complete description of the Genie.

GEORGE SHOT was the world's first thermonuclear explosion. The United States conducted the George Shot on May 8, 1951, at Eniwetok Atoll in the South Pacific. The device exploded in the George Shot was an unwieldy experimental contraption, which could not be used as a weapon. However, the George Shot supplied information that was instrumental in the manufacture of the first THERMONUCLEAR WEAPON in 1952. Thermonuclear weapons, the most powerful nuclear weapons, reproduce the reactions that occur at the center of the sun. The George Shot produced a relatively small thermonuclear explosion.

GLICKUM is the nickname of a GROUND-LAUNCHED CRUISE MISSILE. It is derived from the initials GLCM.

GLOBAL BALLISTIC MISSILE DEFENSE SYSTEM (GBMD) see HIGH FRONTIER

GLOBAL RADIOACTIVE FALLOUT see DELAYED RADIOACTIVE FALLOUT

GO CODE is an official order for U.S. bombers to proceed beyond their last possible turnaround point and to make a final approach to their targets. It is issued by the NATIONAL COMMAND AUTHORITIES (the President and the Secretary of Defense).

GOLD CODES is the nickname of the codes that activate the release of U.S. nuclear weapons. Gold Codes are a random combination of numbers and letters, which are changed daily for security reasons. Gold Codes are submitted to the White House and to all installations where U.S. nuclear weapons are deployed. This has been the procedure since 1962, when President John Kennedy established the Gold Codes to enable a quick presidential decision to launch nuclear weapons.

GOLDEN ARCHES is a U.S. military slang term that describes an attacking nuclear missile's flight path as it streaks over the North Pole. Both American and Soviet nuclear missiles would fly over the North Pole in a nuclear war.

GOLF is a class of Soviet ballistic missile submarines. See BALLISTIC MISSILE SUBMARINE for a complete description of the Golf.

GOMULKA PLAN called for prohibiting any increase in nuclear weapons in central Europe. The Gomulka plan, forwarded by Polish Premier Wladyslaw Gomulka in 1964, specifically called for freezing at existing levels all nuclear weapons deployed in West Germany, East Germany, Poland, and Czechoslovakia. The plan was rejected by the NATO allies on the grounds that it was too limited in scope. The Gomulka Plan did not call for any reductions of the existing number of nuclear weapons. NATO wanted to link this type of partial arms-control plan to broader plans for general disarmament. In addition, NATO allies feared that the plan would seriously limit West Germany's military role in the alliance.

GRADUATED DETERRENCE is the strategy of matching enemy aggression with an equal or slightly higher level of force. Graduated deterrence is intended to prevent or minimize the escalation of a conflict. It aims to restrain enemy provocation by convincing it that any aggression will only invite blow-for-blow retaliation. In the early 1960s, the United States adopted a policy of graduated deterrence in order to counter what was perceived as a growing threat of Soviet aggression in Europe and Asia. Later, however, graduated deterrence was abandoned in favor of MUTUAL ASSURED DESTRUCTION (MAD). Unlike graduated deterrence, MAD relies on the superpowers' ability to inflict enormous damage even after absorbing a nuclear attack. In this way, MAD deters either superpower from introducing nuclear weapons into a conflict. Graduated deterrence is also known as proportional deterrence or controlled deterrence.

GRADUATED RESPONSE   see FLEXIBLE RESPONSE

GRAVITY BOMB   see NUCLEAR BOMB

GREENHAM COMMON is the site of a U.S. Air Force base outside London, England, where a well-known peace camp has been established in opposition to the deployment of new U.S. nuclear weapons. The peace camp, founded in 1981, is now constantly staffed by the so-called Greenham Common Women.

GREEN PARTY is a well-known West German political party that strongly opposes nuclear weapons. Since it was established in 1979, the Green Party has grown steadily and has gained several seats in the Bundestag, the West German parliament. It has given momentum to a rapidly growing West German peace movement, which strongly opposed the deployment of NATO nuclear missiles in West Germany in 1983. The Green Party, which is also very active in environmental issues, has been characterized as a leftist, one-issue political party. It advocates a nuclear-free West Germany as well as a nuclear-free NATO. In 1983, the Green Party held a widely publicized mock court case in which it tried the five nations that deploy nuclear weapons (China, France, Great Britain, the Soviet Union, and the United States) on the charge of conspiring to bring about a nuclear disaster.

GREENPEACE is an international environmental organization. Founded in Vancouver, British Columbia, in 1971, Greenpeace consists of 400,000 members in the U.S. and supports a worldwide ban on nuclear weapons testing. On July 10, 1985, the Greenpeace ship *Rainbow Warrior* was sunk by French intelligence agents in Auckland, New Zealand. A Greenpeace photographer was killed in the affair; the French government subsequently admitted its guilt. The ship was protesting French nuclear testing at Mururoa Atoll in the South Pacific. Greenpeace is headquartered in Lewes, England, and has branches throughout the world.

GREY AREA SYSTEMS are nuclear weapons that are difficult to classify and thus complicate arms-control negotiations. The Soviet Union's BACKFIRE bomber, which can be used for a variety of bombing missions, is an example of a grey area system. See THEATER NUCLEAR WEAPONS.

GROSS ERROR describes a nuclear attack that fails completely. A gross error occurs when a nuclear weapon explodes so far from its target that it causes no damage at all to the target.

GROUND ALERT is a state of readiness in which bombers are fully serviced and armed, ready to take off on short notice. The basic advantage of a ground alert is that bombers on ground alert can be sent into the air very quickly in the event of a nuclear attack. However, bombers on ground alert may be "sitting ducks" for a surprise enemy attack. Both the U.S. and the Soviet Union constantly maintain a number of bombers on ground alert.

Ground alert is distinct from AIRBORNE ALERT, in which bombers and their crews are kept in the air twenty-four hours a day.

GROUND-BASED ELECTRO-OPTICAL DEEP SPACE SURVEILLANCE (GEODSS) is a U.S. RADAR system designed to detect and track attacking nuclear missiles and bombers travelling high in the atmosphere or in space. GEODSS is designed to notify decision-makers if an enemy attack is underway so that they can take appropriate action. GEODSS uses a technology similar to that of television. Rather than store data on film to be processed later, as some less advanced radars do, GEODSS broadcasts its images almost instantly. The time saved with such broadcasting may be crucial if an enemy attack is underway. A GEODSS station was first deployed in New Mexico in 1981.

GROUND-BASED LASER WEAPON is a hypothetical weapon that would shoot a laser beam at an attacking nuclear missile. A ground-based laser weapon would be part of a high-technology system designed to defend against incoming nuclear warheads. Ground-based laser weapons would function like super-concentrated spotlights; they would focus enormous energy on targets in order to destroy them. In a system that uses ground-based lasers, a ground-based laser weapon would fire a powerful beam of highly concentrated light into the sky. This beam would be aimed at a mirror in orbit high above the earth. This mirror, called a RELAY MIRROR, would then reflect the beam at another mirror, positioned in orbit much closer to the earth. This mirror (called the BATTLE MIRROR) would, in turn, reflect the beam of light at an attacking missile. The light beam would burn a hole in the skin of the attacking missile and deactivate the sensitive electronic equipment responsible for guiding it to its target. Ground-based laser weapons are cheaper to build than space-based laser weapons, because their heavy apparatus would not have to be lifted into space. In addition, they are considered to be less vulnerable to an attack than laser weapons permanently suspended in space. The United States is conducting research on ground-based laser weapons under the STRATEGIC DEFENSIVE INITIATIVE, commonly known as "Star Wars."

GROUND BURST is a nuclear explosion on the ground. A ground burst affects only a relatively limited area, but it produces a great deal of deadly radioactive fallout. When a nuclear weapon explodes on the ground, it destroys anything in the area. The resulting debris is drawn up into the atmosphere. As it rises, this FALLOUT is bathed in radiation from the explosion. This radiation is extremely harmful and can cause nausea, hair loss, internal bleeding, genetic damage, and cancer. A ground burst is distinct from an AIR BURST, in which the explosion takes place above the ground. An air burst affects a wider area but causes less fallout than a ground burst. A ground burst is sometimes called a surface burst.

GROUND LAUNCHED CRUISE MISSILE (GLCM) is a CRUISE MISSILE launched from the ground. Cruise missiles are slow, low-flying highly accurate missiles that resemble pilotless airplanes. Unlike BALLISTIC MISSILES, which are powered by BOOSTER ROCKETS, cruise missiles are powered by jet engines. The Soviet Union will deploy one type of GLCM:

- SSC-X-4 is a Soviet GLCM that will be deployed in the mid-1980s. The missile will have a range of 3,000 km and will be deployed within the U.S.S.R. The SSC-X-4 will serve as a THEATER NUCLEAR WEAPON (intended to be used in a broad geographical region, such as Europe or the Far East) and will be launched from a trucklike vehicle.

The United States also deploys one type of GLCM:

- The U.S. GLCM is a modified version of the Navy's TOMAHAWK CRUISE MISSILE. The ground-launched Tomahawk, known popularly as "the Cruise," is one of the controversial EUROMISSILES deployed by NATO in the mid-1980s. It has a range of 2,500 km and delivers a yield of .3 to 80 kilotons.

GROUND RADAR see RADAR

GROUND SHOCKS are waves of energy that travel through the earth after an underground nuclear explosion. When a nuclear device is detonated beneath the surface, the energy travels from the explosion like ripples moving away from a pebble thrown into still water. Since most nuclear weapons tests are conducted underground, ground shocks are an important means of verifying a nuclear weapon's explosions. Both the U.S. and the U.S.S.R. have facilities to detect ground shocks and thus monitor each other's nuclear testing. Ground shocks are also created by earthquakes.

GROUND WAVE EMERGENCY NETWORK (GWEN) is a U.S. communications system network designed to relay messages during a nuclear war. GWEN consists of 300 to 500 large radio towers set up around the United States and Canada. It is specially designed to enable U.S. military leaders to send undisrupted messages in a nuclear war.

GROUND ZERO is the point on the ground directly under a nuclear explosion. Ground zero is the focus of a nuclear weapon's destructive energy. Ground zero is also known as the hypocenter.

GUIDANCE SYSTEM directs a GUIDED MISSILE to its target. Guidance systems detect and correct deviations from the missile's planned flight path. Depending on the sophistication of the guidance system, guided missiles can be very accurate. Two basic systems are used to guide missiles: INERTIAL GUIDANCE and COMMAND GUIDANCE. Inertial guidance is completely self-contained within a missile; command guidance involves transmitting electronic signals through space. This process occurs in a manner similar to the way a child directs a radio-controlled airplane.

GUIDED MISSILE is a general term for a missile whose flight is continually adjusted during its flight. Almost all missiles in the world's nuclear arsenals are guided missiles. GUIDANCE SYSTEMS detect and correct deviations from the missile's planned flight path. Depending on the sophistication of the guidance system, guided missiles can be extremely accurate. Two basic systems are used to guide missiles: INERTIAL GUIDANCE and COMMAND GUIDANCE. Inertial guidance is completely self-contained within a missile; command guidance involves transmitting electronic signals through space. This process occurs in a manner similar to the way a child would direct a radio-controlled airplane.

GUN-ASSEMBLY is one method of detonating an atomic weapon. In a gun-assembly weapon, such as LITTLE BOY (the bomb dropped on Hiroshima in 1945), a small conventional explosion projects one lump of fuel into a second lump, forming a CRITICAL MASS. A critical mass is the minimum amount of nuclear material necessary to fuel a nuclear explosion. When a critical mass is formed, a reaction occurs that leads almost immediately to an atomic explosion. The gun-assembly method is the simplest way to achieve a critical mass.

H

HADES is a French short-range ballistic missile. See SHORT-RANGE BALLISTIC MISSILE for a complete description of the Hades.

HAIR TRIGGER refers to the condition in which both superpowers are poised to launch a nuclear attack at the slightest provocation. The term describes the situation that exists at command and control centers, the locations where nuclear weapons are launched and enemy nuclear attacks are monitored. Because decisions to launch nuclear weapons must be made in a matter of minutes, officials at command and control centers are under a great deal of pressure if they receive an indication of an enemy attack. They may lack time to carefully evaluate options and might thus make a disastrous miscalculation. The hair-trigger notion is often used in scenarios that portray the launching of an accidental nuclear attack.

HALF-LIFE is the amount of time necessary for a radioactive element to lose half of its radioactivity. A nuclear explosion creates many highly radioactive by-products. The half-life indicates the amount of time that these by-products will retain their deadly radioactivity. Half-lives vary greatly from element to element, from a few millionths of a second to billions of years. Many elements produced in a nuclear explosion have extremely long half-lives. Deadly radiation created in a nuclear explosion may thus remain in the environment for thousands or millions of years.

HARDBODY is a slang term for a nuclear missile streaking toward its target that has been identified by a defensive system. A hardbody would be extremely difficult to destroy because the enormous trail of heat it would emit would effectively conceal its precise location from enemy sensors.

HARDENED SILO is an underground missile silo that has been protected against an enemy nuclear attack by reinforcement with concrete, steel, earth, and other materials in order to withstand the effects of a nuclear attack. The term hardened silo is most commonly applied to missiles housed in underground concrete silos mounted on steel springs and fitted with armored blast doors. A hardened silo is also known as a hard missile base.

HARDENING is reinforcing something with layers of concrete, earth, steel, and other materials to make it less vulnerable to a nuclear attack. Underground missile silos are hardened because they are "sitting ducks" and are thus particularly vulnerable to an enemy nuclear strike. Hardening is also used to protect vital command centers where military personnel coordinate the use of nuclear weapons. The NORTH AMERICAN AEROSPACE DEFENSE COMMAND (NORAD), the U.S. command center that monitors for a nuclear attack and would launch U.S. nuclear weapons in a nuclear war, is embedded in a mountain in Colorado. Hardening is also known as base hardening.

HARD KILL occurs when a target, such as a satellite or attacking missile, is blown up. A FUNCTIONAL KILL, also known as a soft kill, is the opposite of a hard kill and involves disabling a target rather than actually destroying it. A hard kill is desirable because it is easily verified. If a hard kill occurs, a defense system can use its time and ammunition on other targets. A functional kill, though harder to verify, can be just as effective in stopping a satellite or missile from performing its function.

HARD MISSILE BASE   see HARDENED SILO

HARD-POINT DEFENSE   see HARD-SITE DEFENSE

HARD-SITE DEFENSE is a system deployed to defend missile sites and other installations that have been fortified (hardened) against a nuclear attack. Probable targets of an enemy nuclear attack are commonly hardened with concrete, earth, steel, and other materials. The United States deployed a hard-site defense (called SAFEGUARD) in the 1970s to defend Minuteman missile silos in North Dakota. Safeguard was dismantled in 1976, however, because of high cost and technical ineffectiveness.

HARD TARGET is a target that has been reinforced to protect against an enemy nuclear attack. Hard targets have been fortified with thick layers of concrete, steel, earth, and other materials in order to withstand the effects of incoming nuclear missiles. Examples of hard targets are missile silos and facilities that control the launching of nuclear weapons. Attacking missiles must be extremely accurate in order to destroy hard targets. Hard targets are less vulnerable than SOFT TARGETS, such as cities, which have not been equipped to resist a nuclear attack.

HARD TARGET KILL CAPABILITY see LETHALITY

HARPOON is a U.S. antiship CRUISE MISSILE that can be launched from planes, submarines, or surface ships. It was originally planned as a dual-capable missile, able to carry both conventional and nuclear warheads. In 1980, however, development of a nuclear-armed Harpoon was abandoned.

HARRY SHOT was a U.S. nuclear test conducted at the NEVADA TEST SITE on May 19, 1953. Nicknamed "Dirty Harry," the test created the most radioactive fallout ever measured in any populated area in the U.S. It contaminated a broad area, including the town of St. George, Utah. Cancer rates of St. George residents are significantly greater than the national average.

H-BOMB see THERMONUCLEAR WEAPON

HEAT SENSOR see INFRARED SENSOR

HEAVY BOMBER is the term used in SALT II to identify the types of aircraft limited in the treaty. Essentially, heavy bombers are the same thing as LONG-RANGE BOMBERS; their range is intercontinental and they can deliver nuclear or conventional weapons. However, SALT II also specifically defines heavy bombers as any bombers that can deliver air-to-surface BALLISTIC MISSILES or AIR-LAUNCHED CRIUSE MISSILES with a range greater than 600 km. Currently, U.S. B-52 and B-1B and Soviet Tu-95 Bear and Mya-4 Bison bombers are classed as heavy bombers.

HEAVY MISSILE is a BALLISTIC MISSILE that is considerably larger and more powerful than other ballistic missiles. Ballistic missiles are propelled into the upper atmosphere by booster rockets. After the rockets burn out, they fall down through the atmosphere, pulled by gravity to their targets. The precise definition of a heavy missile has always been a point of contention between the U.S. and the U.S.S.R. Generally, the main criteria for judging whether a missile is heavy includes the strength of the missile's warhead(s) as well as the missile's size and weight. During the SALT I negotiations both the American TITAN II intercontinental ballistic missile (ICBM) and the Soviet SS-9 ICBM were described as heavy, but no common definition of the term was agreed upon. For SALT II, the Soviet SS-19 ICBM was used as an official measuring stick for whether a missile was heavy or light. Any ICBM that was as large and powerful as the SS-19 was considered a heavy missile, while any ICBM smaller and less powerful was considered a light missile. Traditionally, the Soviet nuclear arsenal has included many more heavy missiles than the U.S. nuclear arsenal. A heavy missile is also known as a modern large ballistic missile.

HEIGHT OF BURST refers to the vertical distance between the target and the point at which a nuclear weapon is exploded. See OPTIMUM HEIGHT OF BURST.

HEN HOUSE is the U.S. name for a Soviet radar system that detects attacking nuclear missiles. First deployed in the 1960s, the Hen House is a highly sophisticated radar that can track many objects simultaneously. Hen House radars are located on the periphery of the Soviet Union.

HIBAKUSHA is the Japanese word for a survivor of the U.S. atomic bombing of Hiroshima during World War II.

HIGH AIR BURST is a nuclear explosion high above the ground. When a nuclear weapon explodes above the ground, its destructive effects are spread over a wider area than if the weapon is detonated on the ground. For example, it may create a surge of radiation that could cripple computers and other sensitive electronic instruments for hundreds or thousands of miles. A high air burst is distinct from a LOW AIR BURST, in which the explosion takes place closer to the surface, and from a GROUND BURST, in which a nuclear weapon explodes on the surface. A high air burst causes significantly less dangerous radioactive FALLOUT (radioactive debris) than a low air burst or a ground burst.

HIGH-ENERGY LASER   see LASER

HIGH FRONTIER is a private organization that promotes the concept of a strategic defense to defend the Unites States against a nuclear attack. In 1982, High Frontier issued a report that urged the U.S. to develop a space-based defense system. They envisioned placing in orbit 432 satellites armed with missiles to destroy attacking nuclear warheads in the event of a nuclear war. High Frontier contends that the technology is available for such a defense system and estimated the cost at $15 billion. This system could violate both the OUTER SPACE TREATY of 1967 and the ANTIBALLISTIC MISSILE TREATY of 1972. High Frontier acts as a lobbying group for the STRATEGIC DEFENSE INITIATIVE, commonly known as "Star Wars."

HIGH-RISK AREAS are areas most likely to be attacked in a nuclear strike. High-risk areas include missile silos, radar tracking installations, and major cities.

HIROSHIMA is the Japanese city that was the target of the first atomic bomb. At 8:16 A.M. on August 6, 1945, the United States exploded the first atomic bomb (called LITTLE BOY) about 600 yards above central Hiroshima. The bomb's destructive power was small by today's standards; nevertheless, it completedly devastated the city. Approximately 130,000 people died in the blast or within the next three months from injuries sustained in the explosion. Eighty percent of Hiroshima's buildings were obliterated in the blast, and Japan surrendered less than one month later. Hiroshima is located on the southeast coast of Honshu, Japan's principal island. It has been almost completely rebuilt and today contains the corporate headquarters of the Mazda Corporation.

HOFFMAN STUDY was one of two reports authorized by President Ronald Reagan in 1983 under the United States' STRATEGIC DEFENSE INITIATIVE. The study addressed the policy implications of building a system for defending against attacking BALLISTIC MISSILES. It concluded that an effective BALLISTIC MISSILE DEFENSE (BMD) SYSTEM would reduce the likelihood of a nuclear war. The Hoffman Study, however, recommended that the U.S. maintain a strong and modern arsenal of nuclear weapons, and at the same time develop a BMD system to protect against a nuclear attack. The Hoffman Study was carried out in conjunction with the FLETCHER COMMISSION's report, which assessed details concerning the technology necessary to build an effective BMD system. The Hoffman Study, led by defense analyst Fred Hoffman, is officially known as the Future Security Strategy.

HOLLANDITIS describes a condition in which popular movements against nuclear weapons gain widespread support among a nation's general public. The term refers to the Netherlands (Holland), the traditional leader of the European antinuclear movement.

HOMING is a technique by which a missile locates and directs itself to its target. In homing, there must be something that attracts the missile to its target. This could be heat, radio waves, or magnetism. Once the missile has noticed this stimulus coming from the target, it moves toward the target. Homing is similar to the technique by which a bloodhound tracks its prey. A bloodhound is sensitive to smell. Once it has picked up the scent of its prey, it moves in the direction where the scent is strongest. This method eventually brings it directly to its prey. Homing is a very effective way of destroying a target and is used with both nuclear and conventional weapons.

HOMING DEVICE is an instrument that allows a missile to locate and travel toward its target. A homing device includes sensors to detect a specific stimulus given off by the target. This stimulus could be heat, radio waves, or magnetism. Once the homing device has picked up the target's "scent," it directs the missile to the source of the stimulus, the target. The nose of a bloodhound can be thought of as a homing device. The dog uses its nose to pick up the scent of its prey and distinguish where the scent is coming from.

HONEST JOHN is a U.S. short-range ballistic missile. See SHORT-RANGE BALLISTIC MISSILE for a complete description of the Honest John.

HORIZONTAL PROLIFERATION is the spread of nuclear weapons to nations that do not currently possess them. Horizontal proliferation is distinct from VERTICAL PROLIFERATION, which refers to a significant expansion of existing nuclear arsenals.

HOTEL is a class of Soviet ballistic missile submarines. See BALLISTIC MISSILE SUBMARINE for a complete description of the Hotel.

HOT LAUNCH is a technique of firing a nuclear missile that damages the underground silo in which the missile is housed. In a hot launch, a missile's booster rockets are ignited while the missile is still in its silo. The rockets, which propel the missile into space and direct it toward its target, damage the silo with their heat and force. The principal disadvantage of a hot launch is that it prevents the reuse of a silo for an additional launch until the silo has been repaired. Hot launch is distinct from a COLD LAUNCH, which leaves the silo undamaged.

HOT LINE is the direct communications link between the United States and the Soviet Union. It enables the leaders of both nations to communicate with one another in order to prevent misperceptions leading to accidental nuclear war. The Hot Line allows one side to notify the other in the event of an accidental nuclear launch or explosion. Established in 1963 and modernized in 1971, the Hot Line consists of two satellite links which connect bilingual teleprinters in Washington and Moscow. A backup land-based link runs via London and Helsinki. The Soviet Union has established similar hot lines with Great Britain and France.

HOT LINE AGREEMENT (1963) is a bilateral agreement between the Soviet Union and the United States that establishes a direct communications link between Moscow and Washington. The Hot Line enables the leaders of both nations to communicate with one another in order to prevent misperceptions leading to accidental nuclear war. Two systems were set up as a result of the Hot Line Agreement, one a radio telegraph circuit and the other a wire telegraph circuit. These systems were improved in the Hot Line Modernization Agreement of 1971. The U.S.S.R. worked out similar agreements with France in 1966 and with Britain in 1967.

HOT LINE MODERNIZATION AGREEMENT (1971) is a bilateral agreement between the Soviet Union and the United States that improves the direct communications link between Moscow and Washington. The Hot Line enables the leaders of both nations to communicate with one another in order to prevent misperceptions leading to accidental nuclear war. Two satellite communications circuits were established as a result of the Hot Line Modernization Agreement. The original wire telegraph circuit remains as a backup. Details for further modernization were established in July 1984, after a year of bilateral negotiations. The capability for more rapid exchange of messages as well as the transmission of graphic material over the system were established in those talks.

HUDSON INSTITUTE is a private research organization that analyzes nuclear weapons issues. Located in Indianapolis, Indiana, the Hudson Institute was founded by American defense analyst Herman Kahn in 1960. The institute specializes in the study of nuclear war-fighting strategies and CIVIL DEFENSE. It has advocated development of defense systems to strike down attacking enemy warheads and measures for protecting civilian populations during nuclear war.

HURRICANE TEST was the detonation of the first British atomic weapon. Conducted on October 31, 1952, at the Monte Bello Islands off Australia, the test involved the detonation of an atomic weapon inside a British naval vessel, the HMS *Plym.*

HYDROGEN BOMB see THERMONUCLEAR WEAPON

HYPERVELOCITY GUN see ELECTROMAGNETIC RAIL GUN

HYPOCENTER see GROUND ZERO

I

IF DETERRENCE FAILS is an expression that refers to a breakdown in the factors that restrain the Soviet Union and the United States from launching a nuclear attack. With limited means for defending against a nuclear strike, both superpowers rely on their ability to inflict enormous damage on each other. In this way, they attempt to deter one another from launching a nuclear attack. Thus, NUCLEAR DETERRENCE between the superpowers is based on each side's capacity to absorb a nuclear strike and then counter with an unacceptably destructive retaliation. If deterrence fails (if either superpower is not deterred from launching a nuclear attack), then a nuclear war would be more likely.

IMAGING RADAR is a hypothetical device that would be part of a high-technology system for protecting against attacking nuclear missiles. As an attacking nuclear missile streaks toward its target, it may release many decoys and other harmless debris in addition to its nuclear warheads. These decoys are intended to enable actual warheads to evade defenses, which cannot normally distinguish between decoys and real warheads and therefore would waste time and ammunition destroying decoys. Imaging radar would be able to solve this problem by distinguishing between decoys and real warheads. It would thus enable defense systems to concentrate on destroying only attacking nuclear warheads. Imaging radar would be based in space. The U.S. is conducting research on imaging radar under the STRATEGIC DEFENSE INITIATIVE, commonly known as "Star Wars."

IMPLOSION is one method of triggering a nuclear explosion. In order for a nuclear explosion to occur, a minimum amount of suitable material (called a CRITICAL MASS) must be present. Implosion accomplishes this by compressing a hollow sphere of nuclear material into a critical mass. Implosion technology was developed by the U.S. during World War II and was used to trigger the atomic bomb dropped on NAGASAKI, Japan, in 1945.

IMPLOSION WEAPON is any nuclear weapon that is triggered by implosion.

IMPULSE KILL involves destroying attacking nuclear warheads or enemy satellites by striking the target's surface with a powerful pulse of energy. After initial impact, a shock wave would travel through the target and make it collapse. Essentially, this is the same process by which slamming an oven door makes a cake collapse. DIRECTED-ENERGY WEAPONS (DEWS) are theoretical weapons that could be used in a impulse kill. This directed energy can destroy a warhead or disable the sensitive electronics located inside.

INDEPENDENT DETERRENT describes a nuclear arsenal that is not under the control of one of the superpowers. France's nuclear arsenal has been characterized as an independent deterrent since the mid-1960s, when it withdrew from NATO. Although Great Britain maintains its own nuclear arsenal, it is not considered to have an independent deterrent, because its nuclear forces are under the control of NATO. An independent deterrent allows the country possessing it to respond to a nuclear threat independently of the superpowers.

INDIRECT APPROACH is a negotiating strategy of settling major political disputes before discussing nuclear arms control. Indirect approach is distinct from DIRECT APPROACH, which identifies nuclear arms as the central issue in negotiations. An example of indirect approach was the U.S. linkage strategy of the 1970s, which attempted to resolve issues such as Soviet human rights violations as a precondition to nuclear arms-control agreements.

INERTIAL GUIDANCE is a self-contained system that directs a missile as it streaks toward its target. Preprogrammed instruments, called accelerometers, are located within the the missile and determine its proper speed, position, and acceleration. This information is then used to determine in-flight adjustments in the missile's flight path. Because the inertial guidance system is contained totally within the missile and not dependent on outside transmissions, it is not affected by atmospheric conditions or jamming of electronic signals by an enemy. Inertial guidance is sometimes called the "computer brain" of a missile, because it has control over a missile's flight.

INFRARED SENSOR is a device that detects heat. Infrared sensors identify a target by detecting the heat it gives off. Infrared sensors have many uses. First, both the U.S. and the U.S.S.R. use space-based infrared sensors to detect BALLISTIC MISSILE launches. These sensors detect the trail of hot rocket exhaust left in the wake of a ballistic missile after it is launched. Infrared sensors could also be used in a modern defense system to detect attacking warheads as they streak toward their targets. Infrared sensors would notice the heat of an attacking warhead against the cold background of outer space; the warhead would stand out like a hot ember among cold ashes. Finally, infrared sensors can help guide an attacking missile to its target. Certain missiles are designed to hit anything emitting heat. Jet aircraft and missiles emit heat in their engine exhaust. A missile equipped with an infrared sensor could detect this heat and thus fly toward its target. Infrared sensors are also known as thermal or heat sensors.

INITIAL RADIATION see PROMPT RADIATION

INSERTABLE WARHEAD see CLIP-IN WARHEAD

INTEGRATED OPERATIONAL NUCLEAR DETECTION SYSTEM (IONDS) see NUCLEAR DETONATION DETECTION SYSTEM

INTERACTIVE DISCRIMINATION is a theoretical method for distinguishing attacking nuclear warheads from harmless decoys and could be an important component in a high-technology system to defend against a nuclear attack. This technique involves transmitting neutral particle beams, which can penetrate the skin of warheads and decoys and positively identify them from the inside. While warheads and decoys appear identical, warheads are significantly heavier than decoys because they are filled with electronic equipment and nuclear material. A warhead struck by a neutral particle beam also emits telltale gamma rays while an empty decoy does not. The U.S. is conducting research on interactive discrimination as part of the STRATEGIC DEFENSE INITIATIVE, commonly known as "Star Wars."

INTERCEPTOR MISSILE is a missile that homes in on and destroys an attacking nuclear warhead. Currently, all interceptor missiles are deployed on the ground. Examples include the Soviet Union's GALOSH interceptor missile and the United States' GENIE and retired SPRINT and SPARTAN interceptor missiles. Both the superpowers are limited to 100 interceptor missiles by the Antiballistic Missile Treaty of 1972.

INTERCHURCH PEACE COUNCIL (IKV) is one of Europe's largest antinuclear organizations. Established in 1966, the IKV includes all major Christian churches, both Protestant and Roman Catholic, in the Netherlands, consisting of 400 chapters and 20,000 members. Its long-term goal is worldwide nuclear disarmament; its immediate objective is removal of nuclear weapons from Dutch soil. The IKV claims that it is not anti-American or anti-NATO. In 1977, it introduced a campaign against nuclear weapons under the slogan "Help rid the world of nuclear weapons, let it begin in the Netherlands." The Netherlands is considered by many to have the most active antinuclear movement in the world. The initials IKV are derived from the Dutch words for Interchurch Peace Council.

INTERCONTINENTAL BALLISTIC MISSILE (ICBM) is a land-based BALLISTIC MISSILE that can travel between the U.S. and the U.S.S.R. in about 30 minutes. ICBMs are propelled into the upper atmosphere by booster rockets. After the rockets burn out, the missile falls down through the atmosphere, pulled by gravity to its target. ICBMs, commonly housed in underground missile silos, are the most powerful and accurate nuclear weapons. However, because they are immobile, they could be vulnerable to a nuclear attack. They have a range of over 5,500 km and can carry one or many nuclear warheads. ICBMs were developed by the superpowers in the 1950s. The Soviet nuclear arsenal is dominated by ICBMs; the U.S. has balanced its ICBM force with submarine-launched ballistic missiles and strategic bombers. China's nuclear arsenal also contains a small number of ICBMs. The U.S. deploys four types of ICBMs:

- Titan II is the oldest, most powerful, and least accurate U.S. ICBM. Titan missiles will be phased out by the late 1980s. First deployed in 1963, the Titan II has a range of 12,000 km and delivers a single 9-megaton warhead. Because it is not very accurate, the Titan is targeted at vulnerable cities and industrial centers. It is the only liquid-fueled ICBM in the U.S. nuclear arsenal.
- Minuteman II was first deployed in 1966 and is the most powerful and least accurate of the Minuteman missiles. Along with the other Minuteman missiles, it comprises the backbone of the U.S.'s ICBM force. It has a range of 12,500 km and delivers one warhead with a yield of 1.2 megatons.
- Minuteman III was first deployed in 1970 and is the least powerful of the Minuteman missiles. It has a range of 14,000 km and carries 3 warheads, each with a yield of 170 kilotons.
- Minuteman III (Mk 12A) was first deployed in 1979 and is essentially a more powerful version of the Minuteman III. It has a range of 14,000 km and carries 3 warheads, each with a yield of 335 kilotons.

The Soviet Union deploys seven types of ICBMs:

- SS-11 Sego is the oldest Soviet ICBM and was first deployed in 1966 with a single 1-megaton warhead. Modernized versions, which deliver three 100- to 300-kiloton warheads, have been deployed since 1973. Like most Soviet ICBMs, the SS-11 is liquid-fueled. The SS-11 is gradually being replaced in the 1980s by the more advanced SS-19.
- SS-13 Savage has been deployed since 1968 and was the first Soviet solid-fueled ICBM. The SS-13 was a technical failure; only 60 have been deployed. It carries a single 750 kiloton warhead.
- SS-17 has been deployed since 1975 and carries four 750-kiloton warheads. A modernized version, which has been deployed since 1977, carries a single 6-megaton warhead.
- SS-18 is the largest and most powerful Soviet ICBM. The original version of the SS-18, deployed since 1975, carries a massive 20-megaton warhead. A modernized version was first deployed in 1982 and carries up to ten 500-kiloton warheads.
- SS-19 carries either six 550-kiloton warheads or a single 10-megaton warhead. Deployed since 1979, the SS-19 is among the most accurate and powerful Soviet ICBMs. It is gradually replacing older SS-11 and SS-13 ICBMs in the Soviet nuclear arsenal.
- SS-24 will be deployed in the late 1980s. It will be solid-fueled and will carry 10 warheads. The SS-24 will replace the SS-17.
- SS-25 will be deployed in the late 1980s. It will be solid-fueled and will carry a single nuclear warhead. The missile is very controversial. According to the terms of SALT II, both the U.S. and the U.S.S.R. are allowed to develop one new ICBM system. The U.S. argues that the SS-25 is a totally new missile and its development violates SALT II because the Soviets are already developing the new SS-24. The Soviets claim the SS-25 is not a new missile, but a modification of an existing ICBM, the SS-13, and thus does not violate the treaty.

In addition, the People's Republic of China deploys two types of ICBMs:

- CSS-3 was first deployed in 1978 and has a range of 7,000 km. It carries a single 1-megaton warhead.
- CSS-4 was first deployed in 1980 and has a range of 12,000 km. It carries a single 5- to 10-kiloton warhead.

INTERFERENCE is a general term that has two different meanings. First, interference involves hindering a nation's attempts at verifying arms-control agreements. In this sense of the word, interference could include denying another nation information about weapons testing. Under SALT II, which limited the number of nuclear weapons the U.S. and the U.S.S.R. could deploy, both nations agreed to refrain from this type of interference. Second, interference refers to actions taken to render ineffective an opponent's electronic equipment. JAMMING is an example of this type of interference. Jamming involves directing electronic noise at an opponent's radar. Jamming could drown out the opponent's radar signals and make it incapable of detecting attacking nuclear warheads.

INTERIM COMMITTEE advised President Harry Truman on how U.S. atomic weapons should be used in World War II and in the immediate postwar period. The committee was formed in 1945 and chaired by Secretary of War Henry Stimson. The Interim Committee briefly considered detonating the U.S.'s atomic weapons in a deserted area, in order to intimidate the Japanese into surrendering and establish an environment conducive to postwar nuclear arms control. This idea was expressed in the FRANCK REPORT, submitted to the committee on June 11, 1945. Stimson's committee rejected the Franck Report, however, and recommended to Truman that American atomic bombs be dropped on Japan. The committee also rejected sharing the secret of atomic weapons with the Soviet Union.

INTERIM OFFENSIVE WEAPONS AGREEMENT (1972) see
SALT I

INTERMEDIATE-RANGE BALLISTIC MISSILE (IRBM) is a theater nuclear weapon, intended to be used in a broad geographical
region, such as Europe or the Far East. IRBMs are propelled
into the upper atmosphere by BOOSTER ROCKETS. After the
rockets burn out, they fall down through the atmosphere, pulled
by gravity to their targets. IRBMs have a range of 2,750 to
5,500 km. This range is less than that of INTERCONTINENTAL
BALLISTIC MISSILES but greater than that of MEDIUM-RANGE
BALLISTIC MISSILES and SHORT-RANGE BALLISTIC MISSILES. The
United States does not currently deploy any IRBMs. The Soviet
Union, however, deploys two types of IRBMs:

- SS-5 Skean has a range of 5,000 km and carries a single
  1-megaton warhead. The missile was first deployed in 1961
  and was rapidly being replaced in the mid-1980s by the more
  advanced SS-20.
- SS-20, first deployed in 1977, has a range of 5,000 km. It is
  one of the most modern missiles in the Soviet nuclear arsenal
  and is far more accurate than other Soviet missiles. The SS-20
  can carry three 150-kiloton warheads and is transported to
  fixed launch sites on trucklike vehicles in order to increase its
  ability to survive a nuclear attack. The missile is solid-fueled.
  The SS-20 has been viewed as a "wonder weapon" by the
  U.S., considered far superior to existing Soviet systems.
  NATO used the SS-20's deployment as justification for the
  introduction of the controversial EUROMISSILES (TOMAHAWK
  CRUISE MISSILES and Pershing II missiles) into Western
  Europe in the mid-1980s.

In addition, the People's Republic of China deploys one type
of IRBM:

- CSS-2 was first deployed in 1972 and has a range of 2,600 km.
  The missile carries a single 2- to 3-megaton warhead.

France also deploys one type of IRBM:

- S-3 is solid-fueled and was first deployed in 1980. France deploys about eighteen S-3 IRBMs from its Plateau d'Albion launch site in southern France. The S-3 carries a single 1-megaton nuclear warhead and has a range of 3,500 km.

INTERMEDIATE-RANGE BOMBER is any aircraft capable of delivering nuclear and conventional weapons over a broad geographical region, such as Europe or the Far East. Intermediate-range bombers have a range of 3,680 to 9,200 km. Intermediate-range bombers may, if they are equipped for in-flight refueling or if they are sent on a one-way mission, deliver strategic nuclear weapons against the homelands of the superpowers. Intermediate-range bombers are distinct from MEDIUM-RANGE BOMBERS and LONG-RANGE BOMBERS. The Soviet Union deploys one type of intermediate-range bomber:

- Tu-22m/26 Backfire, first deployed in 1974, is among the most advanced Soviet bombers. It has a range of 8,000 km and can carry either gravity bombs or AIR-LAUNCHED CRUISE MISSILES. The Backfire's role is a matter of controversy between the U.S. and the U.S.S.R. The Soviets claim that the bomber is intended for use in Europe and is thus not a strategic bomber. Because the Backfire's range can be increased by in-flight refueling, however, the U.S. argues the bomber can be used for strikes against the continental U.S. and must be classified as a strategic bomber.

The United States also deploys one type of intermediate-range bomber:

- FB-111, first deployed in 1969, is highly effective at penetrating well-defended areas. Its overall effectiveness, however, is limited by its small size and limited range. It can deliver short-range attack missiles and small gravity bombs. Its range can be increased from 5,500 to 8,650 km with midair refueling. The FB-111 will be replaced by the STEALTH BOMBER in the mid-1990s.

INTERMEDIATE-RANGE NUCLEAR FORCES (INF) are nuclear weapons designed for use in specific areas, such as Europe and the Far East. INF could be used to strike deep into Western or Eastern Europe; they are not intended for use over intercontinental distances between the U.S. and the U.S.S.R. Most debate over INF concerns nuclear weapons deployed in Europe. European INF include several types of weapons. U S Pershing II INTERMEDIATE-RANGE BALLISTIC MISSILES (IRBMS) and TOMAHAWK CRUISE MISSILES deployed in Western Europe are INF that pose a direct threat to Soviet territory. In this sense, the Soviets see American INF as partially serving a strategic role, since they can strike the Soviet homeland. Soviet SS-20 and SS-4 IRBMs threaten U.S. allies in Western Europe but do not pose a threat to U.S. territory. The Soviets also deploy SS-20 IRBMs against China and Japan. British and French nuclear forces are also a part of European INF. The exact classification of these weapons has been a point of contention between the U.S. and the U.S.S.R. The Soviets group the British and French forces with the U.S. INF. The U.S. contends, however, that the British and French forces are truly independent and should not be included in the total of U.S. INF. INF are also referred to as longer-range theater nuclear forces (LRTNF) and theater nuclear forces.

INTERMEDIATE-RANGE NUCLEAR FORCES (INF) TALKS were a series of bilateral negotiations between the U.S. and the U.S.S.R. that sought to limit the number of nuclear weapons deployed in Europe. INTERMEDIATE-RANGE NUCLEAR FORCES (INF) are nuclear weapons that can strike deep into Western or Eastern Europe. The INF talks focused on a number of issues. The Soviet Union was concerned with the proposed U.S. deployment of Pershing II MEDIUM-RANGE BALLISTIC MISSILES and TOMAHAWK CRUISE MISSILES in Western Europe because these missiles could hit targets in the Western part of the Soviet Union. The U.S. opposed the Soviet deployment of SS-20 medium-range ballistic missiles that could be used against the homelands of the U.S.'s NATO allies. The nuclear arsenals of Great Britain and France were also major issues during the INF talks. The Soviets grouped the British and French forces with U.S. nuclear weapons deployed in Europe. The U.S. contended, however, that the British and French forces were truly independent and thus should not be included in the total of U.S. INF. Little progress was made in the INF talks and the U.S.S.R. broke off negotiations with the first deployment of Pershing II and cruise missiles in December 1983. The INF talks were initiated by the U.S. as part of the DUAL-TRACK DECISION to simultaneously deploy nuclear missiles in Western Europe and pursue arms-control negotiations. The INF talks were held intermittently in Geneva, Switzerland, between 1981 and 1983.

INTERNATIONAL ATOMIC ENERGY AGENCY (IAEA) is a United Nations agency that promotes cooperation among nations to develop atomic energy for peaceful purposes. The IAEA was first proposed by U.S. President Dwight Eisenhower in 1953 and was established by the U.N. in 1957. One of its purposes is to provide nuclear material to nations for research purposes. The IAEA has drawn up rigid safeguards to prevent the military use of FISSIONABLE MATERIAL that it supplies. These safeguards are outlined in what is known as the IAEA Blue Book. The IAEA also monitors nuclear power plants in nations without nuclear weapons that have signed the Nonproliferation Treaty of 1968. These inspections are conducted in order to verify that fissionable material is not being used to make nuclear weapons. Headquartered in Vienna, Austria, the IAEA also sponsors research projects and conducts studies on the health and safety hazards of atomic energy.

INTERNATIONAL DISARMAMENT ORGANIZATION (IDO)
see GENERAL AND COMPLETE DISARMAMENT

INTERNATIONAL INSTITUTE FOR STRATEGIC STUDIES

(IISS) is a research organization that deals with arms-control and disarmament issues. Established in 1958, the IISS is well known for its principal publication, *Military Balance*, which has been published annually since 1959. *Military Balance* is considered by many to be an authoritative source on nuclear weapons statistics, technology, and information. It is used widely by governments and the media. The IISS also publishes the periodical *Adelphi Papers* eight times each year.

INTERNATIONAL PHYSICIANS FOR THE PREVENTION OF NUCLEAR WAR (IPPNW)

is a federation of different national groups that seeks to publicize the harmful effects of nuclear war. IPPNW, which consists of about 135,000 physicians from over 40 countries, both East and West, was founded by American cardiologist Bernard Lown and Soviet cardiologist Yevgeny Chazov in Geneva in 1980. IPPNW's members aim to prevent nuclear war because of their professional commitment to protect life and preserve health. IPPNW promotes research and discussion of the psychological and medical effects of nuclear war. In 1982, the IPPNW sponsored a historic program on Soviet television featuring three Soviet and three American doctors discussing the medical consequences of nuclear war. IPPNW gained international attention in 1985 when Lown and Chazov were each awarded a Nobel Peace Prize for their efforts. IPPNW has urged nations to use the money they spend on nuclear weapons for health education and the elimination of poverty instead. It has advocated a worldwide ban on the testing of nuclear weapons and has supported a verifiable freeze on the production of nuclear weapons.

INTRAWAR DETERRENCE

is a strategy for limiting the scope of a nuclear war once it has broken out. Intrawar deterrence would involve matching enemy aggression with an equal or slightly higher level of force. Intrawar deterrence aims to compel an enemy to surrender by convincing it that further nuclear attacks will only invite blow-for-blow retaliation. Intrawar deterrence is also called compellence.

INVENTORY is a slang term that refers to the nuclear weapons that a nation has deployed. A nation's inventory are all its weapons that are ready to be used in the event of a nuclear war. Nuclear weapons in storage are not included in a nation's inventory.

IONIZING RADIATION is a type of radiation which is extremely harmful to living cells. Massive amounts of ionizing radiation are created in a nuclear explosion. Ionizing radiation attacks DNA, interferes with cell reproduction, and causes mutations that may be severe. Exposure to large doses of ionizing radiation may cause cancer and death. Ionizing radiation is particularly harmful to cells in the digestive tract and bone marrow. See NUCLEAR RADIATION, THERMAL RADIATION

ISOTOPE is a different variety of a single element. Two different isotopes are essentially the same substance, they just contain a different number of neutrons in their nuclei. For example, uranium-235 and uranium-238 are isotopes of uranium. Uranium-238 contains three more neutrons than uranium 235. Isotopes usually have different physical properties (uranium-235 is much more radioactive than uranium-238). The physical differences of different isotopes are important in a nuclear context for two reasons. First, only a few isotopes are suitable for fueling a nuclear weapon. It is critical to have the correct isotope if the weapon is to work. Second, certain isotopes emit potentially deadly RADIATION. Many of these radioactive isotopes, commonly called RADIOISOTOPES, are created in a nuclear explosion.

J

JACKSON AMENDMENT TO SALT I was a measure to guarantee that the United States would seek numerically equal limits with the Soviet Union in arms-control agreements. In previous arms-control agreements, such as SALT I, the U.S. had allowed the Soviet Union to deploy larger numbers of nuclear weapons as compensation for U.S. technological superiority. The Jackson Amendment maintained that the U.S. would no longer allow this numerical imbalance. The amendment was introduced by U.S. Senator Henry "Scoop" Jackson and approved by the Senate when it ratified SALT I.

JAMMING is a technique for rendering ineffective an opponent's sensitive electronic equipment. Jamming is used specifically against any device that transmits signals. It involves the transmission of a competing signal to drown out a signal transmitted by an opponent's SATELLITES or RADAR. Essentially, jamming works on the same principle as playing two different radio staions at once. A listener cannot clearly distinguish classical music from jazz music if they are both being broadcast at the same time. Jamming can be used to disrupt the communications signals being broadcast from a satellite and to drown out radar signals that detect attacking warheads. Jammers, electronic devices that jam an opponent's signals, are frequently deployed to disrupt radio communications on earth.

JOE I is the American name for the first Soviet atomic explosion, conducted on August 29, 1949. Joe I shocked much of the world because it demonstrated the speed with which the Soviet Union had acquired the secret of atomic weapons. After Joe I, the U.S.'s monopoly on NUCLEAR WEAPONS came to an end. Threatened by this perceived sudden shift in the balance of power (made worse by the success of the communist revolution in China in the same year), the United States decided to pursue development of thermonuclear weapons, the so-called super-bomb project. American physicist J. Robert Oppenheimer named Joe I for Josef Stalin, the leader of the Soviet Union.

JOE 4 is the U.S. name for the first Soviet thermonuclear explosion, conducted on August 12, 1953. THERMONUCLEAR WEAPONS, the most powerful type of nuclear weapons, create the same type of reaction that occurs at the center of the sun. The device exploded in Joe 4 was an unwieldy experimental contraption not adaptable as a weapon. However, Joe 4 supplied information that was instrumental in the manufacture of the first Soviet thermonuclear weapon in 1955. The test was named for Josef Stalin, the leader of the Soviet Union.

JOINT EMERGENCY EVACUATION PLAN (JEEP) is the American plan for evacuating a select number (about 250) of high-level government employees in a nuclear war. These people are selected because they will help run the country during and after a nuclear war.

JOINT STRATEGIC TARGET PLANNING STAFF (JSTPS) is a group of representatives from the United States military services that together choose the targets for America's nuclear war plan. The war plan itself is developed by the JSTPS under guidelines from the Joint Chiefs of Staff. The director of the JSTPS is the commander of the STRATEGIC AIR COMMAND and its deputy director is a naval officer. Established in 1960 and headquartered in Omaha, Nebraska, JSTPS includes repre-sentatives from the air force, navy, marines, and army, as well as from NATO allies.

JOINT SURVEILLANCE SYSTEM (JSS) is a U.S. RADAR system that detects attacking enemy bombers. JSS is designed to notify decision-makers if an enemy attack is underway so they can take appropriate action. JSS is a joint system because it is operated by the air force and the Federal Aviation Administration. It was first deployed in 1982 and consists of 59 stations positioned on the borders of the continental United States.

JUPITER MISSILE   see CUBAN MISSILE CRISIS

K

KEEP-OUT ZONE is the area around a target in which a nuclear warhead must explode in order to destroy the target. An effective defense system would have to keep all attacking warheads out of this zone to protect the target. A keep-out zone can be thought of as a balloon around a target, with the target floating in the middle of the balloon. Any warhead that breaks through the balloon would destroy the target. The more powerful and accurate the attacking warhead, the larger the keep-out zone.

KILL ASSESSMENT is the process of distinguishing destroyed targets from surviving targets. Kill assessment is an important part of any system for defending against incoming nuclear warheads, because it prevents wasting time and ammunition protecting targets that are already destroyed.

KILLER SATELLITE   see ANTISATELLITE WEAPON

KILLIAN PANEL recommended in 1954 that the United States significantly improve its overall military posture. The Killian Panel suggested that the U.S. establish a large force of long-range nuclear missiles, develop defensive missiles to protect against enemy nuclear attack, and construct a high-altitude spy plane (the U-2). The panel also concluded that a stalemate would inevitably result in the nuclear arms race so that "attack by either side would result in mutual destruction." President Dwight Eisenhower adopted most of the Killian Panel's recommendations. The Killian Panel was chaired by M.I.T. President James Killian.

KILL RADIUS is the area around a nuclear explosion within which all people are killed. The kill radius can vary, depending on the size and type of weapon, and on where and how it is used.

KILOTON (kt) is a unit used to measure the amount of energy released in a nuclear explosion. One kiloton is equivalent to the energy released in the detonation of one thousand tons of TNT. One thousand kilotons equal one MEGATON. The bomb dropped on Hiroshima, Japan, released about 13 kilotons of energy.

KILOTON WEAPON is a nuclear weapon with a destructive force of less than one megaton. One megaton is equal to one thousand kilotons and is equivalent to the energy released in the detonation of one million tons of TNT. Kiloton weapons are less powerful than MEGATON WEAPONS; they usually are tactical or THEATER NUCLEAR WEAPONS, intended for use on the battlefield or within a specific geographic region, such as Europe or the Far East. Most weapons built since the early 1970s have been kiloton weapons, which in general are more accurate and easier to deploy than megaton weapons.

KINETIC ENERGY WEAPON (KEW) is a theoretical weapon designed as part of a high-technology shield against attacking nuclear missiles. A KEW would shoot nonnuclear projectiles at attacking warheads. These projectiles, called KINETIC KILL VEHICLES, would disable a warhead by impact. They would not carry an explosive. Instead, the destructive force would come from the collision between the projectile and its target. Kinetic energy weapons would utilize kinetic energy, which is the energy of motion. KEWs could be positioned on the ground or in space. The United States is conducting research on kinetic energy weapons under the STRATEGIC DEFENSE INITIATIVE, commonly known as "Star Wars."

KINETIC KILL VEHICLE (KKV) is a small, high-speed rocket that could theoretically destroy attacking nuclear weapons or satellites. KKVs would be fired from KINETIC ENERGY WEAPONS. They would not carry an explosive. Instead, the destructive force would come from the collision between the projectile and its target. KKVs could be launched either from the ground or from space. They would be used especially to intercept incoming warheads in their final flight phase. The United States is conducting research on kinetic kill vehicles under the STRATEGIC DEFENSE INITIATIVE, commonly known as "Star Wars."

KNEECAP   see NATIONAL EMERGENCY AIRBORNE COMMAND POST (NEACP)

KOKURA is a Japanese city that was the primary target of the atomic bomb dropped on NAGASAKI on August 9, 1945. On that morning, Kokura was shrouded in bad weather, and the mission's commander decided to drop the bomb on the secondary target, Nagasaki.

L

LADAR is a theoretical technique for detecting an attacking nuclear warhead. In ladar, highly concentrated beams of light (LASERS) would be bounced off an attacking nuclear warhead and reflected back to a sensor. The sensor would analyze the laser beam as it returns to determine the warhead's distance and speed. The information revealed by ladar would help aim weapons to destroy an attacking warhead. Ladar is similar to RADAR, but would use laser light instead of radio waves. The word ladar is a combination of laser and radar.

LANCE is a U.S. short-range ballistic missile. See SHORT-RANGE BALLISTIC MISSILE for a complete description of this missile.

LASER is a device that generates a highly concentrated beam of light. Laser beams travel at the speed of light and can retain their intensity over thousands of miles of space. Laser weapons could be part of a high-technology system for protecting against attacking nuclear missiles by generating extremely powerful laser beams, which would burn a hole in the skin of attacking missiles and deactivate the sensitive electronic equipment responsible for guiding them to their targets. Laser weapons would thus function like superconcentrated spotlights; they would focus enormous energy on targets in order to destroy them. Laser beam weapons must be distinguished from PARTICLE BEAM WEAPONS, which generate streams of particles instead of light. The United States is conducting research on laser weapons under the STRATEGIC DEFENSE INITIATIVE, commonly known as "Star Wars." Laser is an acronym for Light Amplification by Stimulated Emission of Radiation.

LASER WEAPON see LASER

LATIN AMERICAN NUCLEAR-FREE ZONE TREATY (1967)   see TREATY OF TLATELOLCO

LAUNCH CONTROL CENTER (LCC) is an American underground command post that coordinates the launching of land-based nuclear missiles. Two officers are placed in each LCC at all times. Safeguards prevent any one crew officer from launching a nuclear attack individually. Instead, the two crew officers must act together to fire a missile. When an encoded launch order, called an EMERGENCY ACTION MESSAGE, is transmitted to an LCC, the crew must decode and validate it. The methods for interpreting and authenticating the code are kept in a double-locked safe, to which each officer has a key.

LAUNCHER is a structure that holds a nuclear missile in position ready for launch. Launchers have been particularly important in arms-control negotiations, where they have served as the means by which the superpowers have assessed and imposed limits on their nuclear arsenals. Launchers may be deployed on land, at sea, or in the air, and may be either moveable or fixed in position. Mobile launchers may be mounted on trucklike vehicles, trains, submarines, or aircraft. Because its exact position is difficult to fix, a mobile launcher would be difficult to destroy in a nuclear attack. A fixed launcher, on the other hand, cannot move around and thus would be a "sitting duck" in a nuclear attack. Most fixed launchers are housed in underground missile silos. Launchers fire many different types of nuclear weapons, from small, battlefield artillery shells to mammoth BALLISTIC MISSILES capable of devastating entire cities.

LAUNCH–ON–IMPACT (LOI) is an order to launch nuclear weapons following the arrival of an enemy nuclear strike. The purpose of a launch-on-impact is to wait for definite confirmation of an enemy nuclear attack before launching a retaliatory strike. It would be used to determine the intent and extent of an enemy attack to help determine how to most appropriately respond. Launch-on-impact is also known as launch-through-attack.

LAUNCH-ON-TACTICAL-WARNING   see LAUNCH-ON-WARNING

LAUNCH-ON-WARNING (LOW) is a nuclear attack launched in response to an indication of incoming enemy nuclear missiles. The decision to inititate a launch-on-warning is made before enemy missiles actually strike their targets. An LOW is launched to ensure that missiles are not destroyed before they can be used. This idea is sometimes referred to as "use 'em or lose 'em." Launch-on-warning is distinct from LAUNCH-THROUGH-ATTACK, which is delayed until enemy nuclear missiles have struck their targets. Launch-on-warning is also known as launch-on-tactical-warning.

LAUNCH-THROUGH-ATTACK (LTA) is a nuclear attack launched in response to an enemy nuclear attack. The decision to launch-through-attack is delayed until after enemy nuclear missiles have struck their targets. It is intended to reduce the risk of accidental nuclear war. Launch-through-attack is distinct from LAUNCH-ON-WARNING, which is launched in response to an indication of an enemy nuclear attack. Launch-through-attack is also known as launch-on-impact.

LAUNCH TUBE is a structure that holds a nuclear missile in position for launch on board a submarine.

LAUNCH-UNDER-ATTACK (LUA) is a nuclear attack launched in response to an indication of incoming enemy nuclear missiles. A launch-under-attack is virtually synonymous with a launch-on-warning. Unlike a launch-on-warning, however, a launch-under-attack involves the launching of land-based nuclear missiles only. Both strategies involve a decision to initiate a nuclear attack before enemy missiles actually strike their targets. An LUA is intended to account for the perceived vulnerability of land-based missiles; it is launched to ensure that land-based missiles are not destroyed before they can be used. This idea is sometimes referred to as "use 'em or lose 'em."

LAUNCH-WEIGHT is the weight of a fully loaded BALLISTIC MISSILE at the moment it is launched. Launch-weight is the sum of all a ballistic missile's components, including its warheads, fuel, electronics, and the booster rockets that lift it off the ground and propel it into space. Launch-weight must be distinguished from THROW-WEIGHT, which does not include the weight of a missile's booster rockets. Launch-weight is one criterion for judging the strength of a ballistic missile, but throw-weight is used more commonly.

LAWRENCE LIVERMORE NATIONAL LABORATORY (LLNL) is one of three major U.S. facilities for the development of nuclear weapons technology. LLNL was founded in 1952 and is located in Livermore, California. LLNL and its rival, the Los Alamos National Laboratory, have designed all the nuclear weapons ever built by the United States. Sandia National Laboratory, the third major U.S. nuclear weapons research facility, designs special features, such as fuses. LLNL was founded partly as a result of the strained relations between physicist Edward Teller and the leadership at Los Alamos. Over the years, LLNL and Los Alamos have engaged in friendly competition. It has been called the Lawrence Livermore laboratory since the death of physicist Ernest O. Lawrence in 1958. LLNL is where much of the research for the American STRATEGIC DEFENSE INITIATIVE (commonly known as "Star Wars") is being conducted. The University of California runs LLNL under contract from the federal government.

LAYERED DEFENSE is a theoretical missile defense system that would be designed to destroy attacking BALLISTIC MISSILES during any of the four stages of a missile's flight. An attacking ballistic missile's flight is divided into BOOST PHASE, POST-BOOST

PHASE, MIDCOURSE PHASE, and TERMINAL PHASE. During each of these phases a layered defense system would attempt to destroy a missile. Each layer acts as a back-up to the previous layer. In this way, each layer acts as a safety measure in case one part of the system is not totally effective. In a layered defense, an attempt would be made to destroy attacking ballistic missiles almost immediately after they are launched in order to relieve the burden on succeeding defense layers. The concept of layered defense is a central component of the United States' STRATEGIC DEFENSE INITIATIVE, commonly known as "Star Wars." Layered defense is also known as multilayered or multitiered defense.

LETHALITY refers to a missile's ability to destroy a target reinforced against nuclear attack, such as a missile silo. Unprotected targets, such as cities, are almost certain to be destroyed by an incoming missile. HARD TARGETS, however, can better withstand the effects of a nuclear blast. Lethality is a complex determination based on a missile's ACCURACY and its destructive power (YIELD). Of these two factors, accuracy is far more important in determining lethality. In recent years, the superpowers have built smaller, very accurate missiles, with a very high degree of lethality. Lethality has many other names, including countermilitary potential, hard target kill capability, silo-busting potential, and warhead lethality.

LEVERAGE refers to the advantage gained in destroying attacking BALLISTIC MISSILES as soon as possible. Time is an important factor in leverage. The sooner ballistic missiles are destroyed, the greater the leverage will be. Leverage is a key aspect of a LAYERED DEFENSE, which attempts to destroy attacking ballistic missiles throughout their flights. In a layered defense, an attempt would be made to destroy attacking ballistic missiles almost immediately after they are launched in order to relieve the burden on a succeeding defense layers.

LIMITED NUCLEAR OPTION (LNO) refers to the choices commanders have for using nuclear weapons in a conflict. Limited nuclear options would be the means by which a LIMITED NUCLEAR WAR would be fought. In such a war, authorities would launch nuclear weapons only at certain carefully chosen military targets, such as railroads, factories, and enemy tank divisions. In theory, it would be possible to confine the use of nuclear weapons to these limited nuclear options. Diplomatic and conventional military efforts would be coordinated with LNOs in a limited nuclear war. Many experts have challenged the notion of LNOs; they contend that once nuclear weapons have been introduced into a conflict, it would be impossible to prevent the fight from escalating into a full-scale nuclear war.

LIMITED NUCLEAR WAR (LNW) is a strategy which holds that a small number of nuclear weapons can be used in a conflict in order to attain specific objectives. Limited nuclear war has its roots in the late 1950s, and was announced as official U.S strategy by Secretary of Defense James Schlesinger in 1974. Essentially, limited nuclear war has three important implications. First, LNW assumes that use of nuclear weapons would be coordinated with diplomatic and conventional military efforts in a conflict. Second, LNW implies that an all-out holocaust is not inevitable if nuclear weapons are introduced into a conflict. Finally, LNW defines a legitimate policy role for nuclear weapons. Without LNW, leaders faced with a crisis (such as a successful Soviet invasion of Western Europe) have only two real options: accepting defeat or launching a massive, suicidal nuclear attack. Limited nuclear war, however, creates a third option—the selective use of nuclear weapons against specific targets. The notion of limited nuclear war has been widely criticized as unrealistic and misleading. Many experts contend that it would be virtually impossible to limit escalation once nuclear war has broken out. Limited nuclear war is also known as protracted nuclear war. See CONTROLLED ESCALATION, SANCTUARY, SCHLESINGER DOCTRINE.

LIMITED TEST BAN (LTB) refers to a partial cessation of NUCLEAR TESTING. A limited test ban generally implies a total ban on testing in certain environments, such as in the air, with continued testing in other environments, such as underground. A limited test ban does not significantly impede the development of new weapons systems; it does, however, drastically reduce the amount of dangerous radioactive material present in the atmosphere. The United States and the Soviet Union signed the Limited Test Ban Treaty in July 1963. Since that time, the number of aboveground nuclear tests has dropped sharply.

LIMITED TEST BAN TREATY (LTBT) (1963) is a multilateral agreement that has been signed by over 100 nations. The treaty prohibits nuclear testing underwater, in the atmosphere, and in outer space. The treaty is "limited," however, because it does not restrict underground nuclear tests. The LTBT is not intended to prohibit nuclear testing; instead, it aims to reduce environmental damage from nuclear testing. The treaty was negotiated in response to worldwide indignation over the dispersal of dangerous radioactive fallout from aboveground nuclear testing in the 1950s. Two nuclear weapons states, France and China, have not signed the treaty and continue to conduct aboveground nuclear tests. The treaty is also known as the Partial Test Ban Treaty.

LINE-OF-SIGHT RADAR is one of two principal RADAR techniques for locating and identifying airborne objects. Line-of-sight radar has a comparatively short range; it cannot "see" objects flying beyond the horizon. Line-of-sight radar is distinct from OVER-THE-HORIZON RADAR, which is not restricted by the curvature of the earth and has a much longer range. Line-of-sight radar is used for a variety of purposes, including detection of enemy nuclear attacks and missile test flights.

LINKAGE is a policy of associating nuclear arms-control negotiations with other unrelated issues in a relationship between two nations. Linkage is often a factor in the relationship between the United States and the Soviet Union. Many supporters of linkage suggest that the United States should link superpower negotiations on limiting and reducing nuclear weapons with the goal of improving Soviet behavior on other issues. They believe that the U.S., for instance, should discuss nuclear arms control and Soviet human rights policy in the same breath. Critics of linkage argue that the nuclear arms race is extremely important as a single issue and thus must be addressed separately from other topics. The Soviet Union has traditionally opposed a policy of linkage. Many analysts claim that when the U.S. Senate failed to approve SALT II, it was linking arms control with the Soviet invasion of Afghanistan in December 1979.

LIQUID-FUELED ENGINE is one type of BOOSTER ROCKET, which propels a BALLISTIC MISSILE into space and directs it toward its target. Liquid-fueled engines are fueled by a liquid mixture of kerosene and an oxidizer. Unlike solid-fueled engines, it is possible to control the rate at which a liquid-fueled engine burns. A liquid-fueled engine is thus similar to an automobile, in which one can increase or decrease speed by pressing down or releasing the gas pedal. In addition, it is possible to steer a liquid-fueled missile by turning the entire engine. Liquid-fueled missiles are less sophisticated and more prone to accidents than solid-fueled engines; they have been almost completely replaced by solid-fueled missiles in the U.S. nuclear arsenal. The U.S.S.R. deploys some liquid-fueled and some solid-fueled missiles.

LITTLE BOY was the first atomic weapon. It was dropped by the U.S. on HIROSHIMA, Japan, on August 6, 1945. Little Boy, which was over ten feet long and weighed about 9,000 pounds, was also the first and only U.S. atomic weapon to be fueled by URANIUM. Uranium is a highly radioactive substance that today fuels most nuclear reactors. Little Boy was designed at Los Alamos, New

Mexico, by a team of scientists led by J. Robert Oppenheimer. Along with Fat Man, the bomb dropped on NAGASAKI, Little Boy was the product of the MANHATTAN PROJECT, the American wartime drive to build the first nuclear weapons.

LOCAL RADIOACTIVE FALLOUT see EARLY RADIOACTIVE FALLOUT

LONDON SUPPLIERS CLUB see NUCLEAR SUPPLIERS GROUP

LONG-RANGE BOMBER is any aircraft that can deliver nuclear and conventional weapons against the homelands of the superpowers. Long-range bombers have a range greater than 9,200 km. Long-range bombers are generally considered STRATEGIC BOMBERS. Long-range bombers can travel farther than medium-range bombers and intermediate-range bombers. The Soviet Union deploys three types of long-range bombers:

- Tu-95 Bear has been widely deployed since 1956. The Bear has a range of 12,300 km and can be equipped with either nuclear or conventional weapons. The Bear-H, which has a range of 12,800 km, is the newest version of the Tu-95 and entered production in 1983. It is capable of carrying the most modern Soviet AIR-LAUNCHED CRUISE MISSILE, the AS-15.
- Mya-4 Bison was first deployed in 1956 and has a range of over 11,200 km. The Bison is similar in size to the American B-52 but carries fewer weapons. The Bison carries gravity bombs and is being replaced in the mid-1980s by the newer Blackjack RAM-P bomber.
- Blackjack RAM-P is the most modern Soviet long-range bomber and is believed to be larger and faster than the American B-1B. U.S. military experts believe the Blackjack will be deployed in 1987 and will carry air-launched cruise missiles and gravity bombs. The Blackjack will replace the older Mya-4 Bison and Tu-95 Bear. The bomber's range is estimated to be 12,800 km.

The United States also deploys three types of long-range bombers:

- B-52G, first deployed in 1959, is a modernized version of the original B-52D. It is equipped to deliver gravity bombs, air-launched cruise missiles, and short-range attack missiles. Its range is 12,000 km and it can carry 24 weapons.
- B-52H, first deployed in 1962, is a modernized version of the original B-52D. It is equipped to deliver gravity bombs, short-range attack missiles, and air-launched cruise missiles. Its range is 16,000 km and it can carry 24 weapons.
- B-1B is a new type of bomber, destined to replace the B-52. It is the descendant of the B-1 bomber, which was canceled by President Jimmy Carter in 1977. The B-1B is equipped to deliver gravity bombs, air-launched cruise missiles, and short-range attack missiles. Its range is 9,600 km and it can carry about 48 weapons. The B-1B was revived by President Ronald Reagan and will be deployed in the mid-1980s.

LONG-RANGE NUCLEAR WEAPONS see STRATEGIC NUCLEAR WEAPONS

LONGER-RANGE THEATER NUCLEAR FORCES (LRTNF) see INTERMEDIATE-RANGE NUCLEAR FORCES

LOOK-DOWN SHOOT-DOWN SYSTEM is a nickname for a system that can identify and wipe out enemy targets. A look-down shoot-down system would include two components: RADAR, for identifying a target; and MISSILES, for destroying it.

LOOKING GLASS see POST-ATTACK COMMAND AND CONTROL SYSTEM

LOP NOR, located in west-central China, is the principal Chinese nuclear test site.

LOS ALAMOS NATIONAL LABORATORY (LANL) is one of three major U.S. facilities for the development of nuclear weapons technology. LANL was founded in 1943 and is located at Los Alamos, New Mexico. LANL and its rival, the Lawrence Livermore National Laboratory, have designed all the nuclear weapons ever built by the United States. The third major nuclear weapons facility, Sandia National Laboratory, designs special components. LANL was established during the MANHATTAN PROJECT and was where a group of eminent scientists, led by J. Robert Oppenheimer, designed and built the first atomic weapons in 1945. Over the years LANL and Lawrence Livermore have engaged in friendly competition. Research for President Ronald Reagan's STRATEGIC DEFENSE INITIATIVE, commonly known as "Star Wars," is being conducted at Los Alamos. The University of California runs LANL under contract from the federal government.

LOW AIR BURST is a nuclear explosion close to the ground. A low air burst produces a great deal of deadly radioactive FALLOUT, but affects a relatively limited area. When a nuclear weapon explodes near the ground, it destroys everything in the area. The resulting debris is drawn up into the atmosphere. As it rises, fallout is bathed in RADIATION from the explosion. This radiation is extremely harmful and can cause nausea, hair loss, internal bleeding, genetic damage, and cancer. A low air burst is distinct from a GROUND BURST, in which a weapon explodes on the surface of the earth, causing less destruction but more fallout than a low air burst, and a HIGH AIR BURST, in which the explosion occurs high above the ground. A high air burst affects a wider area but causes less fallout than a ground burst.

LOW-ALTITUDE DEFENSE SYSTEM (LOADS) is a theoretical defense system that would destroy attacking NUCLEAR WARHEADS in the final seconds of their flight. LOADS would disarm incoming warheads at relatively low altitudes (50,000 to 200,000 feet) above the earth and intercept warheads less than ten seconds before they strike their targets. LOADS would be risky because it would involve intercepting incoming warheads at the last possible moment. Conceived in the early 1970s, LOADS has been considered a possible way of protecting BALLISTIC MISSILE sites. The deployment of LOADS, however, could violate the ANTIBALLISTIC MISSILE TREATY of 1972. It is expected to undergo extensive testing in the late 1980s by the United States.

LUCKY DRAGON was a Japanese fishing boat that was cruising 120 miles from Bikini Atoll when the United States conducted the BRAVO TEST there on March 1, 1954. The Bravo Test was the first explosion of a true THERMONUCLEAR WEAPON and was also one of the worst nuclear accidents ever. The test scattered dangerous radioactive FALLOUT over a wide area of the South Pacific. The *Lucky Dragon*'s entire crew of 23 was seriously contaminated with radioactive fallout from the blast; one crew member died of RADIATION SICKNESS seven months later.

M

MAGNETIC CONTOUR MATCHING (MAGCOM) is an advanced GUIDANCE SYSTEM that directs U.S. CRUISE MISSILES toward their targets. Cruise missiles are slow, low-flying, highly accurate missiles that resemble pilotless airplanes. MAGCOM uses the earth's magnetic field as a reference system to keep a cruise missile on course. Inside a cruise missile is a computer that contains the details of the earth's magnetic field along the missile's intended path. MAGCOM compares the actual magnetic field around the missile with the predicted one in the missile's computers. Any discrepancies are used to make in-flight adjustments in the missile's flight path. MAGCOM was specifically developed for cruise missiles that fly over water. A similar system called TERRAIN CONTOUR MATCHING (TERCOM) uses the physical contours of the earth, rather than the earth's magnetic field, as a reference system.

MANEUVERABLE REENTRY VEHICLE (MARV) is one of several NUCLEAR WARHEADS carried by a single BALLISTIC MISSILE. MARVs, which can be individually aimed and maneuvered, enable a single missile to strike more than one target. MARVs are released by a missile as it streaks toward its target and can turn and dodge to avoid enemy defenses. MARVs released by one missile can thus strike different targets with a high degree of accuracy. MARVs are technologically more advanced versions of the MULTIPLE INDEPENDENTLY TARGETABLE REENTRY VEHICLES (MIRV). Unlike MARVs, MIRVs cannot be guided to their targets. Their flight direction is determined by gravity and wind resistance. Both the U.S. and the U.S.S.R. are conducting research on MARVs. MARVs are also known as evasive reentry vehicles.

MANHATTAN ENGINEERING DISTRICT was the official name of the MANHATTAN PROJECT, the American World War II drive to build the first atomic weapons.

MANHATTAN PROJECT was the massive top-secret U.S. Army program that produced the first atomic weapons during World War II. The Manhattan Project revolutionized science and industry and eventually produced the bombs that leveled the Japanese cities of HIROSHIMA and NAGASAKI in August 1945. A third bomb, exploded in the TRINITY TEST in New Mexico, was also manufactured. Many esteemed scientists from all over the world, including Enrico Fermi, J. Robert Oppenheimer, and Niels Bohr, were associated with the project. Conducted from 1942 to 1945, the Manhattan Project was headed by General Leslie Groves. About $2 billion was spent on the project.

MARV   see MANEUVERABLE REENTRY VEHICLE

MASSIVE RETALIATION is an all-out nuclear attack launched in response to enemy aggression anywhere in the world. The threat of massive retaliation is intended to deter an opponent from aggressive behavior. It relies on a credible commitment to launch a devastating nuclear attack in response to what may be comparatively trivial provocation. U.S. Secretary of State John Foster Dulles announced massive retaliation as U.S. policy in January 1954. Dulles presented massive retaliation as a means of countering what was perceived as a dangerously increasing communist threat in Europe and Asia. Massive retaliation served as the centerpiece of U.S. nuclear strategy until the late 1950s, when the Soviet Union began to challenge U.S. nuclear superiority. As a result, the United States replaced its policy of massive retaliation with FLEXIBLE RESPONSE in the early 1960s. Unlike massive retaliation, flexible response involves countering enemy aggression with a variety of possible responses. In flexible response, using NUCLEAR WEAPONS is generally thought of as a last resort.

MAY-JOHNSON BILL was a Congressional bill that called for military control over U.S. nuclear technology in the period following World War II. It essentially would have institutionalized the MANHATTAN PROJECT, the Army's wartime program to build the first atomic bomb. Generated by the War Department in the fall of 1945, the May-Johnson bill would have perpetuated the military's control over all aspects of American nuclear energy, peaceful as well as military. The May-Johnson bill drew criticism from many scientists, who lobbied to help defeat the bill. In its place, Congress passed the ATOMIC ENERGY ACT OF 1946, which placed control over American nuclear technology in the hands of a five-member civilian board.

McCLOY-ZORIN AGREEMENT (1962) is a U.S.-U.S.S.R. agreement in which the superpowers pledge to pursue U.N. negotiations leading to GENERAL AND COMPLETE DISARMAMENT (GCD). GCD is a United Nations concept that calls for completely eliminating NUCLEAR WEAPONS. The United Nations has established GCD as its goal in the field of disarmament. Approved by the U.N. General Assembly in 1962, the McCloy-Zorin agreement laid the framework for U.N. negotiations on GCD. It established a set of guidelines for abolishing nuclear weapons under an international agency called the International Disarmament Organization. Since the McCloy-Zorin Agreement was signed, both the Soviet Union and the United States have submitted numerous proposals for General and Complete Disarmament. None of these proposals, however, has been adopted.

McMAHON ACT see ATOMIC ENERGY ACT OF 1946

MEDIUM ATOMIC DEMOLITION MUNITION (MADM) see ATOMIC DEMOLITION MUNITION

MEDIUM BOMBER generally refers to any aircraft equipped to deliver nuclear or conventional weapons, but which cannot deliver strategic nuclear weapons against the homelands of the superpowers unless it is refueled in flight. Medium bomber is a general classification that includes intermediate-range bombers and some MEDIUM-RANGE BOMBERS. The Soviet Tu-22m/26 Backfire bomber and the American FB-111 bomber are examples of medium bombers. See INTERMEDIATE-RANGE BOMBER, HEAVY BOMBER.

MEDIUM-RANGE BALLISTIC MISSILE (MRBM) is a BALLISTIC MISSILE intended to be used in a broad geographical region, such as Europe or the Far East. MRBMs are propelled into the upper atmosphere by BOOSTER ROCKETS. After the rockets burn out, they fall down through the atmosphere, pulled by gravity to their target. MRBMs have a range of 1,100 to 2,750 km. This range is greater than that of SHORT-RANGE BALLISTIC MISSILES and less than that of INTERMEDIATE-RANGE BALLISTIC MISSILES and INTERCONTINENTAL BALLISTIC MISSILES. MRBMs are generally classed as THEATER NUCLEAR WEAPONS. The United States deploys one type of MRBM:

- Pershing II is one of the EUROMISSILES deployed by NATO in the mid-1980s. It was deployed in West Germany in 1983, and is gradually replacing older Pershing Ia short-range ballistic missiles. The Pershing II has a range of 1,790 km and delivers one warhead with a yield of .3 to 80 kilotons. The Pershing II is ten times as accurate as the Pershing Ia; it could thus strike well-defended military targets. See DUAL-TRACK DECISION

The Soviet Union also deploys one type of MRBM:

- SS-4 Sandal, deployed since 1959, has a range of 2,000 km and carries a single 1-megaton warhead. The SS-4 was the Soviet missile introduced into Cuba during the CUBAN MISSILE CRISIS of 1962. It is being replaced in the mid-1980s by the advanced SS-20. See ZERO OPTION.

In addition, the People's Republic of China deploys one type of MRBM:

- CSS-1, deployed in 1966, was the first Chinese ballistic missile. It has a range of 1,100 km and carries a single 20-kiloton warhead.

MEDIUM-RANGE BOMBER is any bomber that can deliver conventional or nuclear weapons over a broad geographical region, such as Europe or the Far East. Medium-range bombers have a range of less than 3,680 km. Medium-range bombers cannot travel as far as INTERMEDIATE-RANGE BOMBERS and LONG-RANGE BOMBERS. Some medium-range bombers may be classified as MEDIUM BOMBERS. The United States does not deploy any medium-range bombers capable of delivering nuclear weapons. The Soviet Union, however, deploys two of these bombers:

- Tu-16 Badger, deployed since 1955, is being replaced in the 1980s by the advanced Backfire intermediate-range bomber. The Badger has a range of 4,800 km and can carry AIR-TO-SURFACE MISSILES.
- Tu-22 Blinder, deployed since 1962, takes off from both land bases and aircraft carriers. The Blinder can carry gravity bombs and air-to-surface missiles and has a range of 4,000 km.

In addition, France deploys two types of medium-range bombers:

- Mirage IVA, first deployed in 1964, will be replaced in the 1980s by the advanced Mirage 2000N. It has a range of 1,500 km and carries two 70-kiloton gravity bombs.
- Mirage 2000N began flight testing in 1983 and will be deployed in 1988. It is the most technologically advanced French fighter-bomber and will replace the Mirage IVA. The Mirage 2000N has a range of 1,400 km.

Finally, Great Britain deploys one type of medium-range bomber:

- Tornado strike aircraft, first deployed in 1982, was developed by a consortium of British, Italian, and West German manufacturers. Nonnuclear versions of the Tornado are deployed by the Italian and West German air forces. The Tornado, which is specially equipped for all-weather operation, has a range of 2,600 km and can deliver two gravity bombs.

MEGATON (mt) is a unit used to measure the amount of energy released in a nuclear explosion. One megaton is equivalent to the energy released in the detonation of one million tons of TNT. One megaton equals 1,000 KILOTONS. A one-megaton weapon is about 76 times as destructive as the bomb dropped on HIROSHIMA, Japan, in 1945. The largest nuclear explosion, carried out by the U.S.S.R. in 1961, was 58 megatons.

MEGATON WEAPON is a nuclear weapon with a yield of more than one megaton. One megaton is equivalent to the energy released in the detonation of 1,000,000 tons of TNT. Megaton weapons are usually classified as strategic weapons, intended to strike deep into the homelands of the superpowers. Although many megaton weapons are still deployed, the superpowers have in recent years moved away from megaton weapons because they are, in general, less accurate and more difficult to deploy than less powerful KILOTON WEAPONS. One megaton equals 1,000 kilotons

MER-SOL BALLISTIQUE STRATÉGIQUE (MSBS) designates a French submarine-launched ballistic missile. The French deploy two types of MSBSs, the M-4 and the M-20. See SUBMARINE-LAUNCHED BALLISTIC MISSILE for a complete description of these missiles.

MÉRY PLAN, formulated by French Chief of General Staff Charles Méry in 1976, was a strategy for the use of French nuclear weapons. The Méry Plan reaffirmed the importance of TACTICAL NUCLEAR WEAPONS, but also emphasized the role of conventional forces in the defense of France. Tactical nuclear weapons are small, low-yield nuclear weapons intended for battlefield use. While France is not a part of the military branch of NATO, the Méry Plan urged close cooperation with NATO forces in the event of an attack on Western Europe. The Méry Plan stressed more cooperation with NATO forces and placed less emphasis on the early use of nuclear weapons than previous French strategies. The Méry Plan replaced the FOURQUET PLAN as official French nuclear strategy.

MIDCOURSE DEFENSE   see MIDCOURSE INTERCEPTION

MIDCOURSE INTERCEPTION is the destruction of attacking nuclear warheads during the longest period (called the MIDCOURSE PHASE) of a missile's flight in space. During the midcourse phase, which lasts 15 to 20 minutes, many warheads and decoys have already been released by a BALLISTIC MISSILE. Because midcourse phase is the longest period of a missile's flight, a BALLISTIC MISSILE DEFENSE SYSTEM has more time to detect and destroy warheads. Midcourse interception could be complicated, however, by the several thousand DECOYS and warheads that could be travelling through space simultaneously. During midcourse interception, it is necessary to distinguish between these warheads and decoys.

MIDCOURSE PHASE is the period of a BALLISTIC MISSILE's flight when it travels through space. During this phase the individual NUCLEAR WARHEADS and DECOYS have already been released, but have not yet entered the atmosphere. The midcourse phase lasts from 15 to 20 minutes. The midcourse phase follows the BOOST and POST-BOOST PHASES and precedes the TERMINAL PHASE of a missile's flight.

MIDGETMAN is a new U.S. INTERCONTINENTAL BALLISTIC MISSILE (ICBM). Recommended by the SCOWCROFT COMMISSION in 1983, the Midgetman will be deployed by the early 1990s. The Midgetman, which carries only one warhead, was conceived for two reasons. First, it is small and mobile and therefore would be easier to deploy than larger, traditional ICBMs. Second, with its single warhead, it would be a less inviting target for an enemy FIRST STRIKE. The Midgetman is a very innovative weapon and has given rise to as new classification: SMALL INTERCONTINEN-TAL BALLISTIC MISSILE. It has a range of 10,000 km and a yield of about 350 kilotons.

MIKE SHOT was the first explosion of a high-yield thermonuclear device. The Mike Shot was conducted by the United States on November 1, 1952, at Elugelab Island in the South Pacific. Like the device exploded in the GEORGE SHOT (the first thermonu-clear explosion), the device detonated in the Mike Shot was an unwieldy experimental contraption that could not be used as a weapon. The Mike Shot, however, was much more powerful than the George Shot. Despite the fact that it could not be adapted as a weapon, it is commonly referred to as the first true "superbomb."

MILITARY NUCLEAR POWER is a nation that possesses nuclear weapons.

MILLIREM (mrem) is one-thousandth of a rem. Millirems measure radiation that occurs naturally in the environment and is not especially harmful. The deadly radiation released in a nuclear explosion, however, is measured in REMS.

MILSTAR SATELLITE is a highly advanced U.S. military SATELLITE that is scheduled for deployment in the late 1980s. MILSTAR is designed to allow better communications between the army, navy, and air force in the event of a nuclear war. It is specifically intended to permit the three services to coordinate the use of nuclear weapons. MILSTAR will be positioned three times deeper in space than existing satellites to make it less vulnerable to enemy attack. Proposed by the Reagan Administration in the early 1980s, the development of MILSTAR is given one of the highest priorities of any defense program.

MINIATURE HOMING VEHICLE (MHV) is a small theoretical weapon designed to disable enemy SATELLITES. An MHV would not carry any type of explosive; instead, it would destroy satellites by impact. It is a small cylinder that would be launched from high-flying fighter planes. MHVs would be propelled by a small rocket and guided to their target by built-in telescopes and small jets. The MHV is nicknamed the "flying tomato can" and has been under development by the United States since 1978.

MINIMUM DETERRENCE is a strategy of deploying only the number of nuclear weapons needed to deter enemy aggression. The superpowers have been restrained from fighting a nuclear war by the knowledge that any aggression will be met by an unacceptably destructive retaliation. Minimum deterrence requires that each side deploy a nuclear arsenal powerful enough to ensure that this threat of destructive retaliation remains credible. Under minimum deterrence, however, this would be accomplished by deploying a relatively small nuclear arsenal. France has adopted a policy of minimum deterrence. It has never possessed a nuclear arsenal large enough to destroy all Soviet military targets. Instead, it deploys a minimum number of weapons sufficient only to dissuade the Soviet Union from attacking France. Minimum deterrence is also known as pure deterrence or finite deterrence.

MINIMUM ENERGY TRAJECTORY is the normal path followed by a BALLISTIC MISSILE as it streaks toward its target. Ballistic missiles follow an arching trajectory; they are propelled into the atmosphere by BOOSTER ROCKETS and are then pulled by gravity to their targets. A minimum energy trajectory is distinct from a DEPRESSED TRAJECTORY, in which a ballistic missile flies closer to the ground in order to elude RADAR and reach its target faster.

MINIMUM ESSENTIAL EMERGENCY COMMUNICATIONS NETWORK (MEECN) is an American system that is designed to transmit communications during a nuclear war. Established in 1970, MEECN consists of airborne command posts, satellite systems, and radio transmitters. MEECN is specially designed to enable U.S. military leaders to send undisrupted messages in a nuclear war.

MINIMUM RESIDUAL RADIOACTIVITY WEAPON see CLEAN NUCLEAR WEAPON

MINI-NUKE is an informal term for a small, low-yield nuclear weapon. Mini-nukes are TACTICAL NUCLEAR WEAPONS, designed for battlefield use. Mini-nukes are also known as nominal weapons.

MINOR SCALE was a U.S. conventional weapons test conducted on June 27, 1985, at the TRINITY SITE, near Alamogordo, New Mexico. The Trinity Site is where the first nuclear weapon was exploded in 1945. Minor Scale simulated a nuclear explosion, and was used to test the effects of a nuclear-sized blast on MISSILE SILOS and other potential targets. Minor Scale was the largest nonnuclear explosion ever set off in the U.S.—it released a destructive YIELD of 8 kilotons (equivalent to 8000 tons of TNT) and created a giant mushroom cloud. Aboveground nuclear tests have been prohibited since 1963; conventional simulations must therefore be used to test the effects of a nuclear-sized blast on surface targets.

MINUTEMAN MISSILE is a series of U.S. intercontinental ballistic missiles (ICBMs). The Minuteman II, Minuteman III, and Minuteman III (Mk 12A) are all ICBMs. See INTERCONTINENTAL BALLISTIC MISSILE for a complete description of these missiles.

MIRAGE is a series of French bombers. The Mirage IVA and the Mirage 2000N are medium-range bombers. See MEDIUM-RANGE BOMBER for a complete description of these aircraft.

MIRV see MULTIPLE INDEPENDENTLY TARGETABLE REENTRY VEHICLE

MISSILE is an unmanned projectile that is propelled to its target by some sort of engine. Missiles can carry conventional or nuclear explosives. There are essentially two basic types of missiles found in nuclear arsenals: BALLISTIC MISSILES and CRUISE MISSILES. Ballistic missiles are propelled into the upper atmosphere by BOOSTER ROCKETS. After the rockets burn out, the missile falls down through the atmosphere, pulled by gravity to its target. Cruise missiles, on the other hand, are slow, low-flying, highly accurate missiles that resemble pilotless airplanes. Unlike ballistic missiles, which are powered by booster rockets, cruise missiles are powered by jet engines. Both types of missiles are commonly armed with nuclear warheads. Many missiles are equipped with sophisticated GUIDANCE SYSTEMS, which enable them to strike targets with a high degree of accuracy. Missiles may be fired from a variety of LAUNCHERS, including MISSILE SILOS, submarines, and trucklike vehicles.

MISSILE ACCURACY   see ACCURACY

MISSILE DESTRUCT SYSTEM   see COMMAND DISABLE SYSTEM

MISSILE EXPERIMENTAL   see MX MISSILE

MISSILE GAP is a condition in which one superpower has gained a significant advantage in the nuclear arms race. The term was popularized in the 1960 U.S. presidential election, when experts claimed that the U.S.S.R. had attained a dangerous advantage over the U.S. in its arsenal of nuclear missiles. That missile gap was later proven to be completely fictitious. Nonetheless, claims of a missile gap have recurred in U.S. politics through the mid-1980s.

MISSILE SILO is an underground structure that houses a nuclear missile. Because a missile silo cannot be moved, it may be extremely vulnerable to attacking NUCLEAR WARHEADS. In order to improve its chances of surviving a nuclear attack, a missile silo can be constructed deep underground and reinforced with concrete and earth. Most of the nuclear missiles deployed in the U.S. and the U.S.S.R. are housed in missile silos. These missiles are large and powerful, intended to strike deep into the territory of the other superpower. Smaller nuclear missiles intended for battlefield use are rarely housed in missile silos. Instead, they are usually carried by rail cars or trucklike vehicles.

M-MISSILE is the code that designates French submarine-launched ballistic missiles (mer-sol ballistiques stratégiques). France currently deploys two SLBMs, the M-4 and the M-20. See SUBMARINE-LAUNCHED BALLISTIC MISSILE for a complete description of these missiles.

MOBILE LAUNCHER is a moveable structure that holds a nuclear missile in position ready for launch. Mobile launchers may be mounted on trucklike vehicles, trains, submarines, or aircraft. Because its exact position is difficult to fix, a mobile launcher would be difficult to destroy in a nuclear attack. Mobile launchers can fire many different types of nuclear weapons, from small, battlefield artillery shells to mammoth BALLISTIC MISSILES capable of devastating entire cities. A mobile launcher is distinct from a FIXED LAUNCHER, which cannot move around and thus would be a "sitting duck" in a nuclear attack. Most fixed launchers are housed in underground missile silos, but a few are maintained aboveground.

MOBILE MISSILE is a nuclear missile that can be moved around and fired from different locations. Mobile missiles would usually be launched from trucklike vehicles. Because its position is difficult to fix, a mobile missile would be less vulnerable to enemy attack. Its mobility would also make it an effective battlefield weapon. Most mobile missiles are intended to be used on the battlefield or within a specific geographic region, such as Europe or the Far East.

MODERNIZATION is the process of improving an existing weapon by upgrading its technology. An example of modernization, called MIRVing (for MULTIPLE INDEPENDENTLY TARGETABLE REENTRY VEHICLES), involves replacing a missile's single warhead with several warheads. A MIRVed missile, unlike a missile with a single warhead, can destroy several targets. The exact definition of modernization has been a point of contention during arms-control negotiations between the U.S. and the U.S.S.R. The superpowers often disagree on what constitutes modernization and what is in fact the development of a completely new weapon. For example, SALT II, which limited the number of nuclear weapons the superpowers could deploy, allowed both nations to develop one new type of nuclear missile. The Soviets developed the SS-24 and at the same time modernized an existing missile, which they renamed the SS-25. The U.S., however, claimed that the SS-25 was a new weapon and not a modernization of an existing missile.

MODERN LARGE BALLISTIC MISSILE (MLBM) see HEAVY MISSILE

MOLNIYA is a Soviet SATELLITE system for military communications. The Molniya satellites were first deployed in 1965. The Molniya system is also part of the U.S.-U.S.S.R. HOT LINE, which is the direct communications link between Washington and Moscow. The Hot Line enables the leaders of both nations to communicate in an emergency, such as an accidental nuclear missile launch.

MONAD is a nuclear arsenal that is composed of missiles based either on submarines, in underground missile silos, or on bombers. A monad must be distinguished from a TRIAD, which includes missiles deployed on submarines, on aircraft, and in underground silos.

MONITORING SATELLITES survey nuclear facilities and explosions. Operating at a wide variety of altitudes, monitoring satellites perform many extremely important functions. Monitoring satellites collect data through cameras, heat sensors, and radio receivers and are capable of producing highly detailed images. They are said to be capable of taking pictures of individual human faces. The U.S. first used monitoring satellites in 1960; the U.S.S.R. followed in 1962. Monitoring satellites are also called surveillance satellites.

MONTE BELLO ISLAND is located off western Australia. It was the site of the HURRICANE TEST, in which Great Britain detonated its first atomic weapon. Great Britain now conducts its nuclear tests at the NEVADA TEST SITE in the western United States.

MORATORIUM is a decision to stop doing something. Between November 1958 and September 1961, the United States, the Soviet Union, and Great Britain observed a moratorium on nuclear testing. The U.S.S.R. abrogated the moratorium after American pilot Francis Gary Powers was shot down in his U-2 spy plane over Soviet territory in 1961.

MRV   see MULTIPLE REENTRY VEHICLE

MSBS   see MER-SOL BALLISTIQUE STRATÉGIQUE

MULTILATERALISM is the theory that successful arms-control agreements must include all nations that possess or produce nuclear weapons. Multilateralism stresses nations acting in unison. In this way, no nation can take advantage of another nation. The NONPROLIFERATION TREATY of 1968, which aims to prevent the spread of nuclear weapons, is an example of multilateralism. The treaty has been signed by over 140 nations, including the five nations possessing nuclear weapons (China, France, Great Britain, the U.S., and the U.S.S.R.). Multilateralism is distinct from bilateralism, which involves agreements between two nations.

MULTILAYERED DEFENSE   see LAYERED DEFENSE

MULTIPLE AIM POINT SYSTEM (MAPS) is a proposed U.S. method for deploying land-based nuclear missiles. In MAPS, several silos would be provided for each missile that is deployed. The missile would be periodically placed into different silos in order to create a kind of shell game for an attacker, who would then have to guess where it is located. MAPS thus would involve routinely shuttling missiles to reduce their vulnerability to an attack. MAPS has been considered for housing MX and MINUTE-MAN MISSILES. It is also known as Alternate Launch Point System.

MULTIPLE INDEPENDENTLY TARGETABLE REENTRY VEHI-CLE (MIRV) is one of several NUCLEAR WARHEADS carried by a single missile. MIRVs, which enable a single missile to strike more than one target, are released at different points along a missile's flight path and are guided by gravity to their targets. MIRVs released by one missile can thus strike different targets. MIRVs are technologically less advanced versions of the MANEUVERABLE REENTRY VEHICLES (MARV). Unlike MARVs, MIRVs cannot be individually guided and maneuvered to their targets. Instead, they rely upon gravity to reach their targets and are thus less accurate than MARVs. MIRV technology was developed in the early 1970s by the U.S. and the U.S.S.R. MIRVs can complicate arms-control negotiations because it is impossible to tell how many warheads are deployed on a MIRVed missile. In this way, it is difficult to verify negotiated limits on warheads. In recent years, the superpowers have moved away from MIRVs, instead developing smaller, single-warhead missiles, which are easier to deploy and less inviting targets for an enemy nuclear attack.

MULTIPLE PROTECTIVE SHELTERS (MPS) is a hypothetical method for deploying nuclear missiles. A system of multiple protective shelters would involve building several shelters for each missile. Missiles would then be shuttled between different shelters, so that an adversary could never be sure where they were located and their vulnerability to enemy attack would be reduced. An enemy, in turn, would have to destroy every shelter in order to be absolutely certain of destroying all the missiles. MPS was first conceived as a method of deploying the U.S.'s MX MISSILE. The plan was abandoned, however, and the U.S. eventually decided to deploy the MX in existing underground missile silos. MPS has also been referred to as the shell game.

MULTIPLE REENTRY VEHICLE (MRV) is one of several NUCLEAR WARHEADS carried by a single missile. MRVs, which cannot be individually targeted, enable a single missile to bombard a target with more than one warhead. MRVs thus maximize damage to one target by spreading destruction over a large area, rather than concentrating it at one point. This increased target area is called a NUCLEAR FOOTPRINT. An MRV is a technologically less advanced version of the MANEUVERABLE REENTRY VEHICLES (MARV) and the MULTIPLE INDEPENDENTLY TARGETABLE REEN-TRY VEHICLES (MIRV). Unlike MARVs and MIRVs, MRVs cannot strike more than one target. Both superpowers have abandoned MRV warheads for more sophisticated technol-ogy; however, some MRVs remain in use on British Polaris submarines.

MULTIPLE-WARHEAD MISSILE is any missile that carries more than one NUCLEAR WARHEAD. The development of multiple-warhead missiles is a very important breakthrough in nuclear weapons technology. A multiple-warhead missile, unlike a mis-sile with a single warhead, can spread damage over a very wide area. Three types of multiple-warhead technology have been developed. The MULTIPLE REENTRY VEHICLE (MRV) is the old-est, least technologically advanced multiple-warhead missile. Warheads carried as MRVs must all be directed at the same target. Both superpowers have abandoned MRV warheads for more sophisticated technology; however, some MRVs remain in use on British Polaris submarines. The MULTIPLE INDEPEN-DENTLY TARGETABLE REENTRY VEHICLE (MIRV) was developed by the U.S. in the 1960s as a replacement for outmoded MRV technology. As its name suggests, MIRVs can be fired separately from a single missile to hit different targets. The MANEUVERABLE REENTRY VEHICLE (MARV) is similar to the MIRV, but is more technologically advanced. Not only can MARVs be independently targeted, but they can also be independently maneuvered to evade defenses and increase accuracy. The exact number of warheads carried by a multiple-warhead missile is difficult to verify and thus multiple-warhead missiles can complicate arms control. Modern BALLISTIC MISSILES can carry as many as 14 warheads.

MULTITIERED DEFENSE   see LAYERED DEFENSE

MURUROA ATOLL, located in the South Pacific, is the principal French nuclear test site. The French have conducted nuclear tests at Mururoa Atoll since 1966, when they were forced to stop testing in the Sahara Desert. Other countries in the South Pacific, including Australia and New Zealand, have been sharply critical of the continued French testing at Mururoa.

MUSHROOM CLOUD is the cloud of gas, dust, and other debris that forms in the aftermath of a nuclear explosion. The mushroom cloud, whose name is derived from the cloud's distinctive mushroom shape, is composed of everything that is pulverized in a nuclear blast. The mushroom cloud helps spread deadly radioactive by-products created in a nuclear explosion. A mushroom cloud, also known as a nuclear cloud, may be ten miles across and eight to ten miles high. To many, the mushroom cloud is a symbol of the nuclear age.

MUTUAL ASSURED DESTRUCTION (MAD) is a condition in which two nations are restrained from starting a nuclear war. MAD relies on each superpower's ability to completely devastate the other even after absorbing a nuclear attack. In this way, any attack is suicidal, since it means that the enemy will respond with a destructive retaliation. With limited means for defending against a nuclear attack, both superpowers have relied on the threat of mutual assured destruction since the 1960s to deter each other from launching a nuclear attack. Proponents of MAD contend that it is a very effective way of preventing the superpowers from fighting a nuclear war. Critics, however, contend that MAD is immoral, because it relies on the threat of terror to restrain the actions of the superpowers. Another argument against MAD is that it is an all-or-nothing idea: If, for some reason, nuclear war did break out, widespread death and destruction would be inevitable. The phrase "assured destruction" was coined by U.S. Secretary of Defense Robert McNamara in 1964. Defense analyst and MAD critic Donald Brennan later added the word "mutual" in order to create what he considered a suitable acronym. The Soviet Union does not officially accept MAD as a doctrine.

MUTUAL DETERRENCE   see NUCLEAR DETERRENCE

MUTUAL EXAMPLE FORCE RESTRAINT/REDUCTION   see CONDITIONAL RESTRAINT

MX MISSILE, dubbed "Peacekeeper" by the Reagan Administration, is a U.S. INTERCONTINENTAL BALLISTIC MISSILE. Designed to replace the MINUTEMAN MISSILE as the backbone of America's land-based nuclear force, the MX has had a rocky history of deployment dilemmas and Congressional controversy. A variety of complex schemes have been considered for deploying the MX (including DEEP UNDERGROUND MISSILE BASING, CLOSELY SPACED BASING, RACE TRACK, and MULTIPLE PROTECTIVE SHELTERS); all have been abandoned because of technical infeasibility or legislative resistance. A series of extremely close votes in Congress in 1985 determined that a reduced number of MX missiles would be deployed in existing Minuteman silos in the late 1980s. The MX has a range is 13,000 km and carries ten

300-kiloton warheads. It has MIRV capability, and because it is very accurate, it could strike military targets. The abbreviation MX is derived from the original name, Missile Experimental.

MYA-4 BISON is a Soviet long-range bomber. See LONG-RANGE BOMBER for a complete description of the Mya-4 Bison.

N

NAGASAKI is the Japanese city that was the target of the second atomic bomb dropped in the last days of World War II. On August 9, 1945, the United States exploded the bomb (called FAT MAN) above Nagasaki. Nagasaki was the bomb's secondary target; it was attacked because the primary target, Kokura, was shrouded in bad weather. Fat Man's destructive power was small by today's standards; nevertheless, it completely devastated the city. Approximately 60,000 people were killed in the blast or within the next three months from injuries sustained in the explosion. Forty percent of Nagasaki's buildings were obliterated in the blast, and Japan surrendered less than one month later. Nagasaki is located on the northwest coast of Kyushu, one of Japan's southern islands.

NASSAU AGREEMENT (1962) was an arms sale agreement between the U.S. and Great Britain negotiated in Nassau, Bahamas. Under the terms of the agreement, the U.S. sold Polaris SUBMARINE-LAUNCHED BALLISTIC MISSILES to Great Britain. In return, Great Britain agreed to use the missiles as part of NATO's nuclear force. Britain reserved the right, however, to make the final decision on whether the missiles would be used. The Nassau Agreement reflected a middle way between a unified Western alliance and an independent British nuclear force and solved a fundamental British military dilemma: The British had the capability to manufacture nuclear weapons but didn't have an effective way of delivering them to their targets.

NATIONAL COMMAND AUTHORITIES (NCA) are the President and the Secretary of Defense of the United States. They are responsible for making final decisions about the use of U.S. nuclear weapons.

NATIONAL EMERGENCY AIRBORNE COMMAND POST (NEACP) is a set of airplanes that would carry the U.S. President and top military leaders aloft in a nuclear war. The President could issue orders from NEACP during a nuclear war. The NEACP, pronounced and referred to as "kneecap," is used as a backup to command centers on the ground. NEACP consists of several Boeing 747 aircraft that have been converted into flying command bunkers. NEACP is kept on constant alert at Andrews Air Force Base, near Washington, D.C. NEACP, which is code-named Nightwatch and also known as the Doomsday Plane, was made operational in 1975.

NATIONAL MILITARY COMMAND CENTER (NMCC) is a United States military command post where decisions could be made to launch a nuclear attack. Nicknamed "the Tank," the NMCC was established in 1959 as the Joint War Room Annex. The NMCC serves as both a peacetime and wartime command post, with direct communications with the White House and U.S. military installations around the world. Located on the second and third floors of the Department of Defense outside Washington, D.C., it is a primary U.S. military command center. This installation assesses indications of enemy attack and makes recommendations to the NATIONAL COMMAND AUTHORITIES (the President and Secretary of Defense). The Joint Chiefs of Staff operate the NMCC, which contains the Washington, D.C., terminal of the HOT LINE, the direct communications link between Moscow and Washington. Because the Pentagon is considered vulnerable to nuclear attack, the NMCC is backed up by the ALTERNATE NATIONAL MILITARY COMMAND CENTER, which has been hardened (reinforced) to withstand a nuclear attack.

NATIONAL MILITARY COMMAND SYSTEM (NMCS) is the official name of the American system for controlling its nuclear weapons during a nuclear war. NMCS is intended to gather information, transmit communications, and order the launching of U.S. NUCLEAR WEAPONS. To accomplish this, it encompasses a vast network of satellites, communications systems, and other technical equipment. NMCS was established by Secretary of Defense Robert McNamara in 1962.

NATIONAL STRATEGIC DATA BASE   see NATIONAL STRATEGIC TARGET LIST

NATIONAL STRATEGIC TARGET LIST is a U.S. list of enemy cities, missile bases, and factories that would be targeted in a nuclear war. It includes thousands of targets in the U.S.S.R. and other countries, such as China, that could be potential adversaries in a nuclear war. This list, which is frequently revised and expanded, is also called the National Strategic Data Base. The U.S.S.R. maintains a similar list of targets in the U.S. and Western Europe.

NATIONAL TECHNICAL MEANS OF VERIFICATION (NTM) is the technological network used to ensure compliance with nuclear arms-control agreements. NTM incorporates a variety of technical instruments, including SATELLITES, RADAR, and SEISMIC STATIONS, which detect earth tremors that can be caused by underground nuclear explosions. NTM does not involve active cooperation between nations. However, NTM does depend upon an agreement not to hinder another country's monitoring operations by, for example, concealing nuclear facilities. National technical means are distinct from COOPERATIVE MEANS OF VERIFICATION (such as ON-SITE INSPECTIONS), which rely on active collaboration between nations.

NATIONAL TEST BED refers to a sophisticated computer system that simulates high-technology nuclear battles conducted in space. The national test bed is an important tool used in research on the STRATEGIC DEFENSE INITIATIVE, commonly known as "Star Wars."

NATO (NORTH ATLANTIC TREATY ORGANIZATION) is a military alliance, established in 1949, which provides for the collective security of the Western democracies. NATO's primary purpose is to protect its members against Soviet aggression in Western Europe and the North Atlantic. The alliance stresses joint action to counter any possible military threat posed by the Soviet Union and its Eastern European allies (known as the Warsaw Pact). NATO is a comprehensive military alliance that includes conventional and nuclear forces. NATO's nuclear arsenal is comprised of thousands of NUCLEAR WEAPONS, including small artillery shells intended for battlefield use and powerful missiles capable of striking deep into Soviet territory. The majority of NATO's nuclear weapons are deployed by the United States, but they are stationed throughout Western Europe. NATO's nuclear strategy is formulated by the NUCLEAR PLANNING GROUP, which meets twice a year. The Nuclear Planning Group formulates the NUCLEAR OPERATIONS PLAN (NOP), NATO's blueprint for fighting a nuclear war. While the NOP is revised to keep current with changes in weapons and world events, the basic NATO strategy of "first use" remains in effect. In this policy, NATO officials have stated that they will use nuclear weapons before the Soviets in the event that NATO conventional forces cannot withstand a Soviet attack. NATO's members include Belgium, Canada, Denmark, Federal Republic of Germany, Great Britain, France, Greece, Iceland, Italy, Luxembourg, the Netherlands, Norway, Portugal, Spain, Turkey, and the United States. In 1966, France withdrew its military forces from the command of NATO officers.

NATURAL RADIATION   see BACKGROUND RADIATION

NAUTICAL MILE is a unit of length commonly used in the United States to measure the ranges of missiles and bombers. One nautical mile equals 1.15 statute miles and 1.84 km.

NAVIGATION SATELLITE is a satellite used to fix the position of a variety of weapons and other moving objects. Located in space, navigation satellites have many important uses. They help accurately guide attacking nuclear missiles to their targets. Ships, submarines, aircraft, and tanks can fix their exact position with information provided by navigation satellites. Both the U.S. and the U.S.S.R. deploy many sophisticated navigation satellites.

NAVSTAR is a U.S. navigation satellite system that will be deployed in the late 1980s. NAVSTAR, which will be comprised of 18 to 24 individual satellites, will have many important applications for the U.S. military. First, it will greatly increase the accuracy of U.S. NUCLEAR MISSILES. NAVSTAR will provide highly accurate navigational information to a missile's on-board computer throughout the missile's flight. Using this information, the computer will be able to continually adjust the missile's direction and keep it on target. NAVSTAR will be used to supplement a missile's existing GUIDANCE SYSTEM. In addition, U.S. ships, aircraft, and tanks will be able to use NAVSTAR to determine their exact position.

NEUTRAL PARTICLE BEAM WEAPON is a hypothetical weapon that would be part of a high-technology system for protecting against attacking nuclear missiles. Neutral particle beam weapons would generate a concentrated, high-speed beam of energy that would burn a hole in the skin of an attacking missile and deactivate the sensitive electronic equipment responsible for guiding it to its target. Neutral particle beam weapons are unique because the beams that they generate are not obstructed by the earth's magnetic field. Neutral particle beams were first conceived by the U.S.S.R. and are being researched by the United States under the STRATEGIC DEFENSE INITIATIVE, commonly known as "Star Wars."

NEUTRON BOMB is a NUCLEAR WEAPON that kills chiefly through RADIATION, rather than blast and heat. The neutron bomb represents a different approach to nuclear weapons. It is specially modified to produce limited destructive effects, except for deadly radiation. In this way, it can kill people but leave surrounding buildings and land relatively undamaged. The neutron bomb has been justified in the U.S. as an antitank weapon, whose deadly radiation could penetrate tank armor and kill the tank's crew without any of the significant blast damage associated with traditional antitank weapons. The neutron bomb became a controversial issue in the late 1970s when U.S. President Jimmy Carter planned to deploy the bomb in Europe. Opponents saw the bomb as immoral because it seemed to place a higher value on property than life. President Reagan began adding the bomb to the U.S. nuclear arsenal in 1981 but made no plans for future deployment. France reported a successful neutron bomb explosion in 1980 and the U.S.S.R. has also tested its own version of the neutron bomb. Work began on the neutron bomb in the U.S. in 1958 and the first successful test was conducted in 1962. The neutron bomb is also called the enhanced radiation weapon (ERW).

NEVADA TEST SITE is the principal United States nuclear test site. Great Britain also conducts its nuclear tests at the Nevada Test Site. Established in the early 1950s, it is located 180 km northwest of Las Vegas and covers about 800,000 acres of desert terrain. The Nevada Test Site was established because of the expense and logistical problems associated with conducting American nuclear testing in the South Pacific. Since 1963, all tests at the Nevada Test Site have been conducted underground. The area surrounding the Nevada Test Site has been plagued by deadly radioactive fallout. Thousands of sheep deaths and disproportionate rates of leukemia and other cancers among local residents have resulted from the tests conducted there.

NEW LOOK PROGRAM was U.S. military policy in the 1950s, during the Eisenhower Administration. Essentially, the New Look used nuclear weapons as an inexpensive substitute for conventional forces, giving rise to the expression "more bang for the buck." After World War II and the Korean War, President Eisenhower felt considerable pressure to reduce the size of the military. At the same time, however, the Cold War was at its height and American leaders were wary about signaling weakness to the Soviet Union. The New Look attempted to resolve this dilemma by enabling conventional forces (such as troops in Europe) to be replaced by nuclear weapons. The New Look also incorporated the policy of MASSIVE RETALIATION, which held that the U.S. would respond to communist aggression anywhere in the world with a devastating, all-out nuclear attack.

NIGHTWATCH   see NATIONAL EMERGENCY AIRBORNE COMMAND POST

NIKE-HERCULES is a U.S. surface-to-air missile. See SURFACE-TO-AIR MISSILE for a complete description of the Nike-Hercules.

NIKE-ZEUS was a proposed U.S. system for defending against a nuclear attack. Nike-Zeus would have consisted of RADARS and defensive missiles. Nike-Zeus was the first such system, and is the ancestor of the ANTIBALLISTIC MISSILE SYSTEMS of the 1960s and '70s and the STAR WARS weapons of the 1980s. Research on Nike-Zeus began in 1956, and continued into the early 1960s as policymakers argued about whether it would work. President Kennedy concluded in 1961 that Nike-Zeus would be ineffective, and abandoned the project. Research and development continued, however, and in 1974 the U.S. deployed the SAFEGUARD antiballistic missile system in North Dakota. Safeguard was dismantled in 1976 for the same reasons that Nike-Zeus was never built. It was costly and ineffective.

NO-CITIES DOCTRINE   see COUNTERFORCE

NO FIRST USE is a pledge never to introduce NUCLEAR WEAPONS into a conflict. At the United Nations Special Session on Disarmament II in 1982, the Soviet Union issued a no-first-use pledge. The United States, however, has rejected a policy of no first use because it has asserted that the conventional forces of the Warsaw Pact grossly outnumber NATO conventional forces in Europe. The United States therefore has retained the option of using nuclear weapons if Soviet conventional forces attack its allies or military installations abroad.

NOMINAL WEAPON   see MINI-NUKE

NONCENTRAL SYSTEM   see ALLIANCE/REGIONALLY ORIENTED SYSTEM, FORWARD-BASED SYSTEMS

NONNUCLEAR WEAPON   see CONVENTIONAL WEAPON

NONPROLIFERATION TREATY (1968) is a multilateral treaty which aims to control the spread of NUCLEAR WEAPONS. The treaty, which has been signed by over 140 nations, obligates nuclear weapons states to refrain from transferring nuclear weapons or the technology for their development to nonnuclear weapons states. Nonnuclear weapons states agree not to acquire nuclear weapons technology. The treaty also requires that the three signatories who are allowed in the treaty to maintain nuclear weapons (Britain, the United States, and the Soviet Union) pursue NUCLEAR DISARMAMENT. Peaceful use of nuclear technology is not covered in the agreement. Three nuclear weapons states, France, India, and China, have not signed the treaty.

NO NUKES is a popular battlecry of those who oppose nuclear power and weapons.

NORTH AMERICAN AEROSPACE DEFENSE COMMAND (NORAD) is a joint U.S.-Canadian military installation that receives indications of enemy nuclear attacks and coordinates efforts to determine an appropriate response. NORAD is a major nerve center in the U.S. system for commanding its nuclear weapons. It has a direct link to a variety of RADAR and SATELLITE monitoring installations, and is instantly alerted of any potential enemy attack. After receiving this information, NORAD alerts the President and the Secretary of Defense. NORAD would also perform a variety of other functions if a nuclear war were underway. Located deep inside Cheyenne Mountain, Colorado, NORAD is fortified to withstand the effects of a nuclear attack. NORAD was established in the 1960s.

NORTH ATLANTIC TREATY ORGANIZATION   see NATO

NTH COUNTRY is the latest nation to acquire nuclear weapons. See NTH COUNTRY PROBLEM.

NTH COUNTRY PROBLEM refers to a situation in which an increasing number of nations acquire nuclear weapons so as to increase the likelihood of nuclear war. The nth country problem suggests that as more and more countries join the nuclear club, a point will be reached when nuclear war is inevitable.

NUCFLASH is a U.S. military code name for the message that would tell the U.S. President and Secretary of Defense of an accidental or unauthorized launch of a nuclear weapon.

NUCLEAR ACCIDENT is a general term that describes a number of unintended situations involving NUCLEAR WEAPONS or reactors. The U.S. military identifies five possible events as nuclear accidents: the accidental launch of a nuclear missile, the destruction of a nuclear weapon, the radioactive contamination of a nuclear installation, the loss or theft of a nuclear weapon, or any incident involving a nuclear weapon that causes a public danger. A nuclear accident, code-named a broken arrow, is more serious than a NUCLEAR INCIDENT. Unlike a nuclear incident, a nuclear accident poses an immediate danger to life or property.

NUCLEAR AIR BURST   see AIR BURST

NUCLEAR ARMS   see NUCLEAR WEAPONS

NUCLEAR ARMS CONTROL (NAC) encompasses a wide variety of
measures intended to limit or reduce the number of nuclear
weapons throughout the world. Nuclear arms control is a broad
term, which includes two general categories: arms limitation
and arms reduction. Arms limitation involves only restricting
future deployment of nuclear weapons. During the nuclear era,
numerous arms limitation agreements have restricted the proliferation, accumulation, and improvement of nuclear weapons.
Arms reduction, however, is more ambitious and seeks to actually cut the number of nuclear weapons deployed by nations. It
thus involves dismantling existing weapons. No nation has ever
signed an arms reduction agreement to actually eliminate some
of its existing nuclear weapons. Nuclear arms control has been
a central issue in the nuclear era; innumerable groups and individuals have professed arms control as their goal and have
devoted considerable effort toward achieving it. The U.S. and
the U.S.S.R. have engaged intermittently in nuclear arms-control negotiations since the first atomic bomb was dropped on
HIROSHIMA, Japan, in 1945. Virtually every nation in the world
has participated in efforts to control nuclear weapons.

NUCLEAR ARMS LIMITATION   see NUCLEAR ARMS CONTROL

NUCLEAR ARMS RACE refers to an extended competition between
two nations, in which each continually improves the size and
capability of its nuclear arsenal. An arms race is a complex
phenomenon, involving many weapons and many different
types of improvements. Some experts, noting this complexity,
have commented that perhaps arms race is an inappropriate
metaphor. Instead, they suggest, we should think of the arms
race as a track meet, with many different events and a complicated scoring system. The term arms race usually refers to the
U.S.-U.S.S.R. nuclear arms buildup, which has been going on

for over thirty years. Almost all observers agree that the arms race is an undesirable phenomenon, because it consumes tremendous resources and because it perpetuates tensions between the superpowers.

NUCLEAR ARMS REDUCTION   see NUCLEAR ARMS CONTROL

NUCLEAR ARTILLERY refers to small, mobile cannons and tanks that can fire small, tactical NUCLEAR WEAPONS. Nuclear artillery is designed for use over short, battlefield distances. Artillery-fired atomic projectiles, the nuclear weapons fired from nuclear artillery, outnumber all other types of nuclear weapons. Most nuclear artillery is deployed in Europe. The United States deploys many types of nuclear artillery. Among the more prominent are:

- M110 (203mm), which first became operational in 1961. It is a tanklike vehicle capable of delivering nuclear warheads with a yield of 5 to 10 KILOTONS. The M110 can deliver neutron (enhanced radiation) warheads. It is deployed in the U.S., Western Europe, South Korea, and Okinawa.
- M109 (155mm), which first became operational in 1969. It is a tanklike vehicle capable of delivering nuclear warheads with a yield of .1 kilotons. It is deployed in the U.S., Western Europe, South Korea, and Okinawa.
- M198 (155mm), which first became operational in 1979. It is towed by a truck and is capable of delivering nuclear warheads with a yield of .1 kilotons. It is deployed in the U.S., South Korea, and Okinawa.

The U.S.S.R. is known to deploy only one type of nuclear artillery. Other systems might exist, but very little is known about them. The Soviets are believed to be developing new systems in this area.

- S-23 (180mm) is towed by a truck and is capable of delivering a conventional warhead or a 1-kiloton nuclear warhead.

NUCLEAR BALANCE   see STRATEGIC BALANCE

NUCLEAR BLACKMAIL is a situation in which a group or nation uses the threat of a nuclear attack in order to extract political concessions from its adversaries. If a terrorist group, for example, was able to acquire nuclear weapons, it could decide to use them in nuclear blackmail to coerce an opponent into meeting its demands.

NUCLEAR BOMB is an unpropelled nuclear weapon dropped from an aircraft. Nuclear bombs are commonly called gravity bombs. A nuclear bomb must normally be dropped directly over its target. More modern nuclear bombs incorporate parachutes to slow them down and enable them to hit their targets more precisely. The U.S. deploys five types of nuclear bombs (and is developing a sixth), with yields ranging from 5 KILOTONS to 9 MEGATONS. Nuclear bombs can be dropped from tactical aircraft and strategic bombers. The atomic weapons dropped on HIROSHIMA and NAGASAKI, Japan, in World War II were nuclear bombs.

NUCLEAR BONUS EFFECTS consist of unplanned, desirable damage caused by NUCLEAR WEAPONS. A great deal of uncertainty surrounds the use of modern nuclear weapons; no one is sure exactly what would happen if they were launched. Defense planners project a certain amount of damage resulting from a nuclear attack; nuclear bonus effects would be damage over and above these projections. A cloud of deadly fallout unexpectedly drifting over enemy troops would be a nuclear bonus effect.

NUCLEAR BUDDY SYSTEM is a nickname for the complex safeguards that prevent one person from launching a nuclear attack individually. See TWO-MAN RULE, DUAL KEY, PERMISSIVE ACTION LINKS.

NUCLEAR CHAIN REACTION is the process that releases nuclear energy and makes nuclear weapons and power work. As heavy, unstable atoms (such as URANIUM) are split, tremendous energy is released. A nuclear chain reaction involves the splitting of millions of these atoms in a very short time. The energy released when one uranium atom is split is thus multiplied millions of times, releasing a fantastic amount of energy. A nuclear chain reaction sustains itself. As an atom is split it, in turn, causes other atoms to split. In this way, once an uncontrolled nuclear chain reaction is begun, it can proceed almost immediately to a nuclear explosion. A nuclear chain reaction is triggered when a sufficient amount of nuclear material (known as a CRITICAL MASS) is present. A nuclear chain reaction is the essential mechanism of atomic weapons. A nuclear chain reaction can also be controlled, however, by utilizing devices that limit the number of atoms being split. This process is used in nuclear power plants. The possibility of a nuclear chain reaction was first theorized in the 1930s, and the process was adapted to nuclear weapons near the close of World War II.

NUCLEAR CHARGES is a general term for NUCLEAR WARHEADS and bombs. The U.S. and the U.S.S.R. have not agreed on an exact definition for nuclear charges. The U.S. defines nuclear charges as all warheads carried by BALLISTIC MISSILES and CRUISE MISSILES. The Soviet Union's definition is broader and also includes nuclear weapons carried by aircraft.

NUCLEAR CLOUD   see MUSHROOM CLOUD

NUCLEAR CLUB consists of all nations known to possess or to be able to build nuclear weapons. In the mid-1980s, the members of the nuclear club were China, France, Great Britain, India, the Soviet Union, and the United States.

NUCLEAR COLUMN is the hollow pillar of water formed as the result of an underwater nuclear explosion. A nuclear column is the underwater equivalent of the MUSHROOM CLOUD, the cloud of hot air and debris that is formed in the aftermath of an aboveground nuclear explosion. The nuclear column is composed of water, gases, and hot air.

NUCLEAR CONTROL ORDER (NCO) see EMERGENCY ACTION MESSAGE

NUCLEAR DAMAGE ASSESSMENT see POST-STRIKE ASSESSMENT

NUCLEAR DEFENSE see BALLISTIC MISSILE DEFENSE SYSTEM

NUCLEAR DELIVERY SYSTEM encompasses all the components that help transport a NUCLEAR WARHEAD to its target and includes the ballistic missile. It also includes the delivery vehicle —the device that actually carries the warhead to its target—as well as all the equipment that the delivery vehicle depends on. Missiles and bombers are two types of nuclear delivery vehicles. A typical delivery system also includes the silo that houses the missile and the RADAR that guides the missile to its target.

NUCLEAR DELIVERY VEHICLE is a device that carries a NUCLEAR WARHEAD to its target. There are many types of nuclear delivery vehicles, including missiles, aircraft, submarines, and artillery shells. Nuclear delivery vehicles are often classified as strategic, theater, or tactical. This classification relates directly to the nuclear weapon's purpose. Strategic nuclear delivery vehicles, such as BALLISTIC MISSILES, can cover thousands of kilometers and strike deep into the homelands of the superpowers. Theater nuclear delivery vehicles are intended for use within a specific geographical area, such as Europe or the Middle East. Slow, low-flying CRUISE MISSILES, as well as shorter-range ballistic missiles, are theater nuclear delivery vehicles. Tactical nuclear delivery vehicles are used over battlefield distances. Nuclear artillery shells fired from tanks are examples of tactical nuclear delivery vehicles.

NUCLEAR DEPTH CHARGE is a nuclear bomb, dropped from a tactical aircraft, that is detonated underwater and used in antisubmarine warfare. The U.S. currently deploys one type of nuclear depth charge.

NUCLEAR DETECTION SYSTEM   see NUDETS

NUCLEAR DETERRENCE is a condition in which nations are restrained from fighting a nuclear war. The threat of MUTUAL ASSURED DESTRUCTION (MAD) has been the basis of nuclear deterrence between the superpowers since the 1960s. With limited means for defending against a nuclear strike, both superpowers have relied on their ability to inflict enormous damage on each other. In this way, they have attempted to deter one another from launching a nuclear attack. Thus, nuclear deterrence between the superpowers is based on each side's capacity to absorb a nuclear strike and then counter with an unacceptably destructive retaliation. Critics of nuclear deterrence contend that it is immoral, since it forces the superpowers to rely on the threat of terror to restrain themselves. Further, critics claim that nuclear deterrence is a risky, all-or-nothing proposition. If deterrence fails and nuclear war does break out, nothing will prevent the conflict from becoming a devastating, all-out war. Proponents, however, have argued that deterrence is a very effective means of avoiding nuclear war in an uncertain and tension-filled international arena. Nuclear deterrence is sometimes called stable deterrence or mutual deterrence.

NUCLEAR DETERRENT is a nuclear arsenal built and maintained in order to deter an enemy from starting a nuclear war. A true nuclear deterrent is established with the hope that it will never be used. Instead, its existence is intended only to restrain an enemy from aggressive behavior. NUCLEAR WEAPONS deployed as part of a nuclear deterrent would be used only in response to enemy attack.

NUCLEAR DETONATION DETECTION SYSTEM (NDDS) is a United States SATELLITE system designed to locate and report nuclear explosions during a nuclear war. It consists of sensors placed atop satellites, and can determine the size and location of nuclear detonations anywhere in the world. NDDS is not intended for use during peacetime, but would be used only during a nuclear war in order to help military leaders redirect their missiles away from targets that have already been blown up. NDDS, which was formerly known as the Integrated Operational Nuclear Detection System, is code-named Forest Green and was first deployed by the United States in the mid-1980s. NDDS replaced an older system called NUDETS.

NUCLEAR DEVICE is a mechanism that produces a nuclear explosion used for testing or peaceful purposes, such as mining. A nuclear device is distinct from a NUCLEAR WEAPON, which is designed to be used in an attack on an enemy.

NUCLEAR DIPLOMACY   see ATOMIC DIPLOMACY

NUCLEAR DISARMAMENT encompasses a wide variety of measures intended to eliminate nuclear weapons throughout the world. Nuclear disarmament seeks to actually cut (and eventually eliminate) the number of nuclear weapons deployed by nations. Although numerous arms limitation agreements have restricted the proliferation, accumulation, and improvement of nuclear weapons, no nation has ever signed a disarmament agreement to actually eliminate some of its existing nuclear weapons. Nuclear disarmament has been a central issue in the nuclear era; innumerable groups and individuals have professed disarmament as their goal and have devoted considerable effort toward achieving it. In particular, the United Nations has identified nuclear disarmament as one of its fundamental objectives. The U.S. and the U.S.S.R. have engaged intermittently in nuclear disarmament negotiations since the first atomic bomb was dropped on HIROSHIMA, Japan, in 1945.

NUCLEAR DISENGAGEMENT is the removal of opposing nuclear forces that are located in areas of direct confrontation. Some analysts advocate nuclear disengagement in central Europe to reduce the danger of a nuclear war resulting from accidents and border incidents. NATO critics of nuclear disengagement claim that Western bloc defenses would be weakened by the removal of NATO nuclear forces in West Germany. One of the most well-known nuclear disengagement proposals was the RAPACKI PLAN, presented before the United Nations General Assembly by Polish Foreign Minister Adam Rapacki in 1957. The Rapacki Plan called for the elimination of nuclear weapons in East and West Germany, Poland, and Czechoslovakia. The United States rejected the plan, partly because it would have eliminated West Germany's central role in NATO's defense of Western Europe.

NUCLEAR DUD is a nuclear weapon that fails to explode.

NUCLEAR ENERGY is released when atoms are split or are combined with other atoms. Nuclear energy is extremely potent; relatively small reactions can produce a tremendous amount of energy. Nuclear energy is the key to nuclear weapons and nuclear power. Nuclear energy is used to propel submarines, generate electricity, and fuel nuclear bombs. See NUCLEAR CHAIN REACTION.

NUCLEAR ERA refers to the period of time in which nuclear weapons have played a major role in world issues. From the moment the first atomic bomb was dropped by the United States on HIROSHIMA, Japan, in August 1945, nuclear weapons have played a monumental role in international affairs. During the nuclear era, six nations (China, France, Great Britain, India, the Soviet Union, and the United States) have exploded nuclear devices and together they have accumulated a total of about 50,000 nuclear weapons. In addition, the nuclear era has been marked by an intense arms race between the Soviet Union and the United States. During the nuclear era, several nuclear arms-control agreements have limited the proliferation, accumulation, and improvement of nuclear weapons. But no nuclear weapons state has ever signed an agreement to eliminate some of its nuclear weapons.

NUCLEAR EXOATMOSPHERIC BURST is a nuclear explosion that occurs in space, outside the earth's atmosphere. At this altitude, at least 100 kilometers above the earth's surface, the effects of the explosion on the earth are limited.

NUCLEAR FISSION is a type of nuclear reaction. In a fission reaction, one large, unstable atom (such as URANIUM) is split into two smaller atoms, releasing tremendous energy. Fission occurs naturally when a sufficient quantity of nuclear material (known as a CRITICAL MASS) is present. Fission must be distinguished from NUCLEAR FISSION, in which two small hydrogen atoms are combined. Fission is much less potent than fusion. It is the essential mechanism of atomic weapons and nuclear power and is used to trigger THERMONUCLEAR WEAPONS. Unlike fusion, many forms of harmful radiation are released in fission reactions.

NUCLEAR FLASH   see THERMAL PULSE

NUCLEAR FOOTPRINT is the pattern formed by the detonation of several NUCLEAR WARHEADS. Many missiles carry several nuclear warheads. This technology, known as MULTIPLE INDEPENDENTLY TARGETED REENTRY VEHICLE (MIRV), allows a single missile to release more than one nuclear warhead. These warheads can be aimed individually at a single target but made to land at slightly different points and times. A nuclear footprint implies that one missile causes damage over a wide area and leaves a distinctive pattern.

NUCLEAR FREEZE is a ban on the testing, production, and deployment of nuclear weapons. During the early 1980s, a "mutual and verifiable" nuclear freeze for the U.S. and the U.S.S.R. was commonly discussed in the United States. It generated widespread public interest and sparked considerable discussion in government and among peace groups. At that time, the Soviet Union officially supported a nuclear freeze. In 1982, however, "the freeze" was narrowly defeated in Congress. Advocates contend that a nuclear freeze would halt the arms race and give the superpowers breathing room to pursue further arms-control measures. Critics, however, argue that it would be impossible to verify Soviet compliance with a nuclear freeze. Critics also believe that a freeze would leave the superpowers unable to remedy existing inequalities in their nuclear arsenals.

NUCLEAR-FREE ZONE (NFZ) is a region in which nuclear weapons are prohibited. Several arms-control agreements have established nuclear-free zones, including the ANTARCTIC TREATY of 1959 and the Latin American Nuclear Free Zone Treaty of 1967. A nuclear-free zone is also known as a denuclearized zone.

NUCLEAR FUSION is a type of nuclear reaction. In a fusion reaction, two small light hydrogen atoms are forcibly combined into one larger atom, releasing tremendous energy. Fusion is triggered by tremendous heat, such as that released in a fission reaction. Fusion must be distinguished from NUCLEAR FISSION, in which one large, unstable atom is split. Fusion is much more potent than fission. Fusion is the essential mechanism of THERMONUCLEAR WEAPONS, but has never been harnessed as a peaceful source of electricity. Unlike fission, fusion reactions do not release much harmful radiation.

NUCLEAR HALF-LIFE   see HALF-LIFE

NUCLEAR HOLOCAUST is the tremendous toll of death and destruction that would result from an all-out nuclear war. The inevitability of a nuclear holocaust if nuclear weapons are launched is a matter of some controversy. Proponents of LIMITED NUCLEAR WAR argue that it is possible to restrict the use of NUCLEAR WEAPONS in a conflict. Others, however, argue that any use of nuclear weapons would quickly escalate into a devastating nuclear holocaust.

NUCLEAR HOT SPOTS are geographical regions in which a crisis leading to a nuclear war could occur. The Middle East is commonly referred to as a nuclear hot spot.

NUCLEAR INCIDENT is a general term that describes a number of unintended situations involving NUCLEAR WEAPONS or reactors. The U.S. military identifies two possible events as nuclear incidents: damage to a nuclear weapon requiring repair or replacement of the weapon, or any event involving nuclear weapons which causes an adverse public reaction. A nuclear incident, code-named a bent spear, is less serious than a NUCLEAR ACCIDENT. Unlike a nuclear accident a nuclear incident does not pose an immediate danger to life or property. An insignificant nuclear incident is code-named a dull sword.

NUCLEAR MATERIAL   see FISSIONABLE MATERIAL

NUCLEAR MATERIAL CONVENTION (1977–1980) aims to prevent the military use of nuclear material that is intended for peaceful purposes. Nuclear material, such as radioactive PLUTONIUM, could be used either to make nuclear weapons or to generate electricity in nuclear reactors. The convention also establishes standards of protection for nuclear material during storage and transport. It calls for international cooperation in the recovery and return of stolen nuclear material. The convention document has been signed by over 30 nations.

NUCLEAR MINE   see ATOMIC DEMOLITION MUNITION

NUCLEAR NATION is any country that possesses technology for developing either nuclear weapons or peaceful nuclear reactors.

NUCLEAR NONPROLIFERATION encompasses measures designed to prevent the acquisition of NUCLEAR WEAPONS by nations that do not already possess them. The Nuclear Nonproliferation Treaty of 1968 prohibits the spread of nuclear weapons. In addition, the International Atomic Energy Agency and the nations that supply nuclear materials have adopted strict controls to limit the transfer of technology and materials that might enable nations to acquire nuclear weapons.

NUCLEAR OPERATIONS PLAN (NOP) is the top-secret NATO strategy for fighting a nuclear war. Established in 1968, the NOP is drawn up by military leaders representing all the nations that belong to NATO. In the NOP, NATO follows a policy of FLEXIBLE RESPONSE, which enables NATO to match enemy aggression with a variety of responses. The official name of the NOP is the Supreme Allied Command Europe Supplementary Plan.

NUCLEAR PARITY see PARITY

NUCLEAR PLANNING GROUP (NPG) is an organization that acts as a forum for planning NATO's nuclear strategy. While the NPG seeks to involve all NATO members in formulating strategy, the ultimate decision to use a nuclear weapon remains with the country that owns it. The NPG was established in 1966 and includes both permanent and rotating members. The U.S., Great Britain, West Germany, and Italy are the permanent members of the NPG since NATO's nuclear weapons are deployed in all four of these countries. In addition, three to four other alliance members serve on the NPG on a rotating basis for 9 to 18 months. The NPG meets twice a year and discussions are carried out by national defense secretaries as well as permanent representatives to NATO.

NUCLEAR PLENTY refers to a military arsenal that contains a large number of NUCLEAR WEAPONS capable of striking many different targets. A nation with nuclear plenty maintains a capacity to strike a virtually unlimited number of enemy targets.

NUCLEAR POWER has two different meanings. First, it refers to a nation that possesses NUCLEAR WEAPONS. Nuclear powers are known most commonly as NUCLEAR WEAPONS STATES. Five countries currently possess nuclear weapons: China, France,

Great Britain, the Soviet Union, and the United States. Second, nuclear power refers to electricity produced when atoms are split. Nuclear power is created in a NUCLEAR REACTOR and supplies a significant portion of the world's electricity.

NUCLEAR-POWERED BALLISTIC MISSILE SUBMARINE (SSBN)   see BALLISTIC MISSILE SUBMARINE

NUCLEAR-POWERED CRUISE MISSILE SUBMARINE (SSGN)
see CRUISE MISSILE SUBMARINE

NUCLEAR PROLIFERATION is the spread of NUCLEAR WEAPONS to nations that do not already possess them. Many experts agree that nuclear proliferation is a very alarming prospect. As more nations acquire nuclear weapons, these experts contend, it becomes more likely that they will eventually be used. While knowledge of how to build nuclear weapons is not hard to acquire today, the accessibility of material needed to build nuclear weapons has been stiffly regulated. The Nuclear Nonproliferation Treaty of 1968 has been signed in an effort to prohibit the spread of nuclear weapons. In addition, the INTERNATIONAL ATOMIC ENERGY AGENCY and the nations that supply nuclear materials have adopted strict controls to limit the transfer of technology and materials which might enable nations to acquire nuclear weapons. See VERTICAL PROLIFERATION, HORIZONTAL PROLIFERATION.

NUCLEAR-PUMPED X-RAY LASER   see X-RAY LASER WEAPON

NUCLEAR RADIATION is a general term for all of the deadly RADIATION emitted in the aftermath of a nuclear explosion. Exposure to nuclear radiation may cause radiation sickness, genetic damage, cancer, or death. Nuclear radiation includes two basic types of radiation: PROMPT RADIATION and FALLOUT RADIATION. Prompt radiation is the energy released by a nuclear explosion itself. Fallout radiation, on the other hand, consists of debris that has been contaminated by radioactive by-products of a nuclear explosion. Prompt radiation, though extremely intense, affects a very limited area for a short time only. Fallout radiation, however, may affect the entire earth for months or years.

NUCLEAR REACTOR is a device in which atoms are split at a controlled rate. Unlike nuclear weapons, nuclear reactors cannot blow up. Nuclear reactors could, however, be very dangerous. If a meltdown (runaway reaction) occurred, radioactive waste could be dispersed over a wide area. Nuclear reactors have three principal applications: to produce PLUTONIUM to fuel NUCLEAR WEAPONS, to generate electricity, and to power naval vessels. Most of the submarines that carry nuclear missiles are powered by nuclear reactors. The technology needed to build and operate nuclear reactors has been carefully controlled in accordance with the Nuclear Nonproliferation Treaty and INTERNATIONAL ATOMIC ENERGY AGENCY guidelines.

NUCLEAR REPROCESSING   see REPROCESSING

NUCLEAR SAFETY LINE is an imaginary boundary that surrounds the area affected by a nuclear explosion. The nuclear safety line is a military term, usually applied to situations where battlefield NUCLEAR WEAPONS are used. The area within the nuclear safety line would be a sort of forbidden zone, off-limits to friendly troops.

NUCLEAR SHOW OF FORCE is the explosion of a NUCLEAR WEAPON by a nation in order to demonstrate resolve and further willingness to use nuclear weapons. To show that it "means business," a nation may explode a nuclear weapon high over an enemy city in order to force an enemy to back down in a crisis. A nuclear show of force that is not acknowledged by an enemy may lead to a more damaging strike. A nuclear show of force is sometimes referred to as an exemplary or symbolic attack.

NUCLEAR STALEMATE is a condition in which two nations are restrained from launching a nuclear attack because they fear that it will invite an unacceptably destructive retaliation. Since the early 1960s, many analysts have characterized relations between the superpowers as a nuclear stalemate. These analysts claim that the ability of both superpowers to absorb a nuclear strike and to then retaliate in kind has prevented them from starting a nuclear war.

NUCLEAR STOCKPILE contains NUCLEAR WEAPONS that are in storage but not actually deployed. Nuclear weapons in a stockpile are several steps away from DEPLOYMENT. Before they can be used in battle, they may have to be assembled and tested. In addition, weapons in a nuclear stockpile must be transported to launch facilities, such as air force bases or missile sites. A nuclear stockpile can contain many different types of weapons, ranging from large, powerful BALLISTIC MISSILE warheads to small artillery shells.

NUCLEAR SUPERIORITY refers to a situation in which a nation's nuclear arsenal is significantly stronger than any other nation's nuclear force. Nuclear superiority (or the perception of nuclear superiority) could be very destabilizing. If a nation perceives itself to have nuclear superiority over an opponent, it may feel confident enough to launch a nuclear attack. On the other side of the coin, a nation that perceives itself to be in a position of nuclear inferiority may feel threatened and, in desperation, launch a nuclear attack. In the late 1940s and early 1950s, the United States maintained overwhelming nuclear superiority in the world. By the early 1960s, however, the Soviet Union had built a nuclear arsenal that challenged U.S. nuclear superiority. Because NUCLEAR WEAPONS technology is much more sophisticated today than it was forty years ago, it is now extremely difficult to determine whether any nation possesses overall nuclear superiority. Today, nuclear superiority is usually considered more narrowly, in terms of a particular category of nuclear weapons, such as land-based missiles.

NUCLEAR SUPPLIERS GROUP is a 15-nation organization that aims to prevent the proliferation of nuclear weapons by restricting exports of sensitive technology and material. The Nuclear Suppliers Group, also known as the London Suppliers Club, enforces strict international guidelines intended to prevent nations from using sophisticated technology and material to make nuclear weapons. In this way, the Nuclear Suppliers Group seeks to promote the peaceful use of NUCLEAR ENERGY. The Nuclear Suppliers Group was established partly in response to India's "peaceful" nuclear explosion in 1974. In defiance of existing guidelines, India had used technology and materials supplied by the U.S. and Canada to detonate a nuclear device. India's explosion made nuclear suppliers more aware of the difficulty of distinguishing between military and peaceful nuclear technology. The Nuclear Suppliers Group first met in London in November 1975, and includes fifteen nations from both East and West, including the Soviet Union and the United States.

NUCLEAR TABOO describes a situation in which the use of NUCLEAR WEAPONS is not welcome or advised.

NUCLEAR TERRORISM is the use or threatened use of NUCLEAR WEAPONS for coercive purposes.

NUCLEAR TESTING involves closely monitored explosions of experimental nuclear devices. Testing is a vital stage in the development of new NUCLEAR WEAPONS and is important for two reasons. First, it is the only real means of proving that a bomb design works. In addition, it is the best way to demonstrate a system's power to other nations. Because nuclear testing disperses deadly radioactive FALLOUT in the environment, it has been sharply curtailed. The LIMITED TEST BAN TREATY of 1963 prohibits nuclear testing above the ground, underwater, and in outer space. Thus virtually all nuclear tests since 1963 have been conducted underground, where they do not cause as much damage to the environment. In addition, the U.S., the U.S.S.R., and Great Britain have held negotiations to completely prohibit nuclear tests, but these talks were suspended in 1979 after a general deterioration in superpower relations. Finally, since 1976, the U.S. and the U.S.S.R. have observed a 150-kiloton limit on their nuclear tests, as mandated by the THRESHOLD TEST BAN TREATY. In recent years, Great Britain, France, and China have also observed this limit in their nuclear tests.

NUCLEAR TEST SITE is the location at which a nation conducts nuclear tests. Nuclear test sites are sophisticated installations, equipped to carefully analyze the explosion of experimental nuclear devices. Every nation that currently deploys NUCLEAR WEAPONS maintains a nuclear test site. See LOP NOR, MURUROA ATOLL, NEVADA TEST SITE, SEMIPALATINSK.

NUCLEAR UMBRELLA refers to one nation's nuclear arsenal when it is used to provide protection for other nations. U.S. nuclear weapons form a nuclear umbrella for the NATO countries of Western Europe.

NUCLEAR UTILIZATION THEORY (NUT) is a doctrine that emphasizes using NUCLEAR WEAPONS in a conflict. Also known as Nuclear Utilization Target Selection, NUT encompasses various doctrines that seek to employ nuclear weapons against specific targets in a variety of NUCLEAR WAR-FIGHTING situations.

NUCLEAR VULNERABILITY ASSESSMENT is an estimate of the probable effects of a nuclear attack on a nation's civilian population, military forces, and industry. Military strategists would use a nuclear vulnerability assessment to determine the damage that would be caused by a nuclear war.

NUCLEAR WAR-FIGHTING encompasses those measures taken by a nation to prepare to engage in a nuclear war. Nuclear war-fighting strategy does not necessarily advocate war; rather, it comprises the actions a nation takes to decide how to use its nuclear forces. A NUCLEAR WEAPONS STATE may have several types of nuclear war-fighting strategies. In particular, it may plan to target enemy population, industrial, or military centers. The central United States nuclear war plan is called the SINGLE INTEGRATED OPERATIONAL PLAN.

NUCLEAR WARHEAD is the part of a NUCLEAR WEAPON that contains the mechanism that explodes. A nuclear warhead is the part of a weapon that actually blows up and inflicts damage. A nuclear warhead is contained in any nuclear weapon, including CRUISE MISSILES, artillery shells, BALLISTIC MISSILES, and bombs carried by aircraft. The term is often used as a synonym for REENTRY VEHICLE, but this usage is only applicable to ballistic missiles. A reentry vehicle is a warhead that is designed to reenter the atmosphere from space. It thus includes specific components, such as a heat shield, to protect it from the great heat and pressure it faces upon reentry.

NUCLEAR WARNING SHOT is a single nuclear explosion, ordered to demonstrate resolve to an enemy in a crisis. A nuclear warning shot would be used as a means of demonstrating a nation's willingness to use NUCLEAR WEAPONS without actually launching a nuclear attack. Critics contend that a nuclear warning shot would be extremely dangerous, since it could be perceived as an actual nuclear attack.

NUCLEAR WEAPON is a general term which refers to two types of arms: ATOMIC WEAPONS and THERMONUCLEAR WEAPONS. The key to nuclear weapons is the nucleus, the tiny, compact core of an atom. In atomic weapons, one nucleus is split; in thermonuclear weapons, two nuclei are combined. Nuclear weapons are different from other weapons in many ways. First, the magnitude of the explosion created by a nuclear weapon may be tremendous. Many nuclear weapons are equivalent to thousands or millions of tons of TNT, although less powerful nuclear weapons do exist. Second, nuclear weapons produce deadly RA-DIATION, which can cause genetic damage, cancer, radiation sickness, and death. The effects of this radiation could linger for thousands of years after a nuclear explosion. Finally, the true effects of nuclear weapons are shrouded in mystery, since modern nuclear weapons have never been used in an attack. Effects such as OZONE DEPLETION and NUCLEAR WINTER could extinguish life on earth. In the mid-1980s, a total of about 50,000 nuclear weapons were in the possession of the United States, the U.S.S.R., Great Britain, France, and China. Atomic weapons were first built in 1945; thermonuclear weapons, in 1952. The term nuclear weapon refers to all atomic and thermonuclear weapons, with yields ranging from fractions of a kiloton to many megatons. Nuclear weapons are deployed on ships, in submarines, in aircraft, and in underground missile silos. A nuclear weapon is designed to be used to attack an enemy. It is thus distinct from a NUCLEAR DEVICE, which creates a nuclear explosion used for tests and other peaceful purposes.

NUCLEAR WEAPON-FREE ZONE   see NUCLEAR-FREE ZONE

NUCLEAR WEAPONS EMPLOYMENT PLAN (NUWEP) is a document that outlines American nuclear strategy. Developed by the Secretary of Defense, NUWEP contains all the plans, objectives, and options for using U.S. nuclear weapons. NUWEP sets broad guidelines for the SINGLE INTEGRATED OPERATIONAL PLAN, America's detailed, top-secret plan for nuclear war. The first NUWEP was established by Secretary of Defense Robert McNamara in the early 1960s.

NUCLEAR WEAPONS STATE is a nation that possesses nuclear weapons. Nuclear weapons states are also referred to as NUCLEAR POWERS. Currently there are five nuclear weapons states: China, France, Great Britain, the Soviet Union, and the United States. India exploded a "peaceful" nuclear device in May 1974. While it contends that the device was not a nuclear weapon, some experts have claimed that it was exploded in order to demonstrate India's capability to build nuclear weapons.

NUCLEAR WEAPONS TEST   see NUCLEAR TESTING

NUCLEAR WEAPONS TEST BAN refers to a partial or complete cessation of nuclear testing. See COMPREHENSIVE TEST BAN, LIMITED TEST BAN, THRESHOLD TEST BAN.

NUCLEAR WINTER is a possible situation in which the earth would undergo severe and perilous climatic changes immediately following a nuclear war. The term nuclear winter was coined by American physicist Richard Turco and originated in a 1983 article in the journal *Science*. In the article, written by Turco and his colleagues Thomas Ackerman, James Pollard, Carl Sagan, and Owen Toon, the authors describe a nuclear winter in which large areas of the planet would be subjected to prolonged periods of darkness, below-freezing temperatures, violent windstorms, and persistent radioactive fallout. The authors attribute these freezing temperatures to a large blanket of dust and smoke thrown up in the aftermath of many nuclear explosions, which would prevent the sun's rays from reaching the earth. These lowered temperatures, the authors assert, would last for several months and threaten to ruin crops and freeze human beings and animals. They also claim that a toxic smog, loaded with the debris of burned cities, could circle the Northern Hemisphere and possibly have disastrous effects for the entire earth. While most scientists agree that nuclear winter is possible, many disagree over the extent to which it would occur and exactly how many weapons would need to be exploded in order to cause nuclear winter. Scientists in 1986 claimed that original predictions of temperature variations were too great and that the actual temperature decline during a nuclear winter would be less severe. In any case, the idea of nuclear winter implies that a nation would be endangering itself by launching a nuclear attack.

NUCLEAR YIELD   see YIELD

NUCLEON is an extremely small particle that, together with other nucleons, makes up the nucleus, the tiny, compact core of an atom. Nucleons are protons and neutrons, the two types of particles that combine to form the nucleus. The nucleus is the key to NUCLEAR WEAPONS. In ATOMIC WEAPONS, one large nucleus is split; in thermonuclear weapons, two small nuclei are combined. Both types of reactions release tremendous energy.

NUDETS (NUCLEAR DETECTION SYSTEM) is a combination of U.S. SATELLITES and SENSORS which are used to detect and assess nuclear detonation during a nuclear war. They assess damage in order to allow authorities to make decisions in a nuclear war. NUDETS is a general term for these systems, which include the American NUCLEAR DETONATION DETECTION SYSTEM.

NUKE is the shortened form of the word nuclear. In the verb form, it means to destroy or annihilate an area in a nuclear war. As a noun, it refers to NUCLEAR WEAPONS or power plants.

O

OAK RIDGE, Tennessee, is the site of a massive installation built as part of the MANHATTAN PROJECT during World War II. The Manhattan Project was America's World War II drive to build the first atomic weapons. The plants at Oak Ridge produced the enriched URANIUM that fueled LITTLE BOY, the bomb dropped on the Japanese city of HIROSHIMA. The Oak Ridge facilities are today used chiefly for the production of fuel for nuclear reactors.

OBSERVABLE DIFFERENCES (ODs) are any observable structural features of an aircraft that determine its military role. A refueling probe on an aircraft is an example of a observable difference. With a refueling probe, an aircraft can refuel other aircraft in flight; it is thus regarded as a tanker rather than a bomber. ODs were particularly important during the SALT II negotiations. They were an attempt by negotiators to distinguish between those types of aircraft limited by the treaty and those that were not. ODs were not considered precise enough to classify aircraft, however, and FUNCTIONALLY RELATED OBSERVABLE DIFFERENCES (FRODs) were used instead. In the example above, an aircraft with a refueling probe might still have bomb bay doors, allowing it to serve as either a bomber or a tanker. FRODs account for this variable, while ODs do not.

OFFENSIVE NUCLEAR WEAPON is a general term for a NUCLEAR WEAPON that is designed to attack and destroy enemy targets. Offensive nuclear weapons may be used either to initiate or respond to a nuclear attack. The world's nuclear arsenal consists of about 50,000 offensive nuclear weapons. Because nations are virtually prohibited from using nuclear missiles to defend against a nuclear attack (the ANTIBALLISTIC MISSILE TREATY of 1972 between the U.S. and U.S.S.R. limits missile defense systems), they must rely on their ability to launch an unacceptably destructive retaliation with offensive nuclear weapons in order to deter an enemy attack. Most currently deployed nuclear weapons are classified as offensive nuclear weapons.

OFFSETTING ASYMMETRIES describes the relationship between the nuclear forces of the Soviet Union and the United States. An example of offsetting asymmetries is the notion that the Soviet Union's advantage in large, land-based BALLISTIC MISSILES is offset by the United States' superiority in submarines and bombers. Many strategists claim that offsetting asymmetries constitute a balance in nuclear forces between the superpowers.

ON-SITE INSPECTION (OSI) is a visit to a nation's nuclear facilities conducted in order to verify nuclear arms-control agreements. The Soviet Union has traditionally rejected OSI in nuclear arms-control negotiations because it claims OSI is unnecessary and tantamount to "legalized espionage." The United States has continually made OSI a prerequisite for the verification of any arms-control agreement.

ON THE BEACH is a 1959 American film about the destruction of the earth in a nuclear war. Originally a best-selling book by Nevil Shute, *On the Beach* gives a blunt, powerful account of what life might be like following a nuclear war. The details of the actual war are not dealt with; instead, the film focuses on how a group of survivors in Melbourne, Australia, deal with their final days. In general, most of the survivors accept death with unusual calmness and continue with their lives as if nothing had happened. The normalcy of life following the nuclear holocaust shocked many viewers. Despite the war, people continue to fish for relaxation: A country club rations its best wines to its members. Nevertheless, knowing that life will be impossible in a world destroyed by nuclear war, many people begin to commit suicide rather than face a bleak existence and uncertain future. Gregory Peck stars as a nuclear submarine commander who brings his crew to Melbourne to seek refuge. The film was directed by Stanley Kramer.

OPANAL (Organismo para la Proscripcion de las Armas Nucleares en America Latina) is an organization that enforces the ban on NUCLEAR WEAPONS in Latin America. OPANAL was established to supervise compliance with the TREATY OF TLATELOLCO of 1967, which prohibits nuclear weapons from being deployed in Central or South America. OPANAL's headquarters are in Mexico.

OPEN SKIES PROPOSAL called for a U.S.-Soviet exchange of military information and the opening of all national airspace (even the sky above missile sites) to aerial reconnaissance flights. The proposal, extended as a means of reducing tension in the arms race and verifying arms-control agreements, was rejected by the Soviets because it was seen as a threat to national security. The Open Skies Proposal was forwarded by President Dwight Eisenhower in 1955.

OPERATIONAL FEASIBILITY addresses the issue of whether a nuclear weapon can be actually tested and deployed. The United States, for example, is considering the operational feasibility of building a missile defense shield as part of its STRATEGIC DEFENSE INITIATIVE, commonly known as "Star Wars." Operational feasibility is a major issue in the construction of any NUCLEAR WEAPONS system. It is considered in conjunction with SCIENTIFIC FEASIBILITY, TECHNICAL FEASIBILITY, and ECONOMIC FEASIBILITY.

OPERATION BUSTER-JANGLE was a series of U.S. nuclear tests conducted at the NEVADA TEST SITE in 1952. During one of the tests, a group of 5,000 American soldiers was intentionally exposed to the blast in order to study the effects of a nuclear explosion on nearby troops. The leukemia rates of soldiers exposed to this and other nuclear tests in the 1950s is about 400 times greater than the national average.

OPERATION RANGER was the first series of nuclear tests conducted within the continental United States. Operation Ranger was held at the NEVADA TEST SITE in 1951. All U.S. nuclear tests are now held at the Nevada Test Site.

OPERATION TEAPOT was a series of American nuclear tests conducted at the NEVADA TEST SITE in 1955. During Operation Teapot, a group of 9,000 American soldiers were intentionally exposed to the blast in order to study the effects of a nuclear explosion on nearby troops. Cancer rates of soldiers exposed to nuclear tests during the 1950s is about 400 times greater than the national average.

OPTIMUM HEIGHT OF BURST refers to the height at which a nuclear weapon is detonated in order to cause maximum damage to a target. See HEIGHT OF BURST.

ORBITAL BOMBARDMENT SYSTEM (OBS) was a theoretical Soviet method for deploying a nuclear warhead in orbit above the earth. OBS involved launching a BALLISTIC MISSILE armed with a NUCLEAR WARHEAD into space. Once in space, the missile would have placed the warhead into orbit. The warhead would have remained in orbit indefinitely, rotating around the earth like the moon. In the event of a nuclear war, the warhead would have dropped from orbit and reentered the atmosphere en route to its target. A similar system, called FRACTIONAL ORBITAL BOMBARDMENT SYSTEM (FOBS), was also tested by the Soviets. FOBS involved placing the warhead in orbit for a shorter time than the OBS plan. OBS was tested in the mid-1960s but never deployed. It was banned by the Outer Space Treaty of 1967.

OSIRAK was an Iraqi experimental nuclear reactor destroyed in a highly publicized Israeli attack in June 1981. The Osirak reactor was under construction when it was destroyed; the role it would have played is unclear. Iraq contends that it would have been used for peaceful research. Israel, on the other hand, asserts that it would have been used to supply materials to fuel NUCLEAR WEAPONS.

OUTER SPACE TREATY (1967) prohibits the deployment of NUCLEAR WEAPONS, as well as any weapons of mass destruction in outer space. The treaty, which has been signed by over 80 countries, outlaws the establishment of any military fortifications in space and limits use of all celestial bodies (such as the moon) to strictly peaceful purposes. SPACE-BASED DEFENSE systems, which both the United States and the Soviet Union are researching, could violate the Outer Space Treaty.

OVERKILL occurs when more nuclear weapons are used than are necessary to accomplish desired objectives.

OVERPRESSURE refers to the wall of compressed air created in the aftermath of a nuclear explosion. Overpressure can collapse buildings, uproot trees, and crush people. In addition, the high winds that accompany overpressure can hurl deadly debris, such as bits of broken glass. Overpressure is measured in pounds per square inch, and varies according to the size and type of the weapon that is exploded. The overpressure caused by the explosion of a one-megaton bomb over the center of New York City would collapse all buildings within 61 square miles of GROUND ZERO, the point at which the weapon is detonated. There are two types of overpressure: STATIC OVERPRESSURE and DYNAMIC OVERPRESSURE.

OVER-THE-HORIZON (OTH) RADAR is one of two principal RADAR techniques for locating and identifying airborne objects. OTH radar has a comparatively long range; it can "see" objects flying beyond the horizon. OTH radar is distinct from LINE-OF-SIGHT RADAR, which is restricted by the curvature of the earth and has a much more limited range. OTH radar is used for a variety of purposes, including detection of enemy nuclear attacks and missile test flights.

OZONE DEPLETION is one possible effect of nuclear war. A thin layer of ozone (a form of oxygen) blankets the earth's atmosphere and filters out harmful ultraviolet rays emitted by the sun. Exposure to too much ultraviolet radiation can cause sunburn, blindness, and skin cancer. When a nuclear weapon explodes, it creates and disperses many substances that can deplete the protective ozone layer. The actual extent of large-scale ozone depletion is a matter of controversy, since the phenomenon has never occurred. Some experts estimate, however, that a number of nuclear explosions within a short period could cause blindness and skin disease for all humans and animals in the Northern Hemisphere. Further, some scientists have postulated that it could take as long as 30 years for the ozone layer to be reconstituted once it is destroyed.

P

PARITY is a condition in which two nations' nuclear arsenals are roughly equivalent in capabilities and effectiveness. Parity is a professed goal of both superpowers in nuclear arms-control negotiations. Parity is also a fundamental element that helps restrain nations from fighting nuclear war. With limited means for defending against a nuclear strike, both superpowers rely on their ability to inflict enormous damage on each other. In this way, they attempt to deter each other from launching a nuclear attack. This arrangement works only as long as both sides perceive their nuclear arsenals as equally capable of absorbing a nuclear strike and then countering with an unacceptably destructive retaliation. Thus, parity (or at least the perception of parity) is essential if the superpowers are to be deterred from initiating a nuclear war.

PARTIAL TEST BAN (PTB) see LIMITED TEST BAN

PARTIAL TEST BAN TREATY (PTBT) (1963) see LIMITED TEST BAN TREATY

PARTICLE BEAM WEAPON is a hypothetical weapon that would be part of a high-technology system for protecting against attacking nuclear missiles. Particle beam weapons would generate a concentrated, high-speed beam of energy that would burn a hole in the skin of an attacking missile and deactivate the sensitive electronic equipment responsible for guiding it to its targets. Particle beam weapons must be distinguished from LASER beam weapons, which generate a stream of light instead of particles. Several types of particle beam weapons are currently under development, including ELECTRON BEAM WEAPONS and NEUTRAL PARTICLE BEAM WEAPONS. The United States is

conducting research on particle beam weapons under the STRA-
TEGIC DEFENSE INITIATIVE, commonly known as "Star Wars."

PASSIVE DEFENSE is a general term for certain measures intended
to protect against nuclear attack. Passive defense includes only
measures that do not involve the use of defensive weapons.
Reinforcing probable targets with concrete and earth and evacuating cities are examples of passive defense measures. Passive
defense is distinct from ACTIVE DEFENSE, which involves the use
of defensive weapons to protect against enemy attack.

PASSIVE DETECTION is a general term that describes certain types
of monitoring operations. Passive detection involves locating an
object by noticing light (or other energy) it emits, such as
locating an airplane at night by noticing its wing lights. Passive
detection thus depends on energy which is internal to the object. Passive detection is distinct from ACTIVE DETECTION, which
involves locating an object by noticing light (or other energy)
it reflects, such as locating an airplane by transmitting high-
frequency radio waves and recording them as they are reflected
off the plane. Active detection thus depends on energy which
is external to the object. Passive detection is commonly used to
locate objects such as missiles, aircraft, and submarines.

PASSIVE DETERRENCE is the strategy of threatening a nuclear
attack in order to restrain an opponent from itself launching a
nuclear attack. Passive deterrence requires a credible commitment to use nuclear weapons in response to a direct enemy
attack. It is distinct from ACTIVE DETERRENCE, which is intended more broadly to deter a direct enemy attack on a nation
or on its allies or military forces stationed abroad.

PASSIVE PENETRATION AID   see PENETRATION AID

THE PAUSE   see FIREBREAK

PAVE PAWS is a U.S. RADAR system that detects attacking nuclear
missiles launched from enemy submarines and ships. Pave Paws

is designed to notify decision-makers if an enemy attack is underway so that they can take appropriate action. Pave Paws consists of two stations that use PHASED ARRAY RADAR, a technologically advanced type of radar that can monitor many different objects simultaneously. First deployed in 1979, Pave Paws stations are located in Massachusetts and California and can detect attacking missiles launched from the Pacific Ocean, the Atlantic Ocean, or the Gulf of Mexico. Paws is an acronym for phased array warning system.

PAYLOAD is the weight of the explosive material contained in a NUCLEAR WARHEAD. Payload is often mistaken for THROW-WEIGHT. Payload, however, incorporates the weight of explosive material only. Unlike throw-weight, it does not include other components that add to a missile's weight, such as fuel, electronics, or the casing of the warhead. Payload is one criterion for determining the strength of a nation's nuclear arsenal.

PD-59 (PRESIDENTIAL DIRECTIVE-59) see COUNTERVAILING STRATEGY

PEACE AGENCY see UNITED STATES ARMS CONTROL AND DISARMAMENT AGENCY (ACDA)

PEACEFUL NUCLEAR EXPLOSION (PNE) is any detonation of a nuclear device that is not for a military purpose. Peaceful nuclear explosions could be used for a number of purposes, including mining or altering the course of rivers. The U.S. and the U.S.S.R. have each conducted several peaceful nuclear explosions. The destructive power of peaceful nuclear explosions is limited by the PEACEFUL NUCLEAR EXPLOSION TREATY of 1976.

PEACEFUL NUCLEAR EXPLOSION TREATY (PNET) (1976) is a bilateral treaty that prohibits the United States and the Soviet Union from setting off peaceful nuclear explosions that release a destructive force greater than 150 kilotons. Peaceful nuclear explosions are carried out for nonmilitary purposes such as mining. The treaty is similar to the THRESHOLD TEST BAN TREATY of 1974, which establishes similar restrictions for NUCLEAR WEAPONS explosions. The U.S. Senate has not approved the treaty but both countries have agreed to abide by its terms.

PEACEKEEPER   see MX MISSILE

PENETRABILITY is the capacity of a NUCLEAR WEAPON to penetrate enemy defenses. Because of their mobility and flexibility, bombers can effectively break through enemy barriers and deliver nuclear weapons. The Soviet Union and the United States, however, possess antiaircraft defenses that are designed to reduce a bomber's penetrability. In general, nuclear missiles are virtually assured penetrability, because the ANTIBALLISTIC MISSILE TREATY of 1972 limits the use of systems for defending against ballistic missiles. Penetrability is a major factor in the design of new nuclear weapons.

PENETRATION AID (PEN-AID) is a general term for a device or technique that helps an attacking NUCLEAR MISSILE or bomber reach its target. Pen-aids are divided into two categories: active penetration aids and passive penetration aids. Active pen-aids are more destructive than passive pen-aids; they actually blow up defenses. AIR-TO-AIR MISSILES, carried by bombers and designed to shoot down enemy interceptor fighters, are active pen-aids. Passive pen-aids, on the other hand, confuse enemy defenses. DECOYS, which resemble attacking warheads and are released along with warheads, are passive pen-aids. Pen-aids are widely deployed by the U.S. and the U.S.S.R.

PERIMETER ACQUISITION RADAR ATTACK CHARACTERIZATION SYSTEM (PARCS) is a U.S. RADAR system that detects attacking nuclear missiles and then determines their probable targets. PARCS is designed to notify decision-makers if an enemy attack is underway so they can take appropriate action. First deployed in 1976, PARCS is located in North Dakota.

PERMISSIVE ACTION LINK (PAL) is a safety device that restrains the firing of a NUCLEAR WEAPON. PALs are electrically coded locks that prevent the launching of U.S. nuclear weapons without presidential authorization. In order to unlock PALs, a crew officer must insert a proper code. PALs are installed in most modern nuclear weapons.

PERSHING MISSILE is a type of U.S. BALLISTIC MISSILE. The Pershing Ia is a short-range ballistic missile (see SHORT-RANGE BALLISTIC MISSILE for a complete description of the Pershing Ia); the Pershing II is a medium-range ballistic missile (see MEDIUM-RANGE BALLISTIC MISSILE for a complete description of the Pershing II). See DUAL-TRACK DECISION.

PERSONNEL RELIABILITY PROGRAM (PRP) is the U.S. program of monitoring military personnel who are assigned to work with NUCLEAR WEAPONS. In order to receive such an assignment, an individual must demonstrate that he or she is emotionally stable. Any history of drug or alcohol abuse makes an applicant immediately ineligible for an assignment with a nuclear weapons facility. In addition, qualified personnel undergo frequent physical and psychological screenings under the PRP to ensure that they remain in satisfactory condition.

PHASED ARRAY RADAR is a sophisticated type of radar that can detect and identify airborne objects. RADAR beams radio waves into the sky, which bounce off airborne objects. When they are reflected back, the radio waves are analyzed and reveal the object's size, speed, position, etc. Phased-array radar is a very advanced type of radar that can track hundreds of objects simultaneously. The U.S. and the U.S.S.R. have developed phased array radar as a means of monitoring for enemy nuclear attacks. In this way, phased array radar can notify decision-makers if an enemy attack is underway so that they can take appropriate action. Phased-array radar has been restricted by the ANTIBALLISTIC MISSILE (ABM) TREATY of 1972, which stipulates that phased array radars must be deployed only on the periphery of a nation's territory and must point outward, so that their only function would be to warn of enemy attack. In this way, phased array radar could not be used as part of a defensive system to identify and shoot down attacking missiles.

PHASING is a method of gradually reducing nuclear arms over a period of years. Arms-control experts disagree whether it is wiser to reduce nuclear weapons all at once or through a phasing process. Phasing would enable nations to assess incrementally the consequences of arms control in order to determine future reductions.

PHYSICIANS FOR SOCIAL RESPONSIBILITY (PSR) is an organization of U.S. doctors that aims to increase public awareness of the threat of nuclear war. PSR seeks to promote public and professional education of the psychological and medical consequences of nuclear war. Founded in 1961 by cardiologist Bernard Lown, PSR consists of over 150 chapters and 30,000 members from the medical profession nationwide. PSR lobbied heavily for the LIMITED TEST BAN TREATY of 1963, which severely restricted nuclear testing. PSR became dormant in the 1960s and was revived in the 1970s by Dr. Helen Caldicott.

PHYSICS PACKAGES is a nickname for NUCLEAR MISSILES and NUCLEAR WARHEADS.

PINETREE is a joint U.S.-Canadian radar system that detects attacking enemy bombers. Pinetree is designed to notify decision-makers if an enemy attack is underway so they can take appropriate action. Pinetree forms a chain of radar stations that stretch through the pine forests just north of the U.S.-Canadian border. The Pinetree line was built in the late 1950s.

PLATEAU D'ALBION is the location where French land-based NU-CLEAR MISSILES are deployed. The Plateau d'Albion contains the land-based component of the FORCE DE FRAPPE, France's independent nuclear arsenal. The Plateau d'Albion is located in southern France, near the city of Avignon. Eighteen S-3 INTER-MEDIATE-RANGE BALLISTIC MISSILES are deployed at the Plateau d'Albion. The system is maintained on permenant alert so that all eighteen missiles can be fired after a one-minute warning.

PLUTON is a French short-range ballistic missile. See SHORT-RANGE BALLISTIC MISSILE for a complete description of this missile.

PLUTONIUM is an element that is a basic raw material for many types of nuclear weapons and reactors. It is a by-product of fission (atom-splitting) reactions, which take place in nuclear reactors. In a fission reaction, URANIUM atoms are split, release energy, and decompose into a complex mixture containing plutonium atoms. A technique called REPROCESSING separates these plutonium atoms. Plutonium is a heavy, unstable element that can easily be split. As it is split, tremendous energy is released. Plutonium is highly radioactive—exposure to even a tiny particle is very dangerous. Large amounts of plutonium are created in a nuclear explosion and are dispersed throughout the environment in FALLOUT. Strict controls have been imposed upon the transfer of plutonium in an effort to limit the spread of nuclear weapons.

PLUTONIUM SEPARATION   see REPROCESSING

PLUTONIUM WEAPONS are NUCLEAR WEAPONS fueled by plutonium. Plutonium does not occur in nature; it is a highly radioactive substance created in nuclear reactors. Plutonium weapons comprise the vast majority of the atomic weapons in existence today.

POINT DEFENSE is designed to protect a specific site, such as an underground missile silo, from enemy nuclear attack. Point defense is distinct from AREA DEFENSE, which protects a large region, such as a city.

POINT TARGET is a specific site, such as an underground missile silo, which is targeted in a nuclear attack. A point target is distinct from an AREA TARGET, which encompasses a large region, such as a city.

POKARAN, a town in the Rajasthan Desert in India, is where India conducted its first and only nuclear explosion in May 1974.

POLARIS MISSILE, modernized under the CHEVALINE program, is a British submarine-launched ballistic missile. See SUBMARINE-LAUNCHED BALLISTIC MISSILE for a complete description of the Polaris missile.

POLARIS SUBMARINE is a class of British ballistic missile submarines. See BALLISTIC MISSILE SUBMARINE for a complete description of the Polaris submarine.

POP-UP DEFENSE SYSTEM is a hypothetical system for protecting against attacking nuclear missiles. A pop-up defense system would shoot a concentrated, high-speed stream of light into the sky. This beam could burn a hole in the skin of an attacking missile and deactivate the sensitive electronic equipment responsible for guiding it to its target. These beams would be shot from submarines stationed as close as possible to enemy shores. In this way, they could pop up and intercept enemy missiles soon after they are launched. Proponents of pop-up defense argue that, since it could move around, it would be less vulnerable to an enemy strike than a defense system permanently suspended in space. Opponents, however, contend that it would be more vulnerable to attack because it would have to be deployed very close to enemy territory. See X-RAY LASER WEAPON.

POP-UP LAUNCH   see COLD LAUNCH

POP-UP X-RAY LASER   see X-RAY LASER WEAPON

PORCUPINE is a small, theoretical satellite that could protect nearby satellites. A porcupine would detect and destroy antisatellite weapons. It could shift orbits to destroy a variety of targets. It is called a porcupine because it bristles with small, heat-seeking rockets, called KINETIC KILL VEHICLES, which are fired at attacking antisatellite weapons. The United States is conducting research on porcupine satellites under the STRATEGIC DEFENSE INITIATIVE, commonly known as "Star Wars."

POSEIDON MISSILE is a U.S. submarine-launched ballistic missile. (See SUBMARINE-LAUNCHED BALLISTIC MISSILE for a complete description of the Poseidon missile.)

POSEIDON SUBMARINE (*Lafayette* class) is a U.S. ballistic missile submarine. See BALLISTIC MISSILE SUBMARINE for a complete description of the Poseidon submarine.

POSITIVE CONTROL refers to a nation's ability to recall NUCLEAR WEAPONS that have already been launched. Under positive control, bombers can be recalled or retargeted unless they receive orders to proceed to their targets. In this way, authorities have additional time to verify the validity of an EARLY WARNING of a nuclear attack. Missiles, however, cannot be recalled once they are fired. Positive control, also known as fail-safe, is distinct from FAIL-DEADLY control, which refers to systems that may be activated without final confirmation of orders.

POST-ATTACK ASSESSMENT   see POST-STRIKE ASSESSMENT

POST-ATTACK COMMAND AND CONTROL SYSTEM (PACCS) is a system of airplanes that could serve as U.S. command posts during a nuclear war. Established in February 1961, PACCS would function as a backup to control centers on the ground, which may be destroyed in a nuclear attack. Code-named Cover All or Looking Glass, PACCS consists of specially modified Boeing 707 airliners. The planes, which are supervised by the STRATEGIC AIR COMMAND, are in the air twenty-four hours a day. PACCS aircraft maintain a direct communications link with the Joint Chiefs of Staff in Washington, D.C., and contain

facilities to order the launch of NUCLEAR WEAPONS. PACCS
primarily serves as an airborne command post for the Commander of the Strategic Air Command. PACCS is distinct from the
NATIONAL EMERGENCY AIRBORNE COMMAND POST, which would
operate as a flying command post for the NATIONAL COMMAND
AUTHORITIES (the President and Secretary of Defense) during
a nuclear war.

POST-ATTACK RECOVERY is a nation's ability to rebound from
a nuclear war. Post-attack recovery plays a major role in military
strategy; it is the final measure of whether a nation can truly
"survive" a nuclear war. Post-attack recovery takes many factors
into account beyond the estimated number of survivors. The
quality of life following a nuclear attack, the ability of the
government to function, and the effects on the national econ-
omy are all elements of post-attack recovery.

POST-BOOST PHASE is the period of a ballistic missile's flight
when the POST-BOOST VEHICLE separates from the BOOSTER
ROCKETS and releases the missile's warheads and DECOYS. The
post-boost vehicle is the part of a BALLISTIC MISSILE that contains the missile's warheads. Individual warheads and decoys are
fired from the post-boost vehicle at different points during a
missile's remaining flight path. The post-boost phase, which
lasts five to six minutes, follows the BOOST PHASE and precedes
the MIDCOURSE and TERMINAL PHASES.

POST-BOOST PHASE DEFENSE   see POST-BOOST PHASE INTER-
CEPTION

POST-BOOST PHASE INTERCEPTION is the destruction of attacking NUCLEAR WARHEADS during the period (called the POST-
BOOST PHASE) of a BALLISTIC MISSILE's flight when it releases
warheads and decoys. During the post-boost phase, which lasts
five to six minutes, the POST-BOOST VEHICLE separates from the
ballistic missile and releases many warheads and DECOYS. An

effective post-boost phase interception would destroy the post-boost vehicle before it releases its warheads and decoys. The principle behind a post-boost phase interception is that it is easier to destroy a single post-boost vehicle rather than its numerous warheads and decoys.

POST-BOOST VEHICLE (PBV) is the part of a BALLISTIC MISSILE that contains the missile's warheads. Modern nuclear missiles can deliver more than one NUCLEAR WARHEAD. Individual warheads are released from the PBV as the missile streaks through the upper atmosphere toward its target. The individual warheads are fired from the post-boost vehicle at different points along a missile's flight path. This process occurs similarly to the way a bus lets passengers off at different stops along its route. For this reason, the PBV is commonly known as a bus.

POST-EXCHANGE RECOVERY SCENARIO see POST-ATTACK RECOVERY

POST-LAUNCH SURVIVABILITY is the ability of a NUCLEAR WEAPON to penetrate enemy defenses and strike assigned targets. A defender could use defensive systems to destroy incoming warheads.

POST-STRIKE ASSESSMENT is an evaluation of the results of a nuclear attack. A post-strike assessment provides information necessary for decision-making during a nuclear war. It is also known as a post-attack assessment or a nuclear damage assessment.

PRECISION GUIDED MUNITION (PGM) refers to very accurate, technically advanced weapons that can home in on and destroy their targets. PGM is a very general term, encompassing an entire range of nuclear and conventional weapons. PGMs have been developed in recent years as advanced technology has been applied to weapons development. PGMs are also called smart bombs.

PRECURSOR BURST refers to a nuclear explosion triggered in space by a nation that has just initiated a nuclear attack. A precursor burst would be intended to camouflage attacking missiles from enemy defenses by creating a cloud of heat, magnetic signals, and radiation. This huge cloud would confuse sensors designed to identify attacking missiles by detecting the heat and other signals they emit. In this way, a precursor burst would create a sort of smokescreen for attacking missiles.

PRE-DELEGATION allows U.S. military personnel to authorize the launch of NUCLEAR WEAPONS without consulting civilian leaders. Pre-delegation could occur in a nuclear war if civilian leaders were killed in an enemy attack. In such a scenario, military officers would be empowered to launch nuclear weapons on their own initiative.

PREEMPTIVE ATTACK is a nuclear strike launched on the presumption that an enemy attack is imminent. A preemptive attack is launched before any indication is received that an enemy attack is underway. Instead, it is initiated only on the suspicion that an enemy is preparing to attack. A preemptive attack can have two purposes. First, it could be intended as a preventive attack, to ensure that an ability to retaliate would not be nullified by an enemy attack. This idea is sometimes referred to as "use 'em or lose 'em." Second, it could be launched as an offensive attack, with the hope of effectively destroying an enemy's ability to retaliate and thus winning a nuclear war. See FIRST STRIKE.

PREFERENTIAL DEFENSE see COMPLETELY PREFERENTIAL DEFENSE, SEMI-PREFERENTIAL DEFENSE

PRE-LAUNCH SURVIVABILITY is the ability of a nation to absorb a surprise nuclear attack and to respond with effective retaliation.

PREVENTION OF NUCLEAR WAR AGREEMENT (1973) is a bilateral agreement between the U.S. and the U.S.S.R. that obligates both parties to establish policies that reduce the danger of nuclear war. In the agreement the two superpowers pledge to practice restraint in their relations with each other and to work towards stability and peace.

PREVENTIVE WAR is a war initiated by one side on the assumption that an enemy attack is inevitable, but not imminent. A nation would begin a preventive war because it believes that an enemy is about to attack, and that further waiting could lead to disaster.

PRIMARY ALERTING SYSTEM (PAS) is the telephone hookup that would carry orders from Washington to missile installations and bomber bases to launch U.S. NUCLEAR WEAPONS. The Primary Alerting System is also called the Red Phone. See EMERGENCY ACTION MESSAGE.

PRODUCTION is the stage of weapons development when weapons are actually built. Production follows DEVELOPMENT and NUCLEAR TESTING, and precedes DEPLOYMENT.

PROGRAM FOR USE OF COMMERCIAL UNDERGROUND NUCLEAR EXPLOSIONS   see PROJECT PLOWSHARE

PROJECT PLOWSHARE was an American campaign to demonstrate the peaceful use of nuclear explosions. Introduced in 1957, Project Plowshare resulted in a series of experiments designed to prove the peaceful and economic benefits of nuclear devices. Project Plowshare examined the feasibility of using nuclear explosions for purposes such as building water reservoirs in dry regions, moving mountains, redirecting rivers, and digging harbors and canals. Project Plowshare became part of the ATOMS-FOR-PEACE PLAN, which was U.S. President Dwight Eisenhower's plan to promote cooperation among nations leading toward the peaceful use of atomic explosions. The Soviet counterpart to Project Plowshare was called the Program for Use of Commercial Underground Nuclear Explosions. The name Project Plowshare is derived from the Biblical passage, "they shall beat their swords into plowshares" (Isaiah 2:4).

PROLIFERATION   see NUCLEAR PROLIFERATION

PROMPT RADIATION consists of deadly radiation emitted within the first minute after the detonation of a NUCLEAR WEAPON. Prompt radiation affects the area near GROUND ZERO, the point at which the weapon explodes. Prompt radiation is most significant for very small nuclear weapons, whose other destructive effects are extremely limited, and the NEUTRON BOMB, which is designed to kill through prompt nuclear radiation. Prompt radiation is distinct from FALLOUT radiation, which may not affect the earth for weeks, months, or even years after a nuclear explosion. Prompt radiation is released by a nuclear explosion itself; fallout radiation is emitted by the explosion's by-products. Prompt radiation is also known as initial radiation.

PROPORTIONAL DETERRENCE   see GRADUATED DETERRENCE

PROTOCOL is an international agreement that is less formal than a treaty. Protocols are usually used to supplement a treaty. The ANTIBALLISTIC MISSILE (ABM) PROTOCOL of 1974, for example, amplified the ANTIBALLISTIC MISSILE TREATY of 1972. The ABM Protocol reduced the number of defensive systems that could be deployed by the U.S. and the U.S.S.R. from two to one. In the United States, if a protocol is approved by the U.S. Senate, it is regarded as having the force of a treaty.

PROTRACTED NUCLEAR WAR   see LIMITED NUCLEAR WAR

PSI OVERPRESSURE   see OVERPRESSURE

PU-239   see PLUTONIUM

PUGWASH MOVEMENT was founded to bring together scientists from Eastern and Western blocs to discuss the threat of nuclear war. Pugwash is an independent forum of scientists who feel a moral responsibility to reduce the role of science as it relates to military technology. The Pugwash movement began in 1955 in response to an appeal issued by mathematician and philosopher Bertrand Russell and scientist Albert Einstein, who urged scientists from Eastern and Western blocs to meet and assess the growing dangers of nuclear war. Following the RUSSELL-EINSTEIN MANIFESTO, the first Pugwash conference met in 1957 in Pugwash, Nova Scotia, to discuss the risks of nuclear weapons. Attending this conference were 24 eminent scientists from ten countries on both sides of the Iron Curtain. At the first conference, the participants agreed that the goal of all nations must be the "abolition of war and the threat of war hanging over mankind." The Pugwash Conferences on Science and World Affairs have met annually in Geneva since 1957 and remain the only continual forum in which Western and Eastern scientists can discuss problems posed by the arms race.

PURE DETERRENCE   see MINIMUM DETERRENCE

PUSH-BUTTON WAR is a nuclear war in which all weapons are fired from isolated command and control centers. The term push-button war has been used to characterize the technological and automated nature of nuclear warfare.

PUSH THE BUTTON is an informal expression that describes the launching of a nuclear attack.

Q

QUALITATIVE LIMITATION is a restriction on the capabilities of a weapon. Qualitative limitation is a general term and can include many different restrictions relating to a weapon's mission or its technology. Qualitative limitations play an important role in arms-control negotiations. The ANTIBALLISTIC MISSILE (ABM) TREATY of 1972, for example, imposes qualitative limitations on the type of defense systems the U.S. and the U.S.S.R. are permitted to deploy. According to the ABM Treaty, the superpowers may deploy ground-based missile defense systems, but are prohibited from building defense systems deployed in space or at sea. Qualitative limitations are distinct from QUANTITATIVE LIMITATIONS, which limit the actual number of weapons that can be deployed.

QUANTITATIVE LIMITATION is a restriction on the number of weapons that can be deployed. Quantitative limitations play an important role in arms-control negotiations. The ANTIBALLISTIC MISSILE PROTOCOL of 1974, for example, imposes a quantitative limitation on the number of defense systems the U.S. and the U.S.S.R. are permitted to deploy. According to the ABM Protocol, the superpowers may build only one missile defense system. Quantitative limitations are distinct from QUALITATIVE LIMITATIONS, which restrict the capabilities and technology of weapons.

QUICK REACTION ALERT (QRA) is a status on which U.S. missiles and bombers are maintained so that they can be launched on very short notice. A certain number of missiles and planes are always on QRA, which is also known as combat alert status.

R

RACE TRACK is a hypothetical method for deploying nuclear missiles. A Race Track system would involve building several shelters for each missile. These shelters would be scattered along a loop, stretching for thousands of miles. Missiles would then be shuttled between different shelters, so that an adversary could never be sure where they were. In this way, the missiles would be moving targets and their vulnerability to enemy attack would be reduced. An enemy, in turn, would have to destroy every shelter in order to be absolutely certain of destroying all the missiles. Race Track was first conceived as a method of deploying the American MX missile. The plan was abandoned, however, and the U.S. eventually decided to deploy the MX in existing underground missile silos.

RAD, the acronym for radiation absorbed dose, is a unit used to measure the dose of ionizing RADIATION absorbed by people. Ionizing radiation is the deadly radiation released in a nuclear explosion. Unlike rems (a similar unit), rads do not express the medical damage radiation causes to living cells. Equal amounts of radiation may cause different amounts of damage, depending on the type of radiation and where it is absorbed. Rads do not account for these variables and are used to describe only the amount of radiation that people absorb. See REM, ROENTGEN.

RADAR is a device or system for locating and identifying airborne objects. Radar beams radio waves at an object. When they are reflected back, the beams are analyzed and reveal the object's altitude, size, speed, etc. Radar is used for a variety of peaceful and military purposes. Strictly peaceful uses of radar include guiding civilian airliners. Radar is also used to gather information for military purposes including detecting enemy nuclear attacks and missile test flights. Two major types of radar are used: LINE-OF-SIGHT RADAR and OVER-THE-HORIZON RADAR. See NATIONAL TECHNICAL MEANS OF VERIFICATION.

RADIATION refers to the process in which energy is emitted and travels through space. It can also refer to energy itself. Radiation is a very general term—it covers all types of wavelike and particlelike energy, from heat to light to X-rays. Nuclear radiation, which is released when a nuclear weapon explodes, is extremely harmful to living cells. Exposure to large amounts of nuclear radiation may cause radiation sickness, genetic damage, cancer, or death. See NUCLEAR RADIATION, IONIZING RADIATION.

RADIATION DOSE   see ABSORBED DOSE

RADIATION EFFECTS RESEARCH FOUNDATION (RERF)   see ATOMIC BOMB CASUALTY COMMISSION

RADIATION SICKNESS is the malady that results from excessive exposure to ionizing radiation. Ionizing radiation is the deadly radiation released in a nuclear explosion. Radiation sickness is characterized by nausea, vomiting, diarrhea, blood cell changes, and, later, by internal bleeding and hair loss. Typically, initial symptoms of vomiting and loss of appetite appear within a day or two after exposure. After a few days, these symptoms disappear and the victim appears to be well for a week or two. Within three weeks, however, serious symptoms return and death may result. Radiation sickness is concentrated in the bone marrow and the digestive tract, since these areas are the most susceptible to ionizing radiation.

RADIOACTIVE CLOUD is a cloud of gases, vapor, and heavier debris that forms in the aftermath of a nuclear explosion. The radioactive cloud is formed as the MUSHROOM CLOUD is dispersed by winds. It scatters deadly radioactive FALLOUT over the area in which a NUCLEAR WEAPON was detonated. The radioactive cloud is deadly; exposure to it may cause radiation sickness, genetic damage, cancer, or death.

RADIOACTIVE CONTAMINATION see CONTAMINATION

RADIOACTIVE DECAY is a process in which unstable elements release excess energy in order to become more stable. Detonation of a NUCLEAR WEAPON generates many by-products that undergo radioactive decay. These deadly by-products are found in FALLOUT, the particles of debris created by a nuclear blast and sucked into the atmosphere in the MUSHROOM CLOUD. Elements undergoing radioactive decay proceed through a series of steps, changing to a different element each time they release significant amounts of radiation. Uranium-235, for example, undergoes fifteen separate transformations until it finally becomes lead, a nonradioactive element. Radioactive decay is harmful to people and most other living things: The energy it releases can destroy or deform living cells. Exposure to elements undergoing radioactive decay can cause radiation sickness, can ccr, genetic defects, and death. Radioactive decay continues over what may be a very long period, depending on the HALF-LIFE of the element that is decaying. Plutonium-239, for example, takes over 24,000 years to lose just half of its radioactivity. There are three major types of radioactive decay: ALPHA DECAY, BETA DECAY, and GAMMA DECAY.

RADIOACTIVE FALLOUT see FALLOUT

RADIOACTIVE ISOTOPE see RADIOISOTOPE

RADIOISOTOPE is a type of atom that emits dangerous ionizing radiation in order to become more stable. Many by-products of a nuclear explosion are radioisotopes. Exposure to radioisotopes may cause RADIATION SICKNESS, genetic damage, cancer, or death.

RADIUS OF ACTION see COMBAT RADIUS

RAIL GUN see ELECTROMAGNETIC RAIL GUN

RAINBOW WARRIOR, the flagship of the GREENPEACE environmental movement, was sunk by French intelligence agents on July 10, 1985, in Auckland, New Zealand. A Greenpeace photographer was killed in the bombing. France was immediately suspected of sinking the *Rainbow Warrior* because the ship had been protesting French nuclear testing at MURUROA ATOLL in the South Pacific. Initially, France denied any involvement in the affair. Yet suspicions of French involvement persisted, and the French government finally admitted its guilt in October 1985. Both the French Defense Minister and the head of the French foreign intelligence agency resigned as a result of their involvement in the incident. Two French intelligence agents pleaded guilty to manslaughter and were subsequently prosecuted by the New Zealand government. In July 1986 they were extradited to France as part of an agreement in which France officially apologized to the New Zealand government and agreed to pay it $7 million for damages arising from the bombing.

RAJASTHAN DESERT is the site in northwest India where that country conducted its first and only nuclear explosion in May 1974. While India maintains that the explosion was strictly peaceful, some critics believe the test was intended to prove India's capability to manufacture NUCLEAR WEAPONS.

RAM-P BLACKJACK is a Soviet long-range bomber. See LONG-RANGE BOMBER for a complete description of the Blackjack.

RAND CORPORATION is an independent U.S. think tank that has developed much of the United States's nuclear strategy. Established after World War II by Generals Henry Arnold and Curtis LeMay, RAND enjoyed its heyday in the 1950s and early 1960s. During that period, strategists such as Herman Kahn and Bernard Brodie formulated many of the basic strategic concepts of the nuclear era, including LIMITED NUCLEAR WAR and COUN-

TERFORCE and COUNTERVALUE targeting. RAND has also played an important role in the development of new types of NUCLEAR WEAPONS, including THERMONUCLEAR WEAPONS (the so-called superbomb project) and INTERCONTINENTAL BALLISTIC MISSILES. Finally, RAND pioneered several modern analytical techniques, including systems analysis. RAND's name is an acronym for research and development.

RANDOM SUBTRACTIVE is a strategy for defending against incoming enemy warheads. In a random subtractive strategy, a defense system would attempt to destroy as many targets as possible. Unlike a COMPLETELY PREFERENTIAL DEFENSE or a SEMI-PREFERENTIAL DEFENSE strategy, a random subtractive strategy would make no attempt to distinguish and destroy selected BALLISTIC MISSILES. Since targets are chosen at random, a defense system's effectiveness is spread over a greater area. Unlike both preferential defense strategies, random subtractive strategy would provide an equal amount of protection to all targets.

RANGE refers to the total distance a missile or aircraft can cover. Range is distinct from COMBAT RADIUS, which refers specifically to the maximum distance an aircraft can cover and still have enough fuel to return to its departure point.

RAPACKI PLAN called for the elimination of all nuclear weapons in Czechoslovakia, East Germany, Poland, and West Germany. The plan was presented to the U.N. by Polish Foreign Minister Adam Rapacki in 1957. The Rapacki Plan was presented as a step toward establishing a broader collective European security system to replace existing blocs. The Rapacki Plan was never adopted because of strong U.S. and British opposition. The main arguments against it were that it did not link partial arms-control measures with broader plans for general disarmament; it did not address other European security issues such as the general military balance and conventional force levels; and it made no mention of the reunification of Germany. Two other versions of the Rapacki Plan, modified to take into account Western objections, were forwarded in 1958 and 1962. These plans were rejected by the Western allies for similar reasons.

RAPID RELOAD is the ability to reuse a nuclear MISSILE SILO soon after a missile has been launched. Rapid reload can be achieved only if the nuclear missile is ejected by a COLD LAUNCH. In a cold launch, a missile's rockets are not fully ignited until it has left the missile silo. In this way, the tremendous force of the rockets does not destroy the silo. Rapid reload allows an attacker to launch many missiles quickly and easily from the same silo. If missiles are stored near a silo with rapid reload capability, they can be prepared for launch and fired in relatively quick succession.

RAPID RELOAD/REFIRE CAPABILITY   see RAPID RELOAD

RATIFICATION is the formal confirmation of a treaty after it has been signed. Treaties signed by the U.S. President are then sent to the Senate for approval. Contrary to popular belief, however, the Senate does not ratify treaties. Ratification is a presidential act and follows senatorial approval. Approval and ratification can be a complex and controversial process. For example, SALT II, which set limits on the number of nuclear weapons that could be deployed by the U.S. and the U.S.S.R., was not approved by the Senate. Treaties need not be ratified in order to be observed, however. Despite the Senate's refusal to approve SALT II, the U.S. abided by its terms until 1986, when President Ronald Reagan threatened to scrap the treaty.

RATIO PROBLEM is a major obstacle in arms-control negotiations. Essentially, the ratio problem arises as negotiators attempt to arrive at a fair comparison of each other's forces. Because each nation deploys different types of weapons, two nations' arsenals are not structured in the same way. Thus, negotiators must seek to equate what may be vastly differing types of weapons in order to impose fair limits on both sides. The ratio problem has occurred persistently in arms-control negotiations between the U.S. and the U.S.S.R. This ratio problem results from the different structures of the American and Soviet nuclear arsenals. Unlike the U.S., which deploys its nuclear weapons in roughly equal numbers on submarines, bombers, and in underground MISSILE SILOS, the U.S.S.R. relies almost exclusively on land-based missiles. Thus, any attempt to limit land-based missiles while ignoring other types of missiles would have a greater impact on the Soviet arsenal than on U.S. nuclear weapons.

REACTION TIME is the amount of time a nation has to respond to a nuclear attack. It is the elapsed time between initial warning of an enemy nuclear attack and the moment the enemy missiles strike their targets. The increasing technology and accuracy of modern nuclear weapons has threatened to reduce reaction time. Modern submarine-launched nuclear missiles, for example, can strike their targets in a matter of minutes. Some experts claim that these advances have increased the risk of accidental or surprise nuclear attack.

READINESS is the predicted percentage of a nation's nuclear weapons that are ready to be used at any one time. All the nuclear weapons intended for use are not always ready to be used. There are always some missiles or bombs that are out of commission because of breakdowns or general maintenance needs. In addition, the submarines or aircraft that carry nuclear weapons need maintenance. In general, 98% of the nuclear weapons deployed by the U.S. are ready to be used. The corresponding figure for the U.S.S.R. is estimated at 75%, but this figure is extremely difficult to verify.

RECALL CAPABILITY is the ability to recall nuclear weapons after they have been launched. While missiles cannot be recalled after they are launched, STRATEGIC BOMBERS carrying nuclear weapons can be recalled before reaching their targets.

RED ALERT is a warning that an enemy nuclear attack is imminent or already in progress. Red alert denotes the most grave state of emergency. A red alert is more serious than a yellow alert, which warns of a possible enemy attack.

RED BOX is the nickname of the container that holds two essential elements for launching a nuclear attack. In the Red Box are codes necessary for verifying an order to launch a nuclear attack and keys which actually activate the launch of nuclear missiles. Secured with double locks, a Red Box is stored in bombers, submarines, and underground MISSILE SILOS that contain nuclear missiles. In preparing to launch a nuclear strike, crew officers would open the Red Box.

REDOUT is a theoretical method for rendering an opponent's missile defense system ineffective. Redout would be used specifically to prevent heat sensors from detecting attacking nuclear warheads. Redout would involve detonating a NUCLEAR WARHEAD in the sky directly between a heat sensor's line of sight and a second attacking warhead's flight path. Heat emitted by an attacking warhead would not pass through the part of the sky where the explosion took place. Thus, heat sensors would be temporarily blinded, unable to see through this part of the sky. The second warhead could then sneak through the heat sensor's blind spot and proceed toward its target undetected. A similar process that involves blinding RADAR rather than heat sensors is called BLACKOUT. The United States is conducting research on redout under the STRATEGIC DEFENSE INITIATIVE, commonly known as "Star Wars."

RÉDOUTABLE SUBMARINE is a class of French ballistic missile submarines. See BALLISTIC MISSILE SUBMARINE for a complete description of the Rédoutable submarine.

RED PHONE   see PRIMARY ALERTING SYSTEM

RED TEAM is the informal name of a group of U.S. scientists conducting research on a high technology system to defend against attacking nuclear missiles. The Red Team is responsible for analyzing possible Soviet responses to U.S. defenses. The Red Team is part of the U.S. STRATEGIC DEFENSE INITIATIVE, commonly known as "Star Wars."

REENTRY PHASE   see TERMINAL PHASE

REENTRY PHASE INTERCEPTION   see TERMINAL PHASE INTERCEPTION

REENTRY VEHICLE (RV) is a NUCLEAR WARHEAD that is designed to reenter the earth's atmosphere from space. The term reentry vehicle is often used as a synonym for warhead, but there is a difference between the two. Reentry vehicles are distinct from nuclear warheads because they are specifically released in outer space and then reenter the earth's atmosphere en route to their targets. They are protected by heat shields to withstand the great heat and pressure encountered upon reentering the atmosphere. Nuclear warheads that never leave the earth's atmosphere, such as CRUISE MISSILES or bombs dropped from an aircraft, do not require this special protection and are thus not reentry vehicles.

REFIRE CAPABILITY   see RAPID RELOAD

REGGAN is a town in central Algeria where France exploded its first atomic weapon on February 3, 1960. The bomb released a destructive force of between 60 and 70 KILOTONS. Reggan was the site of all French nuclear testing from 1960 to 1966.

REGIONALLY ORIENTED SYSTEMS   see ALLIANCE/REGIONALLY ORIENTED (RELATED) SYSTEMS

RELAY MIRROR is a hypothetical mirror that would reflect a powerful LASER beam at an attacking nuclear missile. A relay mirror would be part of a high-technology system designed to defend against incoming nuclear warheads. In a system that uses relay mirrors, a GROUND-BASED LASER WEAPON would fire a powerful beam of highly concentrated light into the sky. This beam would be aimed at the relay mirror, which would be positioned in orbit high above the earth. The relay mirror would then reflect the beam at another mirror, positioned in orbit much closer to the earth. This second mirror, called a BATTLE MIRROR, would reflect the beam of light at an attacking missile. The light beam would burn a hole in the skin of the attacking missile and deactivate the sensitive electronic equipment responsible for guiding it to its target. Relay mirrors would have to be huge (as big as 90 feet in diameter) and nearly flawless. The slightest imperfection could cause the light beam to scatter and thus lose its effectiveness. The United States is conducting research on relay mirrors under the STRATEGIC DEFENSE INITIATIVE, commonly known as "Star Wars."

RELIABILITY is the predicted percentage of a nation's NUCLEAR WEAPONS that will reach their targets. There are many factors that can prevent a nuclear weapon from reaching its target, including weapon malfunction and interception by enemy defenses. In general, the reliability of American nuclear weapons is 75 to 85%, while that of Soviet nuclear weapons is 65 to 75%.

RELOAD MISSILE is a NUCLEAR WEAPON that is fired in a nuclear war from a LAUNCHER that has already been used. In theory, it is possible to rearm MISSILE SILOS that have already launched their missiles. Some analysts claim that in a nuclear war, this would enable a nation to gain a tremendous advantage. Reload missiles are also known as backup missiles. See THREE RS OF WINNING A NUCLEAR WAR.

REM, the acronym for roentgen equivalent man, is a unit used to measure the dose of ionizing RADIATION absorbed by people.

Ionizing radiation is the deadly radiation released in a nuclear explosion. Unlike other units, rems are expressed in terms of the medical damage that is caused to living cells. Equal amounts of radiation may cause different amounts of damage, depending on the type of radiation and where it is absorbed. Rems account for these variables and provide an indication of the bodily harm caused by exposure to radiation. Rems are very useful in setting limits on how much radiation people can be exposed to safely. A dose of more than 100 rems will cause RADIATION SICKNESS, the malady that results from excessive exposure to ionizing radiation. Symptoms of radiation sickness include vomiting, hair loss, and internal bleeding.

REPROCESSING is the technique for obtaining purified PLU- TONIUM from the mixture of waste products produced by a nuclear reactor. Plutonium is an important raw material for nuclear weapons and reactors. Plutonium is a by-product; it is produced as the element URANIUM is split and decays. Repro- cessing must be distinguished from ENRICHMENT, which is the technique used for obtaining a suitable mix of uranium isotopes. Reprocessing is less cumbersome than enrichment, but is still a complex and expensive operation. Reprocessing technology has been closely monitored in an effort to control access to plutonium and thus to control the proliferation of NUCLEAR WEAPONS. Reprocessing was first developed by the U.S. during World War II.

RETALIATION is a nuclear attack launched in response to an enemy FIRST STRIKE. The threat of an unacceptably destructive retalia- tion deters both superpowers from launching a first strike at- tack. With limited means for defending against a nuclear strike, both superpowers rely on their ability to inflict enormous dam- age on each other. Both superpowers have strengthened their capabilities to retaliate effectively by fortifying (HARDENING) their NUCLEAR WEAPONS against enemy attack.

RHYOLITE SATELLITE is an American intelligence satellite, a series of which monitor Soviet ground communication and intercept technical data transmitted during missile flight tests. In this way, Rhyolite satellites help verify Soviet compliance with nuclear arms-control agreements. Information about Rhyolite satellites became public in the espionage trials of Christopher Boyce and Daulton Lee, described in Robert Lindsey's book *The Falcon and the Snowman.*

RISOP is the U.S. military slang term for the Soviet Union's top-secret master plan for fighting a nuclear war. RISOP stands for Russian Integrated Single Operational Plan. The U.S. nuclear war fighting plan is the SINGLE INTEGRATED OPERATIONAL PLAN, called SIOP.

ROENTGEN is a unit that measures the amount of ionizing RADIATION given off by a substance. Ionizing radiation is the deadly radiation released in a nuclear explosion. Named for Wilhelm Roentgen, the discoverer of X-rays, roentgens measure the amount of radiation to which people are exposed. Other units, such as RADS and REMS, measure the amount of radiation people absorb.

RUBE GOLDBERG is a slang term for a NUCLEAR WEAPON that is extremely complex and appears farfetched. Modern space-based weapons, such as those being considered under the American STRATEGIC DEFENSE INITIATIVE (commonly known as "Star Wars"), are often referred to as Rube Goldbergs. Rube Goldberg was a cartoonist whose drawings depicted zany, wild contraptions.

RUSSELL-EINSTEIN MANIFESTO was a much-publicized appeal to bring together scientists from Eastern and Western blocs to discuss the threat of nuclear war. Drafted in 1955 by English mathematician and philosopher Bertrand Russell, the Russell-Einstein Manifesto warned against manufacturing extremely powerful NUCLEAR WEAPONS. Eminent physicist Albert Einstein signed the manifesto two days before his death in 1955. The manifesto urged scientists to assemble and discuss the perils in the development of modern nuclear weapons. Signed by several Nobel Prize winners in addition to Einstein, the manifesto gave rise to the PUGWASH MOVEMENT, a series of meetings between Eastern and Western scientists.

S

S-23 is a type of Soviet nuclear artillery. See NUCLEAR ARTILLERY for a complete description of the S-23.

SA-5 GAMMON is the NATO code for a Soviet surface-to-air missile. See SURFACE-TO-AIR MISSILE for a complete description of the SA-5 Gammon.

SAFEGUARD was the only missile defense system ever deployed by the United States. Safeguard was designed to protect a MINUTE-MAN MISSILE site near Grand Forks, North Dakota, from an enemy nuclear attack. Originally deployed in 1974, Safeguard was dismantled in 1976 because of high cost and technical ineffectiveness. Safeguard would have used SPARTAN MISSILES and SPRINT MISSILES to intercept and destroy attacking nuclear warheads. President Richard Nixon originally announced the $7 billion Safeguard program in 1969 as a modification of the previous SENTINEL missile defense system proposal. Safeguard was permitted by the ANTIBALLISTIC MISSILE TREATY of 1972, which allows each superpower one missile defense system.

SAINT GEORGE, Utah, nicknamed "Fallout City," is a small town in western Utah, located about 150 miles from the site where the United States conducts all of its nuclear tests. During the DIRTY HARRY test in May 1953, it received the most deadly FALLOUT ever measured in any populated area in the U.S. As a result of their proximity to the test site, Saint George residents are victimized by an extremely high cancer rate. In 1954 the film *The Conqueror* (starring John Wayne and Susan Hayward) was filmed outside Saint George. By 1980, 41% of the cast and crew (including Wayne and Hayward) had contracted cancer.

SALT (STRATEGIC ARMS LIMITATION TALKS) (1969–1979)

provided a forum for the U.S. and the U.S.S.R. to discuss and negotiate many aspects of their STRATEGIC NUCLEAR WEAPONS. SALT aimed to limit rather than reduce strategic nuclear weapons, which are extremely powerful weapons targeted by both the U.S. and the U.S.S.R. at each other's homeland. SALT consisted of two major sets of negotiations. The first set, called SALT I, lasted from 1969 to 1972 and resulted in two agreements: the ANTIBALLISTIC MISSILE TREATY and the Interim Offensive Weapons Agreement. The VLADIVOSTOK ACCORD of 1974 set the guidelines for SALT II, the second set of negotiations, which lasted from 1972 to 1979. SALT II replaced the Interim Agreement with a new treaty that placed broad limits on strategic nuclear weapons. The U.S. Senate, however, has not approved SALT II but both countries agreed to abide by the terms of the agreement through 1986, when President Ronald Reagan threatened to scrap the treaty.

SALT I (STRATEGIC ARMS LIMITATION TREATY) (1972) is the

result of the first set of SALT negotiations between the U.S. and the U.S.S.R. SALT I was the first arms-control agreement in which the superpowers actually limited the number of the NUCLEAR WEAPONS they deploy. The treaty contains two separate agreements, covering offensive and defensive nuclear weapons. Each part of the treaty was approved by the U.S. Senate.

- Antiballistic Missile Treaty (1972) allows each superpower to deploy two weapons systems designed to defend against attacking nuclear missiles. One of these systems is designated to protect the national capital and the other to protect a missile site. The ABM Protocol of 1974 reduced the number of permitted defensive systems from two to one. The Soviet ABM system, GALOSH, surrounds Moscow. The American ABM system, SAFEGUARD, was deployed to protect a missile site in Grand Forks, North Dakota. It was dismantled in 1976 because of high cost and technical ineffectiveness. The ABM Treaty also prohibits technological improvements in these defense systems and forbids new systems based at sea, in the air, or in space. This provision has caused great controversy in the mid-1980s. The United States contends that research for its STRATEGIC DEFENSE INITIATIVE, commonly known as "Star Wars," is not prohibited by the ABM Treaty. Others, however, interpret the ABM Treaty differently and claim that Star Wars research violates the treaty. The treaty calls for reviews every five years and each side must give six months advance notice before withdrawing from the treaty.

- Interim Offensive Weapons Agreement (1972) set numerical limits on the number of strategic missile LAUNCHERS that could be deployed by each superpower over the next five years. The Interim Agreement limited the U.S. to 1,054 and the Soviet Union to 1,618 intercontinental ballistic missile launchers. Its accompanying protocol limited the U.S. to 710 and the Soviet Union to 950 submarine-launched ballistic missile launchers. Unlike later arms-control agreements between the superpowers, the Interim Agreement did not establish numerically equal limits on the number of nuclear weapons deployed by each side. The U.S. agreed to let the Soviet Union deploy larger numbers of nuclear weapons as compensation for U.S. technological superiority. The treaty also did not cover emerging missile technologies, such as CRUISE MISSILES and missiles with more than one warhead (called MIRVs). The VLADIVOSTOK ACCORD of 1974 revised the limits established in the Interim Agreement.

SALT II (STRATEGIC ARMS LIMITATION TREATY) (1979) is a bilateral agreement between the U.S. and the U.S.S.R. that set limits and guidelines on many aspects of the superpowers' nuclear arsenals. SALT II attempts to establish parity between the superpowers by placing numerically equal limits on their nuclear weapons. This characteristic of SALT II was very different from

SALT I (1972), which allowed the Soviets a greater number of weapons because U.S. weapons were considered technologically superior. In addition, each side agreed to limit MODERNIZATION of existing weapons systems under SALT II and each was permitted to develop only one new type of INTERCONTINENTAL BALLISTIC MISSILE. Finally, SALT II was the first arms-control agreement that limited nuclear missiles equipped with more than one warhead. SALT II was not approved by the U.S. Senate following a general deterioration of U.S.-U.S.S.R. relations in the late 1970s. The treaty has been criticized by some experts in the U.S., who claim that it enabled the Soviet Union to move toward an unfair advantage in the arms race. Nonetheless, both sides agreed to abide by its terms through 1986, when President Ronald Reagan threatened to scrap the treaty.

SALTED WEAPON   see DIRTY NUCLEAR WEAPON

SALTNIK is a nickname for someone who favors and endorses the SALT treaties.

SALVAGE FUSING causes a NUCLEAR WEAPON to blow up if it is intercepted by enemy defenses. Salvage fusing is intended as a backup, to ensure that weapons can still inflict some damage even if they are intercepted before they reach their targets. If intercepted very high above the earth, however, even a salvage-fused weapon will not cause any damage to targets on the ground.

SANCTUARY is a region (such as the homelands of the superpowers) that would be unaffected by a LIMITED NUCLEAR WAR. In a limited nuclear war, small numbers of nuclear weapons would be used in order to attain specific objectives. Widespread destruction would not be an inevitable result of limited nuclear war, because the superpowers would observe limits on where and how their nuclear weapons would be used. The notion of sanctuaries has been very controversial. Since most limited nuclear war scenarios occur in Europe, many Europeans have expressed outrage at the notion of sanctuary. They argue that it would be unjust for the U.S. and the U.S.S.R. to fight a devastating nuclear war in Europe while the superpowers' homelands would come out of the war unscathed.

SANDAL is the NATO code for a Soviet medium-range ballistic missile. See MEDIUM-RANGE BALLISTIC MISSILE for a complete description of this missile.

SANDIA NATIONAL LABORATORY is one of three major U.S. facilities for the development of nuclear weapons technology. It was founded in 1948 and is located in Albuquerque, New Mexico. American nuclear weapons are designed at either the LOS ALAMOS NATIONAL LABORATORY (located in Los Alamos, New Mexico) or the LAWRENCE LIVERMORE NATIONAL LABORATORY (located in Livermore, California). At Sandia, special features such as fuses and safety devices are designed for these weapons. Sandia has also engaged in other types of weapons development, including research for the STRATEGIC DEFENSE INITIATIVE, popularly known as "Star Wars." Sandia was originally a branch of the Los Alamos installation; it became independent in 1948. It is run by Western Electric under contract from the U.S. government.

SANE—THE NATIONAL COMMITTEE FOR A SANE NUCLEAR POLICY is an organization that seeks to educate Americans about the dangers of the arms race and nuclear war. SANE was formed in 1957 to promote a ban on the testing of nuclear weapons in the atmosphere. SANE played an active role in the effort to establish the LIMITED TEST BAN TREATY of 1963, which severely restricted nuclear testing. SANE, which is located in Washington, D.C., and has a membership of about 85,000, has in recent years lobbied against the development of the MX MISSILE and the deployment of Pershing and TOMAHAWK CRUISE MISSILES in Western Europe.

SATELLITE is an object that orbits another, larger object. There are almost 5,000 artificial satellites currently in orbit around the earth, deployed by many nations. Satellites are used for a variety of peaceful and military purposes. Strictly peaceful uses of satellites include weather forecasting and relaying television signals. Specific military purposes for satellites include monitoring nuclear tests, detecting enemy nuclear attacks, and helping to guide missiles as they streak toward their targets. Satellites form an essential link in the defense communications system, which transmits emergency orders from central command headquarters to installations where nuclear weapons are deployed. See NATIONAL TECHNICAL MEANS OF VERIFICATION.

SATELLITE EARLY WARNING SYSTEM (SEWS) is a group of U.S. SATELLITES that detect attacking nuclear missiles. SEWS is designed to notify decision-makers if an enemy attack is underway so that they can take appropriate action. One SEWS satellite is positioned over the Indian Ocean and specifically watches for nuclear missiles launched from the U.S.S.R. The other two SEWS are deployed over the Atlantic and Pacific Oceans to detect attacking nuclear missiles launched from submarines. SEWS pinpoints the location of a nuclear missile by detecting the rocket exhaust left in its wake as it streaks across the sky. SEWS was first deployed in 1964.

SATKA is the informal term for the computer system that would monitor an attacking nuclear missile as it streaks toward its target. Satka is the acronym created from the four tasks (surveillance, acquisition, tracking, kill assessment) that such a computer would have to perform.

SATURATION ATTACK is a massive nuclear strike intended to overwhelm enemy defenses and completely wipe out targets. A saturation attack is distinct from a SURGICAL STRIKE, which is a very limited nuclear attack on selected targets only.

SCENARIO is a sequence of events that could, hypothetically, lead to nuclear war between the superpowers. Scenarios are used principally to develop a strategy for fighting a nuclear war. Three basic scenarios are discussed by war planners, including a surprise attack (a so-called bolt from the blue); escalation to nuclear war from a severe nonnuclear crisis (e.g., a Soviet invasion of West Berlin or the Persian Gulf); and isolated, random incidents (such as computer failure or terrorist attacks) flaring unexpectedly into a nuclear war.

SCHLESINGER DOCTRINE, announced by Secretary of Defense James Schlesinger in 1974, established LIMITED NUCLEAR WAR as official U.S. strategy. Schlesinger emphasized "selectivity and flexibility" in choosing where and how nuclear weapons would be used in a conflict. In this way, use of nuclear weapons could be used to attack only specific targets. Limited nuclear war and the Schlesinger Doctrine have been widely criticized as being unrealistic and misleading. Nonetheless, the Schlesinger Doctrine has served as the foundation of contemporary U.S. nuclear strategy. It has been amplified by succeeding administrations; the concepts of limited nuclear war and NUCLEAR WAR-FIGHTING have continued to dominate U.S. strategy.

SCIENTIFIC FEASIBILITY addresses the issue of whether a nuclear weapon can be physically possible. For example, researchers are considering the scientific feasibility of building laser beam weapons in space. Scientific feasibility is an important issue in the building of any nuclear weapon system. It is considered in conjunction with TECHNICAL FEASIBILITY, ECONOMIC FEASIBILITY, and OPERATIONAL FEASIBILITY.

SCOPE LIGHT   see AIRBORNE COMMAND POST

SCOWCROFT COMMISSION was a bipartisan commission created by U.S. President Ronald Reagan in January 1983 to determine the best way to deploy the MX MISSILE. The MX, capable of carrying up to 10 warheads, is the most modern U.S. INTERCON-

TINENTAL BALLISTIC MISSILE (ICBM) and will replace the older Titan and Minuteman ICBMs. The commission recommended building 100 MX missiles with 1,000 warheads and basing them in existing Minuteman silos. The commission also urged a future shift away from nuclear missiles that carry more than one warhead. To accomplish this, the commission advised building 1,000 smaller, single-warhead MIDGETMAN ICBMs. Finally, the commission concluded that the "window of vulnerability"—the danger to the U.S. posed by the Soviet numerical advantage in land-based ICBMs—was not as serious a threat as was previously believed. In November 1983, Congress approved a plan based on the commission's recommendations. Deployment of the MX began in 1986. Despite Congressional approval, debate continued into the mid-1980s over the appropriation of funds for the MX. The commission was chaired by Brent Scowcroft, a retired Air Force lieutenant general who was a high-ranking official under Presidents Nixon, Ford, and Carter. The Scowcroft Commission was officially called the Commission on Strategic Forces.

SCUD is the NATO code for a Soviet short-range ballistic missile. See SHORT-RANGE BALLISTIC MISSILE for a complete description of this missile.

SEA BED TREATY (1971) prohibits the deployment, testing, and storage of nuclear weapons on the sea bed of the world's oceans. The Sea Bed Treaty, signed by over 80 nations, outlaws nuclear weapons deployed on the ocean floor 19 kilometers (12 miles) beyond a nation's coastline. Nuclear weapons carried by ships and submarines are not covered by the treaty.

SEA-LAUNCHED CRUISE MISSILE (SLCM) is a CRUISE MISSILE launched from a submarine or ship. Cruise missiles are slow, low-flying, highly accurate missiles that resemble pilotless airplanes. Unlike BALLISTIC MISSILES, which are powered by

BOOSTER ROCKETS, cruise missiles are powered by jet engines. The U.S. deploys one type of SLCM:

- The navy's Tomahawk cruise missile has been deployed since 1984 in American submarines, cruisers, destroyers, and battleships. The sea-launched Tomahawk has a range of 2,500 km and delivers a yield of 200 kilotons.

The Soviet Union deploys six types of SLCMs.

- SS-N-3 Shaddock, the oldest Soviet SLCM, has been deployed since the early 1960s. The missile has a range of 450 km and carries either a conventional warhead or a single 350-kiloton nuclear warhead. The SS-N-3, which is deployed on submarines, is being replaced in the 1980s by the advanced SS-N-12 SLCM.
- SS-N-7 Siren, deployed since 1968, has a range of 45 km and can carry either a conventional warhead or a 200-kiloton nuclear warhead. It is deployed on submarines.
- SS-N-9, deployed since 1968, has a range of 280 km and carries either a conventional warhead or a single 200-kiloton nuclear warhead. It is deployed on submarines.
- SS-N-12, deployed since 1973, has a range of 1,000 km and can carry either a conventional warhead or a single 350-kiloton nuclear warhead. The missile is replacing the older SS-N-3 on submarines and will also be deployed on aircraft carriers.
- SS-N-14 Silex, deployed since 1974, has a range of 55 km and carries a single 1-kiloton nuclear warhead. The SS-N-14, unlike most Soviet SLCMs, is deployed exclusively on ships, such as frigates and aircraft carriers.
- SS-N-19, first deployed in 1980, has a range of 500 km and can carry either a conventional or a nuclear warhead. It is deployed on both aircraft carriers and submarines.

SEASAT is a NASA monitoring SATELLITE that detects ocean characteristics such as temperature, wave height, and surface winds. Seasat can detect underwater nuclear tests and help locate enemy submarines armed with nuclear missiles. In this way, Seasat can play an important role in antisubmarine warfare, conducted to prevent enemy submarines from launching nuclear missiles in a conflict.

SECOND-GENERATION WEAPON   see GENERATION WEAPONS

SECOND STRIKE is a massive nuclear attack launched in response to an enemy nuclear attack. The doctrine of deterrence is based on each superpower's ability to launch an effective second strike. With limited means for defending against a nuclear strike, both superpowers rely on their ability to inflict enormous damage on each other. In this way, they attempt to deter each other from launching a nuclear attack. This arrangement works only as long as both sides are capable of delivering a second strike—as long as they are capable of absorbing a nuclear strike and then countering with an unacceptably destructive retaliation.

SECOND-STRIKE CAPABILITY is the capacity to launch a massive nuclear attack after absorbing a devastating enemy attack. The existence of a second-strike capability is a fundamental element that helps restrain nations from fighting a nuclear war. With limited means for defending against a nuclear strike, both superpowers rely on their ability to inflict enormous damage on each other. In this way, they attempt to deter each other from launching a nuclear attack. This arrangement works only as long as both sides are capable of delivering a second strike—of absorbing a nuclear strike and then countering with an unacceptably destructive retaliation. Thus, a credible second-strike capability is essential if the superpowers are to be deterred from initiating a nuclear war. Second-strike capability is also called strike-back capability.

SEISMIC DETECTION   see SEISMIC VERIFICATION SYSTEM

SEISMIC STATIONS are unstaffed instruments that detect nuclear explosions by sensing tremors in the earth's crust. They are used to verify compliance with arms-control agreements. Seismic stations are extremely sensitive (they can detect tremors 10,000 km away) and can distinguish between nuclear explosions and natural phenomena, such as earthquakes. Also known as black boxes, seismic stations are the most important means of monitoring underground nuclear tests. A network of seismic stations forms a seismic verification system.

SEISMIC VERIFICATION SYSTEM is a network of sensitive equipment that detects nuclear explosions by sensing tremors in the earth's crust. In this way, a seismic verification system could be used to verify compliance with arms-control agreements. A seismic verification system covers much of the earth, but is far from comprehensive, because the U.S.S.R. has opposed construction of seismic stations on its territory. See SEISMIC STATIONS.

SELF-DETERRENCE   see COUNTERDETERRENCE

SEMIPALATINSK, located in Kazakhstan in the south-central U.S.S.R., is the principal Soviet NUCLEAR TEST SITE.

SEMI-PREFERENTIAL DEFENSE is a strategy for defending against attacking nuclear warheads. In semi-preferential defense, specific incoming warheads are targeted for destruction in flight while others are allowed to continue unchallenged toward their targets. The theory behind such a strategy is to ensure the survival of particularly important targets, while conceding that other targets must be sacrificed. In this way, the survival of certain important targets is guaranteed. A semi-preferential defense resembles a COMPLETELY PREFERENTIAL DEFENSE in that both concentrate on defending only certain target areas at the expense of others. However, they differ in one important respect: In a semi-preferential defense strategy, the targets are selected before an actual attack is launched. In a completely preferential defense strategy, the missiles to be destroyed would be selected after an attack has been launched.

SENSOR is a sensitive electronic instrument that detect a variety of objects. Sensors record energy that objects reflect or emit, and are commonly used to detect NUCLEAR WEAPONS explosions or the launching of BALLISTIC MISSILES. Sensors play a critical role in nuclear weapons technology. They are used to detect attacking warheads as well as to guide warheads to their targets. Sensors are also used to verify arms-control agreements. Essentially, sensors act as an extension of human sense organs; they are electronic eyes, ears, noses, and fingers. There are many different types of sensors that respond to different types of energy. RADAR sensors "see" by detecting radio waves reflected off objects. Seismic sensors "feel" disturbances by detecting shock waves in the earth's crust. Heat sensors "smell" heat being given off by an object.

SENTINEL was a proposed United States missile defense system. Secretary of Defense Robert McNamara announced the Sentinel program in 1967. It was a $5 billion program intended to defend 17 U.S. cities against a Chinese nuclear attack. Sentinel was never deployed, but the program was modified under President Richard Nixon and renamed SAFEGUARD in 1969. Safeguard was eventually deployed in 1974 to protect ballistic missile sites in North Dakota. It was dismantled in 1976 because of high cost and technical ineffectiveness.

SHELF LIFE is the period of time that a NUCLEAR WEAPON can remain effective without being used. Some nuclear weapons, such as U.S. Titan missiles, have been deployed since the early 1960s without being replaced. Military experts debate whether a weapon that has "been on the shelf" for such a long period will be effective if it is actually used.

SHELL GAME   see MULTIPLE PROTECTIVE SHELTERS

SHINING is the process of coating a missile's surface with a reflective substance. Shining would involve painting a sort of mirror onto attacking missiles, so they would reflect high-technology defensive weapons such as laser beams. The United States is conducting research on shining under the STRATEGIC DEFENSE INITIATIVE, commonly known as "Star Wars."

SHOCK WAVE is a wall of compressed air created as the result of a nuclear explosion. The shock wave generates tremendous air pressure and may devastate everything in its path. The shock wave causes destruction in two ways. First, it creates very high winds and pushes objects outward, like a hurricane. Second, it creates STATIC OVERPRESSURE, which crushes everything in its path like a rolling pin flattening dough. The shock wave sucks up any debris left in its wake, and may thus carry all sorts of deadly projectiles, such as broken glass. The shock wave can be one of the most destructive effects of a nuclear explosion. Its intensity depends on the size and type of weapon that is exploded and diminishes as the wave moves outward from the point of detonation. The shock wave is sometimes called the blast wave. See OVERPRESSURE.

SHOOT-LOOK-SHOOT is a strategy for the most efficient use of BALLISTIC MISSILES in an attack. A shoot-look-shoot strategy involves three distinct steps. First, an attack is launched with a small fraction of the total missile arsenal. Hopefully, this attack would destroy undefended targets and in the process reveal those targets most that are heavily defended. Second, an attacker looks to verify which targets are most heavily defended. Third, a second attack is launched against the most heavily defended targets with the bulk of the nuclear arsenal. A shoot-look-shoot strategy avoids wasting warheads against targets that can easily be destroyed and concentrates most of the warheads against those targets that are the most difficult to destroy.

SHORT-RANGE ATTACK MISSILE (SRAM) is a U.S. air-to-surface missile. See AIR-TO-SURFACE MISSILE for a complete description of the SRAM.

SHORT-RANGE BALLISTIC MISSILE (SRBM) is a ballistic missile intended for use over battlefield distances. SRBMs have a range of less than 1,100 km. This range is shorter than MEDIUM-RANGE BALLISTIC MISSILES, INTERMEDIATE-RANGE BALLISTIC MISSILES, and INTERCONTINENTAL BALLISTIC MISSILES. SRBMs are generally classed as TACTICAL NUCLEAR WEAPONS. The United States deploys three types of SRBMs:

- Honest John has been deployed since 1954 in Western Europe. It has been replaced by the Lance missile in all NATO forces except those of Greece and Turkey. Honest John, which must be heated to 77°F for one to two days before launching, can carry either a conventional or a nuclear warhead. Honest John has a range of 30 km and delivers a single .01 to 15 kiloton warhead.
- Pershing Ia was first deployed in West Germany in 1964 and is gradually being replaced by the modern Pershing II. The Pershing Ia has a range of 740 km and delivers a single 60- to 400-kiloton warhead.
- Lance, deployed since 1972 in Western Europe and the U.S., can carry either a conventional or a nuclear warhead. It has largely replaced the older Honest John missile. The Lance missile has a range of 125 km and carries a single 1- to 100-kiloton warhead.

The Soviet Union deploys four types of SRBMs:

- SS-1 Scud, first deployed in 1962, is carried by and launched from trucklike vehicles. With a range of 300 km, the Scud can deliver nuclear or conventional warheads. In the mid-1980s, the Scud is being replaced by the SS-23, which boasts greater range and improved accuracy.

- FROG-7 missile is the NATO code for the Free Rocket Over Ground missile. The Frog 7 has a range of 70 km and carries a 200-kiloton warhead. It is fired from a trucklike vehicle. The Frog has been deployed since 1965 and is being replaced in the mid-1980s by the more advanced SS-21.
- SS-21, deployed since 1978, has a range of 120 km and is replacing the older Frog 7 missile. It is targeted at Western Europe and the People's Republic of China.
- SS-22, first deployed in 1979, carries a single 500-kiloton warhead. The U.S.S.R. has deployed the SS-22 within its own borders. It began deploying the missile in East Germany and Czechoslovakia in 1984 in response to the NATO deployment of TOMAHAWK CRUISE MISSILES and Pershing II missiles in Western Europe. With a range of 900 km, the SS-22 can reach NATO cruise missile sites in England.
- SS-23, with a range of 500 km, is expected to replace the older SS-1 Scud in the mid-1980s. The missile is more accurate than the SS-1 and will feature a single nuclear warhead.

The People's Republic of China deploys one type of SRBM:

- DF-1, first deployed in 1966, has a range of 650 km and delivers one 2- to 10-kiloton warhead.

France deploys two types of SRBMs:

- Pluton has a range of 120 km and first came into service in 1974. The missile is deployed on a trucklike vehicle and carries a single 15- to 25-kiloton warhead.
- Hades is being developed to replace the older Pluton in the French nuclear arsenal. The missile, which is planned for deployment in 1992, will be mobile and have a range of 240 km. The missile will probably be deployed with both conventional and nuclear warheads. The Hades might also carry a neutron bomb.

SHROUD is the covering of the uppermost part of a nuclear missile. The shroud is designed to protect the missile's warhead(s).

SIDEBAR NEGOTIATIONS   see BACK-CHANNEL NEGOTIATIONS

SIGNATURE is an identifying characteristic that allows a defense system to detect an attacking nuclear weapon. A BALLISTIC MISSILE, for example, leaves a signature that is easily detected by RADAR. A ballistic missile is propelled by powerful rockets into space and is then pulled by gravity to its target. While the booster rockets are firing the missile into space, they leave a trail of hot gas and exhaust in the missile's wake. This easily detectable trail of heat and smoke is a ballistic missile's signature. Size, shape, radar image, and noise emitted by a weapon are other possible signatures.

SILK PURSE   see AIRBORNE COMMAND POST

SILO   see MISSILE SILO

SILO-BUSTER is a nickname for a technologically advanced nuclear missile that can destroy underground missile silos that have been reinforced against attack. Missile silos may be fortified with dirt, concrete, steel, and other materials to withstand the effects of silo-busters.

SILO-BUSTING POTENTIAL   see LETHALITY

SINGLE INTEGRATED OPERATIONAL PLAN (SIOP) is the top-secret U.S. master plan for fighting a full-scale nuclear war. SIOP is a comprehensive plan that tries to take into account all the details of waging a nuclear war. It includes plans for the use of the entire U.S. nuclear arsenal; missiles deployed in the U.S. as well as those on submarines and in Europe are included in SIOP. SIOP is said to be integrated because it takes into account all the individual U.S. strategies for waging war in specific areas, such as the Far East, Europe, and the Middle East. Great Britain's war plans are also included in SIOP. SIOP involves more than predicting the ability of U.S. missiles to destroy their targets. It includes plans for coping with the destruction of targets in the U.S. In addition, SIOP attempts to ensure that the U.S. communications network used for coordinating a nuclear war can function properly if under attack. SIOP was first devised in 1960 during the Eisenhower Administration, and has since undergone numerous changes to keep it up-to-date with new developments in weapons and strategy.

SITE DEFENSE see POINT DEFENSE

SKEAN is the NATO code for a Soviet intermediate-range ballistic missile. See INTERMEDIATE-RANGE BALLISTIC MISSILE for a complete description of this missile.

SKYBOLT was a well-known U.S. missile program that was abandoned in 1962 because of technical problems. In 1960, U.S. President Dwight Eisenhower agreed to sell Skybolt missiles to Great Britain. The Skybolt missile would have been deployed on aircraft. Great Britain had previously canceled its plans to develop its own Blue Streak BALLISTIC MISSILE. Under the terms of the sale, Great Britain agreed to make a naval base in Scotland available to U.S. ballistic missile submarines. Skybolt's cancellation left Great Britain without an effective way of deploying its NUCLEAR WEAPONS and reflected Great Britain's dependence on the U.S. for nuclear weapon technology. The 1962 NASSAU AGREEMENT rectified the situation. Under the terms of the Nassau Agreement, the U.S. sold Polaris missiles to Great Britain.

SLBM TUBES are the mechanisms that hold and launch nuclear missiles from submarines. SLBM tubes are the underwater equivalent of MISSILE SILOS.

SLEW TIME is the time needed for a defensive weapon to reaim at a new target after having just fired at a previous target. This term applies to high-technology weapons, such as LASERS, which would be based in space to destroy attacking nuclear warheads. Ideally, defensive systems would contain weapons with very short slew times. The faster a defensive weapon can reaim, the more targets it can destroy.

SLICKUM is the nickname of a SEA-LAUNCHED CRUISE MISSILE. It is derived from the initials SLCM.

SLOW FLYER is a nickname for CRUISE MISSILES. Cruise missiles are slow, low-flying, highly accurate nuclear missiles that resemble pilotless airplanes. They are powered throughout their flight by jet engines. Author Strobe Talbott claims that U.S. President Ronald Reagan coined this term.

SMALL INTERCONTINENTAL BALLISTIC MISSILE (SICBM) is an innovative type of long-range nuclear missile. The principal features of an SICBM are its single warhead and its method of deployment. SICBMs would be deployed so that they could be transported among many different silos. This arrangement is designed to reduce their vulnerability to enemy attack. SICBMs have been recommended for development because they would, in theory, be less inviting targets for an enemy FIRST STRIKE. The U.S. MIDGETMAN is commonly described as an SICBM.

SMALL-SCALE NUCLEAR ATTACK   see LIMITED NUCLEAR WAR

SMART BOMB   see PRECISION GUIDED MUNITION

SMART BULLET   see SMART ROCK

SMART ROCK is a theoretical weapon that could be used to destroy attacking nuclear warheads. A smart rock is a small projectile hurled through space at great speed. Shaped like hockey pucks, smart rocks are said to be smart because they steer themselves toward targets with built-in computers and heat sensors. After sensing and analyzing the target, smart rocks would disarm the warhead by impact. They do not contain an explosive device. Instead, smart rocks destroy a target in the same way as bullets.

Fired from high-technology LAUNCHERS, smart rocks are also known as smart bullets or "hypervelocity footballs." The United States is conducting research on smart rocks under the STRATEGIC DEFENSE INITIATIVE, commonly known as "Star Wars."

S-MISSILE is the code that designates a French surface-to-surface nuclear missile (officially known as sol-sol ballistique stratégique). France currently deploys the S-3, an intermediate-range ballistic missile. (See INTERMEDIATE-RANGE BALLISTIC MISSILE for a complete description of the S-3).

SOFT KILL   see FUNCTIONAL KILL

SOFT TARGET is a target that has not been reinforced to protect against an enemy nuclear attack. Examples of soft targets are oil refineries, airfields, and cities. Because they are not protected against a nuclear attack, soft targets can be severely damaged by relatively inaccurate missiles. Soft targets are more vulnerable than HARD TARGETS, such as MISSILE SILOS, which have been reinforced with concrete, earth, or steel to resist a missile strike.

SOLID-FUELED ENGINE is one type of BOOSTER ROCKET, which propels a BALLISTIC MISSILE into space and directs it toward its target. Solid-fueled engines are fueled by a rubberlike material. Unlike liquid-fueled engines, it is impossible to control the rate at which solid-fueled engines burn. A solid-fueled engine is thus similar to an automobile in which the gas pedal is pressed to the floor. Nonetheless, it is possible to control a solid-fueled engine's speed, by releasing excess energy out of the side of the missile. It is also possible to steer a solid-fueled missile, by deflecting energy out one side in order to push the missile one way or the other. Solid-fueled engines are safer and more sophisticated than liquid-fueled engines; they have almost entirely replaced liquid-fueled engines in the U.S. nuclear arsenal. The U.S.S.R., however, continues to deploy many liquid-fueled missiles.

SOL-SOL BALLISTIQUE STRATÉGIQUE   see SSBS

SOSUS (SOUND SURVEILLANCE SYSTEM) is a U.S. system for locating enemy submarines armed with nuclear missiles. Established in 1957, SOSUS is composed of underwater devices that "hear" submarines as they cruise around the ocean. SOSUS is a sophisticated system, which must deal with the vastness of the ocean and the peculiar qualities of sound travelling through water. SOSUS is part of the U.S. antisubmarine warfare force, developed to prevent enemy submarines from launching their nuclear missiles in a nuclear war.

SOUND SURVEILLANCE SYSTEM   see SOSUS

SPACE-BASED DEFENSE is a system for defending against incoming nuclear warheads. Space-based defense weapons are hypothetical devices based in space which could destroy attacking enemy missiles. Scientists have studied the possibility of using directed-energy (nonnuclear) weapons and beam weapons such as LASERS in space-based defense systems. Two arms-control agreements limit space-based defense. The ANTIBALLISTIC MISSILE TREATY, signed by the Soviet Union and the United States in 1972, prohibits space-based weapons that are designed to destroy attacking nuclear missiles. In addition, the OUTER SPACE TREATY of 1967 more generally forbids the use of space for military purposes. The United States is conducting research into space-based defense under the STRATEGIC DEFENSE INITIATIVE, commonly known as "Star Wars."

SPACE-BASED LASER WEAPON   see LASER

SPACE MINE is a small, theoretical SATELLITE that would be suspended in orbit near an enemy's space-based weapons and satellites. Space mines would contain an explosive charge set to explode by remote control or on impact. They would be used primarily to attack military satellites in low orbits. Space mines would be invisible to radar. The United States is conducting research on space mines under the STRATEGIC DEFENSE INITIATIVE, commonly known as "Star Wars."

SPARTAN MISSILE was a defensive missile designed to destroy incoming enemy warheads. Spartan missiles were deployed in 1974 by the U.S. as part of the SAFEGUARD antiballistic missile system at Grand Forks, North Dakota. Safeguard, which incorporated both Spartan and SPRINT MISSILES, was deployed to protect a nearby cluster of Minuteman missile silos. Safeguard was dismantled in 1976 because of its high cost and dubious efficacy. Spartan missiles were retired in the mid-1980s.

SPASM RESPONSE is the nickname for a massive nuclear retaliation launched in response to an enemy attack.

SPASM WAR is a type of enormously destructive nuclear war in which total resources are employed ruthlessly in a brief conflict.

SPECIAL ATOMIC DEMOLITION MUNITION (SADM) see ATOMIC DEMOLITION MUNITION

SPINNING is a technique for imparting a spin to nuclear missiles as they are launched. Spinning is intended to counter high-technology defensive weapons, such as LASERS. Spinning would, in theory, spread the intensity of defensive beams of energy over the entire surface of a missile. In this way, the beam's effect would be weakened and the missile could continue unimpeded toward its target.

SPRINT MISSILE was a defensive missile designed to destroy incoming enemy warheads. Spartan missiles were deployed in 1974 by the U.S. as part of the SAFEGUARD antiballistic missile system at Grand Forks, North Dakota. Safeguard, which incorporated both Sprint and SPARTAN MISSILES, was deployed to protect a nearby cluster of Minuteman MISSILE SILOS. Safeguard was dismantled in 1976 because of its high cost and dubious efficacy. Sprint missiles were retired in the mid-1980s.

SPUTNIK was the first artificial SATELLITE to be launched into space. Sputnik was unmanned. Developed by the U.S.S.R. and launched on October 4, 1957, Sputnik represented the dawn of modern space and missile technology and prompted the hectic "space race." Sputnik caused an alarmed uproar in the United States; it signaled to the world that the Soviet Union was moving toward parity with the U.S. as a scientific and military power. Sputnik spurred significant increases in U.S. military spending and increased the intensity of the nuclear arms race.

SSBS (SOL-SOL BALLISTIQUE STRATÉGIQUE) designates a French ground-launched ballistic missile. The French deploy one type of SSBS, the S-3 intermediate-range ballistic missile. See INTERMEDIATE-RANGE BALLISTIC MISSILE for a complete description of the S-3.

SSC-MISSILE is the NATO code that designates Soviet ground-launched cruise missiles. The SSC-4 is a GLCM. (See GROUND-LAUNCHED CRUISE MISSILE for a complete description of the SSC-4.)

SS-MISSILE is the NATO code that designates Soviet surface-to-surface nuclear missiles. SS-1 Scud, SS-21, and SS-23 are short-range ballistic missiles. (See SHORT-RANGE BALLISTIC MISSILE for a complete description of these missiles.) SS-4 Sandal and SS-22 are medium-range ballistic missiles. (See MEDIUM-RANGE BALLISTIC MISSILE for a complete description of these missiles.) SS-5 Skean and SS-20 are intermediate-range ballistic missiles. (See INTERMEDIATE-RANGE BALLISTIC MISSILE for a complete description of these missiles.) SS-11 Sego, SS-13, SS-17, SS-18, SS-19, SS-24, and SS-25 are intercontinental ballistic missiles. (See INTERCONTINENTAL BALLISTIC MISSILE for a complete description of these missiles.)

SS-N-MISSILE is the NATO code that designates Soviet submarine-launched ballistic missiles (SLBMs) and sea-launched cruise missiles (SLCMs). The SS-N-5, SS-N-6, SS-N-8, SS-N-17, SS-N-18, and SS-N-20 are SLBMs. (See SUBMARINE-LAUNCHED BALLISTIC MISSILE for a complete description of these missiles.) The SS-N-3 Shaddock, SS-N-7 Siren, SS-N-9,

SS-N-12, SS-N-14, and SS-N-19 are SLCMs. (See SEA-LAUNCHED CRUISE MISSILE for a complete description of these missiles.)

SS-X-MISSILE is the NATO code that designates experimental Soviet nuclear missiles.

STABILITY   see STRATEGIC STABILITY

STABLE DETERRENCE   see NUCLEAR DETERRENCE

STANDARD is a U.S. surface-to-air missile. The Standard is also known as the Aegis. (See SURFACE-TO-AIR MISSILE for a complete description of this missile.)

STANDING CONSULTATIVE COMMISSION (SCC) is a group of American and Soviet officials, appointed by the leaders of each country, that convenes at least twice a year to discuss disputes about compliance with arms-control agreements. The SCC was established by SALT I in 1972 and extended by SALT II.

STAND-OFF BOMB is a general term for a nuclear weapon fired from an aircraft at considerable distance from the target. A stand-off bomb covers the final distance to the target under its own power. Stand-off weapons have been developed to enable aircraft to "stand off" from targets in order to avoid enemy defenses. The U.S. AIR-LAUNCHED CRUISE MISSILE (ALCM) is an example of a stand-off bomb.

STAR WARRIORS is the nickname for scientists who perform research on high-technology weapons designed to protect against a nuclear attack. Star Warriors conduct research under the U.S. STRATEGIC DEFENSE INITIATIVE, commonly known as "Star Wars."

STAR WARS is the nickname for the STRATEGIC DEFENSE INITIATIVE (SDI), a United States research program to determine whether a defensive shield can be built to destroy attacking nuclear warheads. The nickname is derived from the popular American science fiction film *Star Wars*, released in 1977. The film portrays extravagant battles in outer space involving high-technology weapons such as LASERS. In his "Star Wars" speech of March 23, 1983, President Ronald Reagan called for developing a means for rendering nuclear weapons "impotent and obsolete." Following this address, the U.S. embarked upon a long-term, multibillion-dollar program to examine the feasibility of establishing a space "shield" to destroy attacking enemy BALLISTIC MISSILES. SDI proponents contend that, if such a missile defense system could be built, it would eliminate the threat of nuclear war by effectively countering any attempted nuclear strike. Opponents of the program claim that SDI will destabilize the current strategic balance and thereby increase the risk of a nuclear exchange.

STATIC OVERPRESSURE is essentially a strong, crushing wind created in the aftermath of a nuclear explosion. Static overpressure pushes objects down in the same way that a rolling pin flattens a lump of dough. Overpressure can collapse buildings, uproot trees, and crush people. Static overpressure is distinct from DYNAMIC OVERPRESSURE, which is also created in a nuclear explosion. Dynamic overpressure pushes objects outward in the same way a strong wind blows leaves off trees.

STEALTH BOMBER is a high-technology airplane currently under development by the United States. The Stealth bomber will incorporate technology that makes it "invisible" to enemy RADAR. The Stealth, officially known as the Advanced Technology Bomber, will eventually replace the FB-111 bomber. See STEALTH TECHNOLOGY.

STEALTH TECHNOLOGY is intended to make bombers and missiles "invisible" to RADAR. Stealth involves sharp aerodynamic contours and special coating materials that prevent radar from detecting airborne objects. The U.S. is conducting research on stealth technology, and is expected to deploy a STEALTH BOMBER in the early 1990s.

STELLAR GUIDANCE is a technique to improve the accuracy of nuclear missiles. Stellar guidance uses the stars or other celestial bodies as points of reference. With stellar guidance, each missile is equipped with a small telescope. After the missile is launched, the telescope takes readings of stars overhead. These measurements are then compared with a programmed map of the sky stored in a computer within the missile. Any discrepancies between actual and predicted readings are used by the computer to set it on target.

STIMSON INTERIM COMMITTEE   see INTERIM COMMITTEE

STOCKHOLM INTERNATIONAL PEACE RESEARCH INSTITUTE (SIPRI) was established in 1966 as an independent research institute to examine questions of international peace and security. SIPRI was founded by the Swedish government in honor of Sweden's 150 years of continuous peace. Funded entirely by the Swedish government, SIPRI maintains a staff of experts from around the world. SIPRI, however, purposely excludes U.S. and Soviet experts from serving on its board. SIPRI sponsors international conferences and publishes books dealing with current arms-control issues. Its highly respected yearbook, *World Armaments and Disarmament,* published annually since 1968, is considered by many as one of the authoritative sources on nuclear weapons statistics, technology, and information.

STOCKPILE   see NUCLEAR STOCKPILE

STRATEGIC AIR COMMAND (SAC) is the branch of the U.S. Air Force that oversees the bulk of the American nuclear arsenal. SAC controls land-based nuclear missiles and long-range bombers deployed on U.S. soil. These weapons would be used to strike deep in the territory of the Soviet Union or China in the event of a nuclear war. In addition, SAC supervises the POST-ATTACK

COMMAND AND CONTROL SYSTEM, which is a system of airplanes that would serve as a U.S. command post during a nuclear war. Headquartered at Offutt Air Force Base in Omaha, Nebraska, SAC was established following World War II.

STRATEGIC ARMS LIMITATION TALKS AND TREATIES see SALT, SALT I, SALT II

STRATEGIC ARMS REDUCTION TALKS (START) were a series of bilateral negotiations between the U.S. and the U.S.S.R. that sought to reduce the number of STRATEGIC NUCLEAR WEAPONS. Strategic nuclear weapons are targeted by each superpower against the homeland of the other. The talks were held in Geneva, Switzerland, between June 1982 and December 1983. No agreement was ever reached, primarily because neither side could agree on which weapons to reduce. During START, the U.S. wanted to reduce land-based nuclear missiles, which make up the backbone of the Soviet nuclear arsenal. The Soviets, however, wanted to include missiles launched from submarines and aircraft. The U.S. has a numerical advantage over the Soviets in these two categories. The Soviets walked out of START after the U.S. began deploying Pershing II BALLISTIC MISSILES and TOMAHAWK CRUISE MISSILES in Western Europe in December 1983.

STRATEGIC BALANCE is the comparison of the United States' and the Soviet Union's ability to fight a nuclear war. Generally, the strategic balance is thought of in terms of the number of nuclear weapons deployed by each side; it is commonly measured by each side's total number of NUCLEAR WARHEADS. Strategic balance suggests that an equal number of warheads essentially means that each superpower has an equal ability to fight a nuclear war. Critics contend, however, that counting the number of warheads is not adequate for determining the strategic balance. They argue that successfully fighting a nuclear war depends on many other factors, such as the types and technology of nuclear weapons in each nation's nuclear arsenal. Other factors considered in the strategic balance include the geographical position of each country, which affects the vulnerability of a country's weapons, cities, and industry to attack. Finally, some experts emphasize the human factor. They contend that the quality of the people in charge of fighting a nuclear war is as important as the weapons themselves in determining the strategic balance.

STRATEGIC BOMBER is any aircraft that can take off in one superpower's homeland and deliver nuclear weapons against the other superpower's territory. Strategic bombers take about ten hours to reach their targets and, unlike missiles, can be recalled or retargeted during their flight. Strategic bombers are the air-based component of the U.S.'s strategic triad. The triad also includes land- and submarine-based nuclear missiles. LONG-RANGE BOMBERS are strategic bombers; INTERMEDIATE-RANGE BOMBERS can serve as strategic bombers if equipped for in-flight refueling or if they are sent on one-way missions. In general, U.S. strategic bombers are superior to those deployed by the Soviet Union.

STRATEGIC BUILDUP refers to a prolonged, deliberate increase in the size and capability of a country's nuclear arsenal. A strategic buildup is a recurring phenomenon of the nuclear arms race. If one side perceives itself to be at a disadvantage in the arms race, it may embark on a strategic buildup. Perhaps the most notable strategic buildup was undertaken by the Soviet Union from the mid-1950s through the 1970s. In this period, the U.S.S.R. moved from a position of definite nuclear weapons inferiority toward parity with the United States. See NUCLEAR ARMS RACE.

STRATEGIC COUPLING refers to the NATO policy of combining American and Western European defenses. Strategic coupling is an essential part of the NATO alliance. With strategic coupling, forces of all the NATO allies would be combined to counter any enemy attack on Western Europe or North America.

STRATEGIC DEFENSE encompasses defensive weapons designed to protect against a nuclear attack. The ANTIBALLISTIC MISSILE (ABM) TREATY of 1972 between the United States and the Soviet Union limits strategic defense. The ABM Treaty restricts strategic defense systems deployed in the air, at sea, in space, or on the ground. Strategic defense is distinct from STRATEGIC OFFENSE, which encompasses nuclear weapons designed to attack an enemy. In March 1983, U.S. President Ronald Reagan announced the STRATEGIC DEFENSE INITIATIVE (SDI), commonly known as "Star Wars." SDI is a research program to develop an effective strategic defense.

STRATEGIC DEFENSE INITIATIVE (SDI) is the United States research program to determine whether a defensive shield can be built to destroy attacking nuclear warheads. SDI is nicknamed STAR WARS after the popular American science fiction film of the same name that portrays extravagant battles in outer space involving high-technology weapons such as LASERS. In a speech on March 23, 1983, President Ronald Reagan called for developing a means for rendering nuclear weapons "impotent and obsolete." Following this address, the U.S. embarked upon a long-term, multibillion-dollar program to examine the feasibility of establishing a space "shield" to destroy attacking enemy BALLISTIC MISSILES. SDI proponents contend that, if such a missile defense system could be built, it would eliminate the threat of nuclear war by effectively countering any attempted nuclear strike. Opponents of the program claim that SDI will destabilize the current strategic balance and thereby increase the risk of a nuclear exchange.

STRATEGIC DEFENSE INITIATIVE ORGANIZATION (SDIO) is a United States government agency that oversees the STRATEGIC DEFENSE INITIATIVE (SDI), commonly known as "Star Wars."

SDI is a U.S. research program to determine whether a defensive shield can be built to destroy attacking nuclear warheads. SDIO was established in 1984 as a separate agency of the Department of Defense.

STRATEGIC NUCLEAR FORCE   see STRATEGIC NUCLEAR WEAPON

STRATEGIC NUCLEAR PARITY   see PARITY

STRATEGIC NUCLEAR SUFFICIENCY is a U.S. term that refers to the number of nuclear weapons that are necessary for the United States to deter an enemy attack. In the early 1970s, President Richard Nixon used the term to describe what it would take for the U.S. to prevent an enemy nuclear strike. U.S. strategic nuclear sufficiency has usually been based on three requirements. First, it requires that the U.S. must be capable of absorbing an enemy nuclear strike and then launching an unacceptably destructive retaliation. Second, it asserts that the U.S. must not weaken its military forces, so that the U.S.S.R. would not have an incentive to launch a nuclear attack in a crisis. Finally, strategic nuclear sufficiency must aim to prevent a situation in which the Soviet Union could inflict greater damage on U.S. population and industrial centers than the U.S. could on Soviet population and industrial centers.

STRATEGIC NUCLEAR WEAPON is a nuclear weapon that travels over intercontinental distances and is intended to strike the homelands of the superpowers. Strategic missiles are the biggest, most powerful nuclear weapons in the world's nuclear arsenals. They are larger and can travel farther than both THEATER NUCLEAR WEAPONS (intended to be used in a broad geographical region, such as Europe or the Far East) and TACTICAL NUCLEAR WEAPONS (intended for battlefield use). They are particularly relevant to warfare between the U.S. and the U.S.S.R. because of the great distances between the two superpowers. Strategic nuclear weapons can be launched from underground

MISSILE SILOS, submarines, or bombers. Strategic nuclear weapons are sometimes called long-range nuclear weapons.

STRATEGIC OFFENSE encompasses nuclear weapons designed to attack an enemy. With limited means for defending against a nuclear attack, both superpowers have relied on their ability to inflict enormous damage on each other. In this way, they use strategic offense to deter one another from launching a nuclear attack. Strategic offense is distinct from STRATEGIC DEFENSE, which encompasses defensive weapons designed to protect against a nuclear attack.

STRATEGIC RETALIATION see SECOND STRIKE

STRATEGIC STABILITY is a condition in which the superpowers choose not to build or use nuclear weapons. Strategic stability encompasses two complementary ideas: ARMS RACE STABILITY and CRISIS STABILITY. Arms race stability occurs when neither superpower feels compelled to develop major new weapons programs. Crisis stability, by contrast, is a condition in which neither superpower chooses to use nuclear weapons in a conflict. Strategic stability would establish a safe international environment, in which the risk of nuclear war would be greatly reduced.

STRATEGIC TRIAD see TRIAD

STRATEGIC WARNING is a determination that an enemy will launch a nuclear attack very soon. Actions such as sending nuclear submarines out to sea, evacuating cities, or releasing nuclear weapons from storage facilities could lead a nation to believe a nuclear attack is imminent.

STRIKE-BACK CAPABILITY see SECOND-STRIKE CAPABILITY

STRIP ALERT see GROUND ALERT

STRONTIUM-90 is a deadly radioactive substance released in a nuclear explosion. Strontium-90 can cause genetic damage, and is particularly hazardous to the bones and teeth of young children.

During the 1950s and early 1960s, when aboveground nuclear tests were regularly conducted, a great deal of strontium-90 was released into the environment and entered the human food chain. It was drawn into the atmosphere, fell to the earth in rain, settled on grass, was eaten by cows, and finally began showing up in dairy products. The BABY TOOTH SURVEY of 1962 revealed that, because of unbridled nuclear testing, the level of strontium-90 in children's teeth had increased 14-fold between 1949 and 1957. Public outrage over the increasing amount of strontium-90 in the environment was a major force that led to the signing of the LIMITED TEST BAN TREATY in 1963. This treaty banned aboveground nuclear tests.

SUB-KILOTON WEAPON is a small nuclear weapon with a yield of less than one kiloton. A kiloton is equivalent to 1,000 tons of TNT. Sub-kiloton weapons are TACTICAL NUCLEAR WEAPONS, designed for battlefield use.

SUBMARINE-LAUNCHED BALLISTIC MISSILE (SLBM) is a ballistic missile that is transported in and launched from a submarine. SLBMs are propelled into the upper atmosphere by BOOSTER ROCKETS. After the rockets burn out, they fall down through the atmosphere, pulled by gravity to their targets. Submerged deep in the ocean, SLBMs are less vulnerable than other nuclear missiles, and can reach their targets in a matter of minutes. They are also, however, less accurate than land- or air-based missiles. The U.S. SLBM force is far superior to its Soviet counterpart in terms of numbers and technological capability. The Soviets deploy six types of SLBMs:

- SS-N-5, deployed since 1963, forms only a small percentage of the total Soviet SLBM arsenal. It is rapidly being phased out and carries a single 1-megaton warhead.
- SS-N-6 Sawfly has been deployed since 1973 with a single 1-megaton warhead. A modernized version, which carries two 200-kiloton warheads, has been deployed since 1974. Unlike

most Soviet SLBMs, the SS-N-6 has a very short range of 3,000 km and must be fired from submarines stationed relatively close to enemy shores. Because they are deployed far from the security of Soviet territorial waters, submarines carrying the SS-N-6 are particularly vulnerable to antisubmarine warfare.

- SS-N-8, deployed since 1972, has a very long range. It can be fired from submarines safely positioned within Soviet territorial waters. The SS-N-8 carries either a single 1-megaton or a single 800-kiloton warhead.
- SS-N-17, first deployed in 1977, is replacing the older SS-N-6 in the Soviet nuclear arsenal. It carries a single 1-megaton warhead and, like the SS-N-6, it has a relatively short range.
- SS-N-18 has been deployed since 1978. It is replacing the SS-N-8 and carries three to seven warheads.
- SS-N-20, deployed since 1983, has a range of 8,000 km. Because of its long range, the SS-N-20 can reach the U.S. from submarines positioned in Soviet territorial waters. It carries six to nine warheads and is solid-fueled. The SS-N-20 is deployed on new Typhoon submarines.

The U.S. deploys three types of SLBMs:

- Poseidon, first deployed in 1971, is carried in Poseidon submarines. Poseidon missiles comprised the backbone of the U.S.'s submarine-based nuclear force in the 1970s and early 1980s. They are gradually being replaced in the mid-1980s by newer Trident missiles. They have a range of 4,000 km and carry ten 40-kiloton warheads.
- Trident 1 (C4) was first deployed in 1979 in both older Poseidon submarines and new Trident submarines. Trident I has a range of 7,400 km and carries 8 to 14 100-kiloton warheads. Trident I will be replaced by Trident II by the early 1990s.
- Trident II (D5) will be deployed by the late 1980s in Trident submarines. Trident II has a range of 7,400 to 11,000 km and

carries nine or ten 475- to 600-kiloton warheads. Another possible configuration is fifteen warheads, each with a yield of 150 kilotons. Trident II will replace Trident I and any remaining Poseidon missiles by the early 1990s.

Great Britain deploys one type of SLBM:

- Polaris missiles, carried in Polaris submarines, comprise the backbone of the British submarine-based nuclear force. First deployed in 1959 by the United States, Polaris missiles have a range of 4,600 km and carry three to six 200-kiloton warheads. The U.S. replaced its Polaris missiles with Poseidon SLBMs beginning in 1971; the British have modernized their Polaris missiles under the CHEVALINE program. The modernized missiles have a longer range, better accuracy, and an increased number of warheads with smaller yield than unmodified Polaris missiles. The British plan to replace their Polaris missiles with Trident II missiles in the 1990s.

The People's Republic of China deploys one type of SLBM:

- CSS-N-3 was first deployed in 1983 on Xia-class submarines. The CSS-N-3 has a range of 3,300 km and delivers one 200-kiloton or 1-megaton warhead.

France deploys two types of SLBMs:

- M-4 MSBS (mer-sol ballistique stratégique) was first deployed in 1985 on the French submarine *L'Inflexible*. The missile has a range of 6,000 km and carries six 150-kiloton warheads. Both the M-4 and the M-20 are deployed on French Rédoutable-class submarines.
- M-20 MSBS (mer-sol ballistique stratégique) was first deployed in 1977 and is being replaced by the more advanced M-4. The missile has a range of 3,000 km and carries a single 1-megaton warhead.

SUBROC (SUBMARINE ROCKET) is a U.S. antisubmarine missile. See ANTISUBMARINE MISSILE for a complete description of the SUBROC.

SUITCASE BOMB is a nuclear weapon that can be transported and detonated in a suitcase or in a similarly-sized container. A common SCENARIO portrays terrorists sneaking a suitcase bomb into a country and threatening to blow it up if their demands are not met.

SUPER   see SUPERBOMB

SUPERBOMB was the name given to THERMONUCLEAR WEAPONS during the 1950s, when they were developed and first deployed. Thermonuclear weapons, the most destructive type of nuclear weapons, create the same type of reaction that occurs in the center of the sun. On January 31, 1950, President Harry Truman ordered that the United States proceed with development of the superbomb. After two years of frenzied research and experimentation at the LOS ALAMOS SCIENTIFIC LABORATORY in New Mexico, the U.S. exploded the first superbomb on November 1, 1952. The U.S.S.R. followed suit on November 23, 1955. Thermonuclear weapons presently dominate the world's nuclear arsenal.

SUPER EXCALIBUR   see X-RAY LASER WEAPON

SUPERHARDENING is a hypothetical method for deploying nuclear missiles. More extensive and costly than the current technique of HARDENING, superhardening would involve fortifying underground MISSILE SILOS so that they could survive an enemy nuclear attack. Silos could be superhardened with earth, concrete, steel, and other materials. Superhardening was first conceived as a method of deploying the U.S.'s MX MISSILE.

SUPREME ALLIED COMMAND EUROPE SUPPLEMENTARY PLAN   see NUCLEAR OPERATIONS PLAN

SURFACE BURST   see GROUND BURST

SURFACE-TO-AIR MISSILE (SAM) is a missile launched from the ground or from a surface ship at an airborne target. Surface-to-air missiles are primarily defensive weapons, launched at attacking aircraft and missiles. The United States deploys three types of surface-to-air missiles that carry nuclear warheads:

- Nike-Hercules, first deployed in 1958 in Western Europe, is ground-launched and designed to wipe out enemy aircraft. It can also be used as a SURFACE-TO-SURFACE MISSILE against targets on the ground. It can be equipped with either a conventional or a nuclear warhead. The Nike-Hercules is gradually being replaced by conventional missiles. With a range of 160 km, the Nike-Hercules delivers a single 1- to 20-kiloton warhead.
- Terrier, first deployed in 1955, is launched from aircraft carriers, cruisers, and destroyers. Terrier missiles originally delivered nuclear or conventional warheads. All Terrier missiles currently deployed, however, are armed with nuclear weapons. With a range of about 37 km, Terriers deliver a single 1-kiloton warhead.
- Standard (SM-2), which first became operational in 1978, is a missile launched from cruisers and destroyers. The Standard can also be used as a surface-to-surface missile against targets on the ground. The Standard has a range of 104 km and delivers a single, low-yield warhead. It can be armed with either a conventional or a nuclear warhead. The Standard is also called the Aegis.

The U.S.S.R. deploys one type of surface-to-air missile:

- SA-5 Gammon, which first became operational in 1967, carries a single nuclear warhead whose yield is not available. The missile's range is 240 km.

SURFACE-TO-SURFACE MISSILE is a missile launched from the ground or from a ship at a target on land or sea. Most nuclear missiles are surface-to-surface missiles. See GROUND-LAUNCHED CRUISE MISSILE, INTERCONTINENTAL BALLISTIC MISSILE, INTERMEDIATE-RANGE BALLISTIC MISSILE, MEDIUM-RANGE BALLISTIC MISSILE, MIDGETMAN, MX MISSILE, NUCLEAR ARTILLERY, SHORT-RANGE BALLISTIC MISSILE, SMALL INTERCONTINENTAL BALLISTIC MISSILE, and SS-MISSILE.

SURGICAL STRIKE is a very limited nuclear attack on selected targets only. A surgical strike, for example, may involve targeting nuclear weapons specifically at enemy military installations. A surgical strike is distinct from a SATURATION ATTACK, a massive nuclear strike intended to overwhelm enemy defenses and completely wipe out targets.

SURPRISE ATTACK is an unexpected nuclear strike. Both superpowers seek to prevent each other from launching a surprise attack by using SATELLITE systems to provide EARLY WARNING of an enemy attack. A surprise attack is also known as a "bolt from the blue."

SURVEILLANCE SATELLITES see MONITORING SATELLITES

SURVIVABILITY refers to the ability of military and civilian targets to withstand the effects of a nuclear attack. Measures such as HARDENING (reinforcing) military targets and CIVIL DEFENSE are designed to improve the survivability of military and civilian targets, respectively. Though survivability is an important characteristic of nuclear warfare, it is an extremely uncertain concept, because no one knows exactly what the effects of a nuclear war would be.

SURVIVABLE LOW-FREQUENCY COMMUNICATIONS SYSTEM (SLFCS) is a part of the MINIMUM ESSENTIAL EMERGENCY COMMUNICATIONS NETWORK, the U.S. system that is designed to transmit communications during a nuclear war. SLFCS consists of several navy and air force transmitters that are connected to missile launch centers, submarines, and bombers. SLFCS is specially designed to enable U.S. military leaders to send undisrupted messages in a nuclear war.

SWARMJET refers to a theoretical method for destroying attacking nuclear warheads. Swarmjet would involve firing many small interceptor missiles at an incoming nuclear warhead. These missiles would blanket a large region of the sky. This swarm of missiles would have a better chance of destroying an incoming warhead than a single missile. A swarmjet defense would intercept incoming warheads near the end of their flight, when they are relatively close to the earth. Since the swarmjet defense might cause an attacking warhead to explode near the ground, it would be suitable for defending MISSILE SILOS rather than cities. The United States is conducting research on swarmjets under the STRATEGIC DEFENSE INITIATIVE, commonly known as "Star Wars."

SYMBOLIC ATTACK   see NUCLEAR SHOW OF FORCE

T

TACAMO is an airplane that relays emergency messages from Washington to patrolling submarines armed with nuclear missiles. In a nuclear war, TACAMO planes would relay orders to launch submarine-based missiles. A TACAMO plane is aloft twenty-four hours a day, and is designed to be able to relay messages to submarines in a nuclear war. TACAMO planes have had a history of technical problems, however, and many experts doubt that they could be counted on in an emergency. TACAMO is an acronym for "take charge and move out."

TACTICAL AIRCRAFT is any aircraft designed to deliver nuclear or conventional weapons over battlefield distances. Tactical aircraft are distinct from STRATEGIC BOMBERS, which deliver nuclear weapons over intercontinental distances. The United States deploys 13 types of tactical aircraft capable of carrying nuclear weapons. In addition, three types of tactical aircraft built by the U.S. are used exclusively by NATO forces. The Soviet Union deploys eight types of tactical aircraft, Great Britain deploys two types and France deploys three types.

TACTICAL NUCLEAR FORCE   see TACTICAL NUCLEAR WEAPON

TACTICAL NUCLEAR WEAPON is a nuclear weapon that is intended for battlefield use. It is designed to travel relatively short distances and does not threaten the homelands of the superpowers. Tactical nuclear weapons are small, highly specialized nuclear weapons first developed in the early 1950s by the U.S. as a substitute for the deployment of conventional forces in Europe. They are less powerful and cannot travel as far as either STRATEGIC NUCLEAR WEAPONS (intended to strike the homelands of the superpowers) or THEATER NUCLEAR WEAPONS (intended to be used in a broad geographical region, such as Europe or the Far East). Tactical nuclear weapons specially developed to be used in battle include nuclear artillery shells and atomic demolition munitions, which are nuclear mines. Tactical nuclear weapons can also be launched from trucklike vehicles or short-range aircraft. Tactical nuclear weapons are also called battlefield nuclear weapons.

TACTICAL OPERATING RADIUS   see COMBAT RADIUS

TACTICAL WARNING is a determination that an enemy has lauched a nuclear attack.

TALON GOLD is part of a theoretical, high-technology U.S. defense system that will detect and destroy enemy satellites and attacking bombers with a LASER, a highly concentrated beam of light capable of burning through the surface of bombers and satellites. Talon Gold, which would be based in space, will be tested in the late 1980s. The U.S. is conducting research on Talon Gold under the STRATEGIC DEFENSE INITIATIVE, commonly known as "Star Wars."

TAMPER is the blanket of uranium-238 that surrounds the core of a nuclear weapon. U-238 is relatively common in nature, and cannot normally be used to fuel a nuclear explosion. When exposed to the tremendous heat generated by a nuclear explosion, however, the tamper explodes. The tamper is an inexpensive way to enhance a weapon's destructive power, and also absorbs much of the deadly PROMPT RADIATION emitted by a nuclear explosion. Thus a weapon with no tamper, such as the NEUTRON BOMB, would be less destructive but would release a great deal of harmful radiation.

TANK   see NATIONAL MILITARY COMMAND CENTER

TARGET OF OPPORTUNITY is an unplanned target of a nuclear strike. A target of opportunity is a essentially a bonus; by destroying it an attacker would gain an advantage without using extra weapons.

TARGET RESPONSE is the U.S. military term for the effects of a nuclear explosion on the surrounding environment.

TEAL RUBY is a U.S. SATELLITE that is being developed to detect attacking bombers. TEAL RUBY will be designed to notify decision-makers if an enemy attack is underway so they can take appropriate action. TEAL RUBY is scheduled to be deployed in the mid-1980s.

TECHNICAL FEASIBILITY addresses the issue of whether a weapon that is physically possible can be built within a certain amount of time using available technology. Technical feasibility played a major role in the decision to build the first atomic bomb. Scientists knew the process by which atomic energy was created, but they were unsure if it could be adapted in a nuclear weapon. They determined that it could, and the U.S. developed the first atomic weapons during World War II. Technical feasibility is a major issue in the construction of any nuclear weapon. It is considered in conjunction with SCIENTIFIC FEASIBILITY, OPERATIONAL FEASIBILITY, and ECONOMIC FEASIBILITY.

TELEMETRY is the stream of technical data transmitted by missiles during tests. Telemetry is used by analysts to evaluate missile performance. It is also intercepted by satellites and used to verify arms-control agreements. ENCRYPTION (coding) of telemetry would interfere with this process and is prohibited under the terms of SALT I.

TERMINAL GUIDANCE is a series of last-minute adjustments to a missile's direction as it approaches its target. Effective terminal guidance improves the accuracy of a warhead. While a missile's direction is controlled throughout the flight, terminal guidance specifically seeks to home a missile in to its target. One method of terminal guidance uses a map of the area right around the target stored in the missile's computers. Sensors mounted on the missile scan the horizon as it approaches the target and compare the actual terrain under the missile with the programmed map. This technique could be used to positively identify the target and direct the missile unerringly toward it.

TERMINAL PHASE is the final phase of a BALLISTIC MISSILE's flight. It follows the BOOST PHASE, POST-BOOST PHASE, and MIDCOURSE PHASE. During the terminal phase, which lasts 30 to 100 seconds, the nuclear warhead has already entered the atmosphere and is bearing down on its target. The terminal phase is also known as the reentry phase.

TERMINAL PHASE DEFENSE   see TERMINAL PHASE INTERCEPTION

TERMINAL PHASE INTERCEPTION is the destruction of attacking nuclear warheads during the final seconds of a missile's flight. During the terminal phase, which lasts about 30 to 100 seconds, warheads reenter the atmosphere and prepare to strike their targets. Terminal interception is the most critical layer of MISSILE DEFENSE INTERCEPTION. Terminal phase interception would be risky, because missile defense systems would have very little time to detect and destroy incoming warheads. If warheads survive the terminal phase, there is nothing to stop them from destroying their targets. Terminal phase interception is also known as reentry phase interception.

TERRAIN CONTOUR MATCHING (TERCOM) is a guidance system for U.S. CRUISE MISSILES. Cruise missiles are slow, low-flying, highly accurate missiles that resemble pilotless airplanes. TERCOM uses the earth's surface as a reference system to keep a cruise missile on course. Inside a cruise missile is a computer that contains the details of the earth's topographic features (such as mountains and valleys) along the missile's intended path. TERCOM compares the actual terrain under the missile with the predicted information in the missile's computers. Any discrepancies are used to determine in-flight adjustments in the missile's path. A similar system, called MAGNETIC CONTOUR MATCHING (MAGCOM), uses the earth's magnetic field as its reference system.

TERRIER is a U.S. surface-to-air missile. See SURFACE-TO-AIR MISSILE for a complete description of the Terrier.

TEST BAN   see NUCLEAR WEAPONS TEST BAN

TESTING   see NUCLEAR TESTING

TEST RANGE is a location where missiles are flight tested. A test range is distinct from a test site, where nuclear devices are exploded.

TEST SITE   see NUCLEAR TEST SITE

THEATER NUCLEAR FORCE (TNF)   see THEATER NUCLEAR WEAPON

THEATER NUCLEAR WEAPON (TNW) is a nuclear weapon intended to be used in a broad geographical region, such as Europe or the Far East. It is designed to travel over relatively long distances, but is not especially intended to strike the homelands of the superpowers. Theater nuclear weapons are a sort of hybrid of STRATEGIC NUCLEAR WEAPONS (intended to strike the homelands of the superpowers) and TACTICAL NUCLEAR WEAPONS (designed for battlefield use). For this reason, they are somewhat difficult to classify and have been nicknamed "grey area weapons." Theater nuclear weapons can be launched from a variety of devices, including underground MISSILE SILOS, bombers, naval vessels, and trucklike vehicles.

THERMAL KILL is a theoretical method for destroying a target by using heat. Thermal kill would be used against space-based targets, such as SATELLITES or attacking missiles. Thermal kill would require a weapon that could shoot a concentrated beam of heat on the target's surface. The heat would raise the surface temperature of the target and damage its sensitive electronic equipment. Essentially, a thermal kill involves "cooking" the target.

THERMAL PULSE is the burst of intense heat and light released in a nuclear explosion. The thermal pulse is one of the most destructive effects of a nuclear explosion—it can cause burns, blindness, and massive fires over a very wide area. The thermal pulse is also known as the nuclear flash.

THERMAL RADIATION is the intense heat and light released in a nuclear explosion. Thermal radiation is one of the most destructive effects of a nuclear explosion—it can cause burns, blindness, and massive fires over a very wide area. The effects of thermal radiation depend on the size of the weapon and the distance from GROUND ZERO, the point where the weapon is detonated. Thermal radiation must be distinguished from ionizing radiation, which is more energetic and causes effects such as cancer, genetic damage, and RADIATION SICKNESS. See NUCLEAR RADIATION.

THERMAL SENSOR   see INFRARED SENSOR

THERMONUCLEAR WEAPON is the most destructive type of nuclear weapon. One medium-sized thermonuclear weapon is capable of completely destroying a city the size of New York. Thermonuclear weapons derive their tremendous destructive power primarily from the energy released in the forced combination (fusion) of small, light atoms. Essentially, a thermonuclear bomb is detonated in a two-step process. First, an atom-splitting (fission) reaction generates very high temperatures. Second, this heat triggers the combining of atoms (fusion). Fusion, which releases tremendous energy, is the process that takes place in the center of the sun. The fusion reaction then triggers an optional third step, the fission of the TAMPER, the uranium shell that surrounds the core of the weapon. This third step can double the destructive power of the weapon. A thermonuclear weapon that incorporates this third step is commonly called a FISSION-FUSION-FISSION WEAPON; one that does not incorporate the third step is known as a FISSION-FUSION WEAPON or a NEUTRON BOMB. Thermonuclear weapons are much more powerful than atomic weapons, which involve only the initial fission reaction. Thermonuclear weapons were developed by the United States and the Soviet Union in the early 1950s, and presently dominate the world's nuclear arsenals. The first thermonuclear weapon was known as the superbomb; later versions have been called the h-bomb and the hydrogen bomb.

THINKING ABOUT THE UNTHINKABLE is a popular phrase that describes actively considering the horrors of nuclear war. Coined by American analyst Herman Kahn in his 1961 book *Thinking About the Unthinkable,* the phrase urges everyone to open eyes to the possibility of nuclear war. In this way, Kahn argues, we will realize what is at stake and we will work hard to ensure that nuclear war never occurs. By the same token, Kahn asserts, we must be prepared to consider using nuclear weapons in order to prevail if nuclear war breaks out.

THIRD-GENERATION WEAPON   see GENERATION WEAPONS

THREAT AZIMUTH is a U.S. military term that describes an enemy rocket launch that could be a nuclear attack against the United States. U.S. Air Force officers in RADAR stations around the world routinely observe every rocket launch within the Soviet Union and China in order to determine whether it is a test, a civilian space shot, or a possible nuclear attack. If the rocket launch appears to be on a threatening course, then it is considered a threat azimuth. As a result of a threat azimuth, warning officers will transfer confirmation of a nuclear attack to authorities, who ultimately decide how the U.S. should respond.

THREAT CLOUD is an informal name for a swarm of attacking nuclear warheads and DECOYS. A single missile may release many warheads and decoys, in addition to shrapnel and other debris designed to confuse enemy tracking systems. One missile may thus create a "cloud" of warheads, decoys, and debris as it streaks toward its target. The threat cloud may include as many as 100,000 objects.

THREAT CORRIDOR is the route that nuclear missiles would follow as they streak toward their targets. The threat corridor can be thought of as the road leading from the place where nuclear weapons are deployed to the location of their targets. U.S. nuclear missiles launched from the Great Plains would follow a threat corridor over the North Pole to their targets in the Soviet Union.

THREE Rs OF WINNING A NUCLEAR WAR are reload, reconstitution, and refire. The three Rs represent the theory that if one side could store abundant backup (reload) missiles, reassemble its forces after absorbing a nuclear strike, and then fire its remaining missiles from LAUNCHERS that have been used already, it would have a tremendous advantage in a nuclear war.

THRESHOLD COUNTRIES are nations on the brink of developing nuclear weapons.

THRESHOLD DOSE is the minimum amount of IONIZING RADIATION necessary to cause serious damage to living cells. Ionizing radiation is the deadly radiation released in a nuclear explosion. Exposure to levels of ionizing radiation exceeding the threshold dose may cause RADIATION SICKNESS, genetic damage, cancer, or death.

THRESHOLD TEST BAN (TTB) refers to a cessation of nuclear testing above a certain limit. TTBs do not prohibit nuclear testing; they simply restrict the destructive power of the devices that may be exploded in tests. In this way, a TTB seeks to reduce the amount of environmental damage caused by nuclear testing. In 1974, the United States and the Soviet Union signed the THRESHOLD TEST BAN TREATY, which prohibits testing nuclear devices with yields greater than 150 kilotons.

THRESHOLD TEST BAN TREATY (TTBT) (1974) is a bilateral treaty that prohibits the U.S. and the Soviet Union from testing nuclear weapons that release a destructive force greater than 150 kilotons. The Threshold Test Ban Treaty was negotiated to reduce the amount of environmental damage caused by nuclear testing. The treaty is similar to the PEACEFUL NUCLEAR EXPLOSIONS TREATY of 1976. The principal difference between the two is that the Threshold Test Ban Treaty is concerned exclusively with nuclear weapons explosions. The Threshold Test Ban treaty has not been approved by the U.S. Senate, but both nations have agreed to abide by its terms

THROW-WEIGHT is the amount of weight (minus the weight of BOOSTER ROCKETS) that a BALLISTIC MISSILE carries as it streaks into space. Booster rockets lift a missile into space and direct it toward its target. Throw-weight includes the warhead and all the components that deliver the warhead to its target. A number of components that are not carried all the way to the target, such as fuel and DECOYS, are included in throw-weight. Throw-weight is one criterion for determining the strength of a nation's nuclear arsenal. In general, the Soviet Union deploys heavier, larger missiles than the U.S.; the U.S.S.R. thus maintains a considerable advantage over the U.S. in terms of throw-weight. The amount of total permissible throw-weight has been a point of contention between the U.S. and the U.S.S.R. during nuclear arms-control negotiations. Throw-weight is distinct from payload, which is the weight of the explosive material contained in a nuclear warhead.

TIME-SENSITIVE TARGET is any target that can move to avoid being struck in a nuclear attack. It specifically refers to weapons that can be launched or redeployed before enemy aircraft or missiles arrive. An example of a time-sensitive target is a mobile missile, which could be carried and launched on a trucklike vehicle. Time-sensitive targets are generally more vulnerable to high-speed BALLISTIC MISSILES than to relatively slow-flying CRUISE MISSILES and bombers. Time-sensitive targets are also known as time-urgent targets.

TIME-URGENT HARD-TARGET KILL POTENTIAL is the ability to quickly destroy targets that have been reinforced to resist a nuclear attack. Time-urgent hard-target kill potential requires two basic factors: time and destructive power. Specifically, the object is to strike enemy MISSILE SILOS before any weapons can be launched in retaliation. INTERCONTINENTAL BALLISTIC MISSILES possess time-urgent hard-target kill potential because they can destroy their targets in a matter of minutes with tremendous power and accuracy. Strategic bombers do not have time-urgent hard-target kill potential because they may take up to ten hours before arriving at their targets.

TIME-URGENT TARGET see TIME-SENSITIVE TARGETS

TITAN II is a U.S. intercontinental ballistic missile. See INTERCONTINENTAL BALLISTIC MISSILE for a complete description of the Titan II.

TNT EQUIVALENT see YIELD

TOMAHAWK CRUISE MISSILE is a U.S. CRUISE MISSILE deployed in Western Europe and on American submarines. Originally developed by the Navy as an antiship SEA-LAUNCHED CRUISE MISSILE (SLCM), the Tomahawk has been modified so that it can also be launched from the ground and air. The ground-launched Tomahawk (GLCM), known popularly as the Cruise, is one of the controversial EUROMISSILES deployed by NATO in Western Europe in the early 1980s. The Tomahawk, first deployed in 1983, has a range of 2,500 km and carries one warhead with a yield of 10 to 50 kilotons (GLCM) or 200 kilotons (SLCM). The Tomahawk is exceedingly accurate and is thus capable of striking well-defended military targets. See DUAL-TRACK DECISION.

TORNADO STRIKE AIRCRAFT is a British, West German, and Italian medium-range bomber. The British version of the Tornado is capable of carrying nuclear bombs. See MEDIUM-RANGE BOMBER for a complete description of the Tornado.

TRACKING is the process of monitoring an attacking nuclear warhead or bomber. Essentially, tracking reveals the path of an attacking object. Tracking a warhead or bomber has two important purposes. First, if a target can be tracked, it is easier to intercept and destroy. Second, tracking reveals what target the warhead is attacking. For example, if tracking reveals a warhead is approaching a missile site, the missiles could be launched before the warhead arrives. Tracking is carried out by both SATELLITES and ground-based RADARS.

TRANSPORTER-ERECTOR LAUNCHER (TEL) is a trucklike vehicle that carries a missile from storage, raises it to be fired, and serves as the platform from which the missile is launched. The advantage of deploying a missile on a TEL is increased ability to survive a nuclear attack. Missiles deployed on TELs are moving targets and are thus difficult to pinpoint and destroy. In general, TELs are used for tactical and theater missiles, intended for use over battlefield distances or within a specific geographic region, such as Europe or the Far East.

TRAVEL TIME see ARRIVAL TIME

TREATY is a formal agreement between two or more countries. A treaty is the instrument by which many arms-control agreements are formalized. In the United States, a treaty must be approved by the Senate. The U.S., however, may observe the terms of a treaty even if it is not ratified. SALT II, which limits the number of nuclear weapons the U.S. and the U.S.S.R. can deploy, was never ratified. Despite the Senate refusal to approve

SALT II, however, the U.S. agreed to abide by the terms of the treaty, until 1986, when President Ronald Reagan threatened to scrap it. A treaty must be distinguished from a PROTOCOL, which qualifies or supplements the terms of a treaty. If two countries sign a treaty, it is known as a bilateral treaty; if several countries are involved, it is referred to as a multilateral treaty.

TREATY OF TLATELOLCO (1967) bans nuclear weapons in an area spanning more than 7.5 million square miles of Latin America. The treaty, signed by all the Latin American states except Cuba, does not prohibit the development or use of nuclear energy for peaceful purposes. Two important PROTOCOLS accompany the treaty. The first obligates all four outside powers with possessions in the area to abide by the treaty's terms. The U.S. ratified the protocol in 1981 and thus has promised to abide by the treaty in the Panama Canal Zone, Guantanamo Bay naval base, Puerto Rico, and the U.S. Virgin Islands. The protocol was also signed by France, the Netherlands, and Great Britain. All the nuclear weapons states (China, the U.S.S.R., the U.S., Britain, and France) have agreed to the second protocol, which obliges them to respect the zone's status. The Treaty of Tlatelolco is also known as the Latin American Nuclear-Free Zone Treaty.

TRIAD is a U.S. military force structure that relies on three specific types of nuclear weapons. Since the early 1960s, the United States has developed a nuclear arsenal based on separate components on the ground, in the air, and in the water. Defense planners agree that all three legs of the U.S. triad are equally crucial, because each leg has weaknesses that are offset by the strengths of the other two. Land-based missiles, for example, are the most powerful and accurate nuclear weapons in the U.S. arsenal, but they are vulnerable to enemy attack in their fixed underground silos. Submarine-launched missiles, on the other hand, are difficult to detect. However, they are less accurate than ground- or air-launched missiles. And although long-range bombers are the slowest part of the triad, they can be recalled up to the moment they release their nuclear weapons and are thus the most flexible part of the triad.

TRIDENT MISSILE is a series of U.S. submarine-launched ballistic missiles (SLBMs). See SUBMARINE-LAUNCHED BALLISTIC MISSILE for a complete description of the Trident I and Trident II SLBMs.

TRIDENT SUBMARINE (*Ohio* class) is a class of U.S. ballistic missile submarines. See BALLISTIC MISSILE SUBMARINE for a complete description of the Trident.

TRINITY SITE is the exact spot in the desert near Alamogordo, New Mexico, where the U.S. exploded the world's first atomic weapon on July 16, 1945. The Trinity Test was conducted to test the design of the bomb that would be dropped on NAGASAKI, Japan, less than one month later.

TRINITY TEST was the world's first atomic explosion. The Trinity Test was conducted to test the design of the bomb that would be dropped on the Japanese city of NAGASAKI less than one month later. The device exploded in the Trinity Test was one of three bombs produced by the MANHATTAN PROJECT, the U.S.'s World War II program to build the first atomic weapons. The other two, named LITTLE BOY and FAT MAN, were dropped on HIROSHIMA and NAGASAKI. The Trinity Test was conducted near Alamogordo, New Mexico, on July 16, 1945.

TRIP WIRE is the concept of backing up a small, symbolic force with a much larger reserve. A trip wire is thus a sort of hypersensitive trigger. The slightest action against it would set off massive resistance. The U.S. troops deployed on the German frontier have been described by some experts as a trip wire. They are not, by themselves, capable of defending against a massive Soviet invasion. If they were attacked, however, the U.S. and its nuclear arsenal would enter the conflict. A trip wire can thus deter enemy attack.

TRITIUM is a type of hydrogen that contains two extra neutrons. Tritium is used to fuel THERMONUCLEAR WEAPONS. In these weapons, tritium is commonly fused with DEUTERIUM, another variety of hydrogen. This process releases tremendous amounts of energy. Tritium does not occur in nature (it is created in nuclear reactors) and is highly RADIOACTIVE.

TU-BOMBER designates Soviet Tupolev bombers. The Tu-16 Badger and Tu-22 Blinder are medium-range bombers. (See MEDIUM-RANGE BOMBER for a complete description of these bombers.) The Tu-22m/26 Backfire is an intermediate-range bomber. (See INTERMEDIATE-RANGE BOMBER for a complete description of the Backfire.) The Tu-95 Bear is a long-range bomber. (See LONG-RANGE BOMBER for a complete description of the Bear).

TWO-MAN RULE is a security procedure that requires at least two authorized personnel to be present whenever people come in contact with nuclear weapons or the codes for launching them. In accordance with the two-man rule, two officers in underground MISSILE SILOS must act together to fire a missile. Codes that authorize the launching of nuclear missiles are stored in a double-locked safe called the RED BOX. Each crew officer has a key to the Red Box. In an authorized launch of nuclear missiles, each officer would insert a key simultaneously into widely separated keyholes—the distance between them prevents either officer from turning the key alone. Keys must be turned at the same time and left in place for at least five seconds. In this way, it is impossible for one crew member to launch nuclear weapons individually.

TYPES I, II, AND III DETERRENCE were introduced by American defense analyst Herman Kahn:

- Type I deterrence is the strategy of preventing a massive nuclear attack on the United States by threatening the enemy with an unacceptably destructive retaliation. Type I deterrence is sometimes referred to as PASSIVE DETERRENCE, because it requires that the United States act in response to enemy aggression and avoid engaging in any provocations.
- Type II deterrence is the strategy of restraining an enemy from provocative actions that fall short of a large-scale attack on the United States. It relies on the threat of a massive nuclear attack to deter such an enemy strike. Under Type II deterrence, a nation may want to prevent enemy aggression against allies or military bases abroad. Type II deterrence is sometimes referred to as ACTIVE DETERRENCE, because it requires that the United States initiate a nuclear attack in order to restrain enemy aggression against the United States or its allies. Type II deterrence is also called extended deterrence.
- Type III deterrence embodies all the ways, except threatening all-out nuclear war, to deter provocations and encourage acceptable enemy behavior. Type III deterrence is sometimes referred to as tit-for-tat deterrence, because it involves the United States matching an enemy's action with a similar action. For example, the U.S. would launch very small nuclear weapons in response to a limited enemy attack. Type III deterrence is distinct from Type I and II deterrence, which require a massive nuclear attack in response to enemy provocation.

TYPHOON SUBMARINE is a class of Soviet ballistic missile submarines. See BALLISTIC MISSILE SUBMARINE for a complete description of the Typhoon.

U

U-235 see URANIUM

U-238 see URANIUM

UNACCEPTABLE DAMAGE is any amount of destruction deemed intolerable. The concept of unacceptable damage is a key factor restraining the superpowers from fighting a nuclear war. With limited means for defending against a nuclear strike, both superpowers rely on their ability to inflict unacceptable damage on each other. In this way, they attempt to deter one another from launching a nuclear attack. Thus, nuclear deterrence between the superpowers is based on each side's capacity to absorb a nuclear strike and then counter with an unacceptable destructive retaliation.

UNCONTROLLED CHAIN REACTION see NUCLEAR CHAIN REACTION

UNDERGROUND NUCLEAR TEST is any nuclear test conducted below the ground. In 1963, the U.S. and the U.S.S.R. signed the LIMITED TEST BAN TREATY, which prohibits aboveground nuclear testing. Since that time, most nuclear tests have been carried out underground. They must be conducted in suitable environments, i.e., where the geologic structure is exceedingly stable. Underground nuclear tests release some radioactive material into the atmosphere, and are not covered by the Limited Test Ban Treaty.

UNDERWATER NUCLEAR TEST is any nuclear test conducted underwater. In 1963, the U.S. and the U.S.S.R. signed the LIMITED TEST BAN TREATY, which prohibits underwater nuclear testing. Only five underwater nuclear tests have ever been conducted, all between 1946 and 1962.

UNILATERAL ARMS-CONTROL MEASURE is any action taken independently by one nation to limit or reduce its nuclear arsenal. A unilateral arms-control measure requires no action by any other nation. Some theorists claim that it is the only way to overcome a deadlock in arms control. They argue that if one nation showed the courage to adopt a unilateral arms-control measure, it would inspire trust and confidence, leading other nations to follow suit. Critics, however, claim that unilateral arms-control measures would leave a nation vulnerable to attack. The fear of this vulnerability would, critics argue, always discourage a nation from such an action. The Soviet Union's announcement of a moratorium on nuclear testing in the late 1950s is an example of a unilateral arms-control measure.

UNILATERAL DISARMAMENT is any action taken independently by one nation to reduce its nuclear arsenal. Unilateral disarmament requires no action by any other nation. Some theorists claim that it is the only way to overcome a deadlock in arms control. They argue that if one nation showed the courage to unilaterally disarm, it would inspire trust and confidence, leading other nations to follow suit. Critics, however, claim that unilateral disarmament would leave a nation vulnerable to attack. The fear of this vulnerability would, critics argue, always discourage a nation from such an action. No nation possessing nuclear weapons has ever unilaterally disarmed.

UNILATERAL STATEMENTS are proclamations of policy issued by one country acting independently. A unilateral statement can be used to qualify a previously signed nuclear arms-control agreement. A unilateral statement is not binding for other nations; it simply establishes one side's policy.

UNION OF CONCERNED SCIENTISTS (UCS) is an independent federation of scientists and citizens who are concerned about the impact of advancing technology on the arms race. Founded in Cambridge, Massachusetts, in 1969, UCS favors arms control and is one of the leading opponents of U.S. President Ronald Reagan's STRATEGIC DEFENSE INITIATIVE (SDI), commonly known as "Star Wars." SDI is a research program to develop a defensive system for defending against attacking a nuclear warheads. UCS is nonpartisan and maintains a sponsorship of 100,000 members nationwide.

UNITED NATIONS ATOMIC ENERGY COMMISSION was the first United Nations forum for discussing disarmament issues. Founded in 1946, the U.N. Atomic Energy Commission was established in part to implement the ill-fated BARUCH PLAN, which called for placing nuclear weapons under a system of international control. The U.N. Atomic Energy Commission merged with the U.N. Commission on Conventional Armaments in 1952 to become the DISARMAMENT COMMISSION, the current U.N. disarmament forum.

UNITED NATIONS DEPARTMENT OF DISARMAMENT AFFAIRS is the central branch of the United Nations that addresses the issue of disarmament. Since 1976, it has published its annual *Disarmament Yearbook,* which outlines the work of the United Nations in the field of disarmament. The U.N. Department of Disarmament Affairs is responsible for staging the World Disarmament Campaign, which is a U.N. program to generate public understanding and support of U.N. goals in the area of disarmament. Its headquarters is in the United Nations in New York.

UNITED NATIONS DISARMAMENT COMMISSION (UNDC) see DISARMAMENT COMMISSION

UNITED NATIONS SPECIAL SESSION ON DISARMAMENT
(SSD) I   see GENERAL AND COMPLETE DISARMAMENT

UNITED NATIONS SPECIAL SESSION ON DISARMAMENT
(SSD) II   see NO FIRST USE

UNITED STATES ARMS CONTROL AND DISARMAMENT
AGENCY (ACDA) is the U.S. government agency that deals
specifically with the issue of arms control. Founded in 1961 by
President John Kennedy and nicknamed "the Peace Agency,"
ACDA serves three primary purposes. First, it must be prepared
to negotiate arms-control agreements. Second, ACDA is responsible for carrying out research on arms control and disarmament issues. Finally, it has a duty to educate the American
public on arms control. Staffed by physicists and foreign policy
and arms-control experts, ACDA is part of the executive branch
of government under the direction of the President. The director of ACDA is by law the President's principal advisor on arms
control, but in practice, ACDA's director has not always served
as the President's chief advisor on arms control. ACDA does
not have the freedom to advocate policies independent of those
of the President, but it may enjoy the opportunity to influence
policy within an administration. In 1975, Congress enacted
legislation that required ACDA to prepare "arms-control impact statements," which examine the pros and cons of proposed
U.S. weapons programs.

UNITED STATES SPACE COMMAND is the military organization
that oversees all U.S. programs involving military uses of space.
The U.S. Space Command would have control over the high-
technology, space-based system for protecting against attacking
nuclear missiles that the United States is seeking to develop.
Research for these weapons is being conducted under the STRA-
TEGIC DEFENSE INITIATIVE, commonly known as "Stars Wars."
The agency's current responsibilities include intelligence gath-

ering and monitoring for enemy nuclear attacks. The U.S. Space Command was established on September 23, 1985, and is headquartered in Colorado Springs, Colorado.

UNIT OF ACCOUNT is the basic unit used to count nuclear weapons in an arms-control agreement. In order for two nations to decide on a unit of account, they usually take into consideration factors with which they can compare each other's forces. For example, in SALT, LAUNCHERS served as units of account. Limitations placed on nuclear arms were based on the specific number of launchers that each side could deploy. Launchers were chosen as the unit of account in SALT primarily because they were easier to verify than other units. Negotiators often disagree when determining the proper unit of account. Some experts claim that launchers are not a precise unit of account, because the superpowers today can put many warheads on each missile that is deployed on a launcher.

UNK-UNKS, short for "unknown unknowns," are effects that seem likely to occur but are impossible to predict accurately. The ELECTROMAGNETIC PULSE (EMP), a powerful burst of radiation released after a nuclear explosion, is an unk-unk. The exact implications of an EMP are unsure but some experts have theorized that the EMP released by one large nuclear explosion over the central United States would cause an electrical blackout of the entire country.

UNWARNED EXPOSED refers to friendly troops who are accidentally exposed to the effects of a nuclear weapon. Military authorities have debated whether small, battlefield nuclear weapons could be used without posing a threat to friendly troops. Since such weapons have never been used in actual combat, it is difficult to predict their effects. In the 1950s, the United States conducted several nuclear tests of extremely powerful nuclear weapons while troops intentionally maneuvered nearby. These tests were conducted to determine the effects of the blast. The cancer rate of these soldiers is 400 times higher than the national average.

URANIUM is a radioactive element that is the basic raw material for nuclear reactions. Uranium is a heavy, unstable element which can easily be split. As it is split, tremendous energy is released. Uranium exists naturally in two varieties, or isotopes: uranium-238 (U-238) and uranium-235 (U-235). Almost all naturally occurring uranium is U-238, which cannot sustain a nuclear reaction. The percentage of U-235 (in nature about .07%) must therefore be increased in order to make enough suitable nuclear fuel. This process is known as ENRICHMENT. Uranium is RADIOACTIVE—exposure to concentrated quantities of it is very dangerous. Uranium reserves exist in many countries; however, strict controls have been placed on the transfer of uranium in order to prevent nuclear proliferation.

USE 'EM OR LOSE 'EM   see LAUNCH-ON-WARNING, PREEMPTIVE ATTACK

V

VERIFICATION is the process of ensuring that an arms-control agreement is not being violated. Verification is a complex and detailed process. Two different means of verification are commonly discussed: NATIONAL TECHNICAL MEANS OF VERIFICATION and COOPERATIVE MEANS OF VERIFICATION. National technical means relies upon technical devices, such as SATELLITES and RADAR, to gather information about another nation's nuclear weapons installations. It does not depend on active cooperation between nations. Cooperative means of verification, however, depends on very close collaboration between nations. On-site inspections are an example of cooperative means of verification. An effective means of verification has been stressed, particularly by the United States, as a precondition to any nuclear arms-control agreement.

VERIFICATION BY CHALLENGE   see CHALLENGE INSPECTION

VERTICAL PROLIFERATION is the expansion of existing nuclear arsenals. Vertical proliferation is distinct from HORIZONTAL PROLIFERATION, which refers to the spread of nuclear weapons to nations that do not currently possess them.

VLADIVOSTOK ACCORD (1974) addressed nuclear arms-control issues not covered in SALT I. It amplified SALT I by setting new limits on the number of nuclear weapons the U.S. and the U.S.S.R. could deploy. Unlike SALT I, however, the Vladivostok Accord established numerically equal limits on the number of nuclear weapons deployed by each side. This represented a significant change in the approach the superpowers took to arms control. The U.S. no longer agreed to let the Soviet Union deploy larger numbers of nuclear weapons as compensation for

U.S. technological superiority. The Vladivostok Accord also limited for the first time nuclear weapons equipped with more than one warhead. The Vladivostok Accord was signed by U.S. President Gerald Ford and Soviet General Secretary Leonid Brezhnev at the Soviet port of Vladivostok and laid the framework for SALT II.

VLADIVOSTOK AIDE-MEMOIRE (1974) is an addition to the 1974 VLADIVOSTOK ACCORD between the U.S. and the U.S.S.R. The Vladivostok Aide-Memoire covers two issues not addressed in the original accord. The aide-memoire allows the Soviets to continue deploying their heavy missiles without U.S. interference. Heavy missiles, such as the Soviet SS-18, are physically larger and more powerful than other missiles. At the time, the Soviets relied on heavy missiles much more than the U.S. did. In return for this concession, the U.S. was allowed to maintain its nuclear missile force in Western Europe without Soviet contention.

W

WALK IN THE WOODS was a much-publicized tentative agreement reached between two negotiators during the INTERMEDIATE-RANGE NUCLEAR FORCE (INF) TALKS in Geneva, Switzerland. On July 16, 1982, Paul Nitze, head of the United States delegation to the INF Talks, and his counterpart, chief Soviet delegate Yuli Kvitinsky, agreed informally on a major arms-control proposal during a walk in the woods in the Jura Mountains of Switzerland. During the walk, Nitze and Kvitinsky agreed to a proposal in which the U.S.S.R. would reduce by two-thirds its SS-20 missiles in Europe in exchange for the cancellation of the planned U.S. deployment in Western Europe of Pershing II missiles and limited deployment of TOMAHAWK CRUISE MISSILES. When the proposal was separately presented by both negotiators to their governments, it was rejected. As a result of the lack of an agreement at the INF Talks, the United States began deploying Pershing and Tomahawk missiles in Europe in December 1983 and the U.S.S.R. broke off the INF negotiations. This deployment marked the first time that U.S. nuclear missiles had been stationed in Europe since the removal of Mace missiles there in 1969.

WAR GAME is a test of a nation's ability to fight an actual war. War games are practice for a real war and simulate them in a number of ways. Some war games are conducted entirely by computer. Military commanders enter their moves into the computer and in turn react to the computer's moves. Other war games involve mock battles with actual maneuvers of troops and the use of weapons. The purpose of war games varies greatly. Some test the capability of a nation to launch an attack, while others test the nation's ability to defend itself from attack. War games can be used to test strategy or weapons. War games can simulate conventional or nuclear war.

WAR GAMES is a 1984 film that examines the possibility of a nuclear war being started accidentally. In *War Games,* a teenage computer buff accidentally connects with the computer of the NORTH AMERICAN AEROSPACE DEFENSE COMMAND (NORAD). Believing he is hooked up to a computer firm's game rather than the War Operations Plan Response (WOPR, pronounced "Whopper") computer, the teenager plays a game called "Global Thermonuclear War." WOPR mistakes the game for a real nuclear war and proceeds to arrange for launching a nuclear attack against the Soviet Union. With the aid of the computer's disillusioned creator, the teen programs WOPR to play tic-tac-toe simultaneously with Global Thermonuclear War. The computer, unable to win at tic-tac-toe, decides that nuclear war is also unwinnable and cancels the plans for launching a nuclear attack. The U.S. government was particularly concerned about errors in the film's portrayal of NORAD.

WARGASM is a slang term that describes an all-out nuclear war. The term was coined by American analyst Herman Kahn in the 1950s.

WARHEAD   see NUCLEAR WARHEAD

WARHEAD LETHALITY   see LETHALITY

WARHEAD SPONGE is an informal term for a location that is very likely to be targeted in a nuclear war. The term is derived from the fact that such a target would be bombarded with and suck up incoming warheads like a sponge.

WARNING SHOT   see NUCLEAR WARNING SHOT

WARNING SYSTEM   see EARLY WARNING

WARSAW PACT   see WARSAW TREATY ORGANIZATION

WARSAW TREATY ORGANIZATION (WTO) is a military alliance established in 1955 to provide for the collective security of its members. The WTO, commonly known as the Warsaw Pact, is made up of the Soviet Union and most of the socialist nations in Eastern Europe. It was formed as a counterweight to NATO, Western Europe's military alliance, which includes the United States. The Warsaw Pact is a comprehensive military alliance that stresses joint military action in the event of a NATO attack against Eastern Europe. The Warsaw Pact's military arsenal includes both conventional and nuclear weapons. While the U.S. shares responsibility for NATO's nuclear arsenal with the other alliance members, the Soviet Union keeps a tight control over the Warsaw Pact's nuclear arsenal. The Warsaw Pact's nuclear weapons are deployed in the Soviet Union, East Germany, and Czechoslovakia. The members of the Warsaw Pact include Bulgaria, Czechoslovakia, East Germany, Hungary, Poland, Romania, and the Soviet Union.

WEAPON OF MASS DESTRUCTION is any weapon that can kill human beings and destroy property on a massive scale. While there is no precise definition for such weapons, most nuclear weapons except the very smallest are considered weapons of mass destruction. Some chemical and biological weapons are also considered weapons of mass destruction.

WEAPONS-GRADE MATERIAL see WEAPONS-GRADE NUCLEAR FUEL, FISSIONABLE MATERIAL

WEAPONS-GRADE NUCLEAR FUEL is URANIUM that has been refined so that it can fuel nuclear weapons. Uranium exists in nature in two varieties: uranium-238 (U-238) and uranium-235 (U-235). Almost all naturally occurring uranium is U-238, which cannot sustain a nuclear reaction. The percentage of U-235 (which can fuel a nuclear reaction) must therefore be increased. This process is known as ENRICHMENT. Enrichment, a complex and expensive process, yields enriched nuclear fuel.

Uranium enriched to about 90% U-235 is considered weapons-grade nuclear fuel.

WEAPONS MIX is a slang term used to describe all the different weapons making up a country's nuclear arsenal. It refers especially to the different methods of deploying nuclear weapons. The weapons mix of the U.S. and the U.S.S.R. includes nuclear weapons deployed on the ground, on airplanes, and on submarines.

WIMEX   see WORLDWIDE MILITARY COMMAND AND CONTROL SYSTEM

WINDOW OF VULNERABILITY is a perceived weakness in one superpower's nuclear arsenal. The window of vulnerability was first conceived in the 1970s to describe the Soviet Union's apparent superiority over the U.S. in its force of land-based nuclear missiles. Theorists asserted that this advantage would enable the U.S.S.R. to launch a devastating nuclear attack that would overwhelm U.S. land-based missiles. In this way, the Soviet Union would be able to destroy U.S. missiles before they could be launched in retaliation and thus would be able to defeat the U.S. The window of vulnerability is a very destabilizing concept, which might increase the chance that either superpower would start a nuclear war. In the 1980 U.S. presidential election, candidate Ronald Reagan campaigned on the need to close the window of vulnerability. After his election, he proposed deploying the MX MISSILE for this purpose.

WORLD DISARMAMENT CAMPAIGN   see UNITED NATIONS DEPARTMENT OF DISARMAMENT AFFAIRS

WORLDWIDE MILITARY COMMAND AND CONTROL SYSTEM (WWMCCS) is the main communications network for conveying orders to United States conventional and nuclear military forces. In particular, WWMCCS would be used to order the launch of U.S. nuclear weapons deployed throughout the world. WWMCCS is complex and made up of many components including computers, warning sensors, command centers, and communications facilities. It is used by the NATIONAL COMMAND AUTHORITIES (the President and Secretary of Defense), the chairman of the Joint Chiefs of Staff, the STRATEGIC AIR COMMAND, and regional military commanders. Nicknamed WIMEX after the pronunciation of its initials, WWMCCS was established in 1962.

WORLDWIDE RADIOACTIVE FALLOUT   see GLOBAL RADIOACTIVE FALLOUT

WORST-CASE SCENARIO   see SCENARIO

X

XIA SUBMARINE is a class of Chinese ballistic missile submarines. See BALLISTIC MISSILE SUBMARINE for a complete description of the Xia.

X-RAY LASER WEAPON is a hypothetical weapon that would be part of a high-technology system for protecting against attacking nuclear missiles. X-ray laser weapons would, by means of a small nuclear explosion, generate a concentrated, high-speed stream of light. Because they are "pumped," or driven by a nuclear explosion, X-ray laser weapons would generate an extremely powerful laser beam. This light beam could burn a hole in the skin of an attacking missile and deactivate the sensitive electronic equipment responsible for guiding it to its target. X-ray laser weapons could be deployed in two ways, both of which are very controversial. First, they could be based in space. This arrangement, however, would involve keeping nuclear bombs hovering in space over the U.S.S.R. They could also be launched from the ground. If they were deployed on the ground, however, they would have to be fired from submarines stationed very close to enemy shores. Critics contend that these submarines would be extremely vulnerable because of their proximity to enemy territory. X-ray laser weapons are nicknamed "excalibur," after the legendary sword that King Arthur pulled from a stone. The United States is conducting research on X-ray laser weapons under the STRATEGIC DEFENSE INITIATIVE, commonly known as "Star Wars."

Y

YANKEE SUBMARINE is a class of Soviet ballistic missile submarines. See BALLISTIC MISSILE SUBMARINE for a complete description of the Yankee.

YIELD refers to the amount of energy released in a nuclear explosion. Yield is one measure of a nuclear weapon's strength. Yield is measured in KILOTONS and MEGATONS; 1 megaton equals 1,000 kilotons. The explosive energy released in a 1-megaton explosion is equivalent to that released when 1,000,000 tons of TNT are detonated. Yield is also called TNT equivalent.

Z

ZERO OPTION was a much-publicized nuclear arms-control proposal presented to the U.S.S.R. by the U.S. at the INTERMEDIATE-RANGE NUCLEAR FORCE (INF) TALKS in 1981. The zero option called for the elimination of all intermediate-range nuclear weapons deployed by the superpowers in Europe. The plan would have involved the removal of existing Soviet SS-4, SS-5, and SS-20 missiles in exchange for a U.S. pledge not to go ahead with planned deployment of Pershing II and TOMAHAWK CRUISE MISSILES in Western Europe. Announced by President Ronald Reagan prior to the opening of the first round of INF negotiations, the zero option was rejected by the Soviet Union. As a result of the Soviet rejection of the zero option, the U.S. went ahead with the deployment of its missiles in December 1983. The deployment marked the first time that intermediate-range U.S. missiles had been stationed in Europe since the removal of Mace missiles in 1969. The idea of a zero option was first conceived by West German Chancellor Helmut Schmidt. The zero option is also known as the zero-zero option or the zero solution.

ZERO SOLUTION   see ZERO OPTION

ZERO-ZERO OPTION   see ZERO OPTION

Abbreviations and Acronyms

AAM	air-to-air missile
ABCC	Atomic Bomb Casualty Commission
ABM	antiballistic missile
ACD	arms control through defense
ACDA	Arms Control and Disarmament Agency
ACIS	arms-control impact statement
ACMT	advanced cruise missile technology
ADM	atomic demolition munition
AEC	Atomic Energy Commission
AEDS	Atomic Energy Detection System
AFAP	artillery-fired atomic projectile
AFSATCOM	Air Force Satellite Communications System
AGM	air-to-ground missile
AIRS	advanced inertial reference sphere
ALBM	air-launched ballistic missile
ALCM	air-launched cruise missile
ALCS	airborne launch control system
ALPS	Alternate Launch Point System
ANMCC	Alternate National Military Command Center
ASAT	antisatellite weapon
ANZUS	Australia, New Zealand, United States
ASM	air-to-surface missile
ASROC	antisubmarine rocket
ASW	antisubmarine warfare
ATB	advanced technology bomber
AWACS	Airborne Warning and Control System
BMD	ballistic missile defense
BMEWS	Ballistic Missile Early Warning System
C^3	command, control, and communications
C^3I	command, control, communications, and intelligence
CBM	confidence building measure
CCD	Conference of the Committee on Disarmament
CD	Committee on Disarmament
CD	Conference on Disarmament
CDI	Center for Defense Information

CDS	command disable system
CEP	circular error probable
CLW	chemical laser weapon
CLW	Council for a Livable World
CMC	cruise missile carrier
CMP	countermilitary potential
CND	Campaign for Nuclear Disarmament
CNI	Committee for Nuclear Information
CPD	Committee on the Present Danger
CSB	closely spaced basing
CSBM	confidence and security building measure
CTB	comprehensive test ban
DC	Disarmament Commission
DEFCON	Defense Readiness Condition
DEW	directed energy weapon
DEW	Distant Early Warning
DNA	Defense Nuclear Agency
DSP	defense support program
DUMB	deep underground missile basing
EAM	Emergency Action Message
ECCM	electronic counter-countermeasure
ECM	electronic countermeasure
EMP	electromagnetic pulse
EMT	equivalent megatonnage
ENDC	Eighteen-Nation Committee on Disarmament
EP	earth penetrator
ERCS	emergency rocket communication system
ERW	enhanced radiation weapon
FAS	Federation of American Scientists
FAS	Force Aérienne Stratégique
FAT	Force Aérienne Tactique
FBS	forward-based systems
FEL	free electron laser
FEMA	Federal Emergency Management Administration
FOBS	Fractional Orbital Bombardment System
FROD	functionally related observable difference
GBMD	global ballistic missile defense
GCD	general and complete disarmament
GEODSS	Ground-based Electro-Optical Deep Space Surveillance
GLCM	ground-launched cruise missile

GPS	global positioning system
GWEN	Ground Wave Emergency Network
IAEA	International Atomic Energy Agency
ICBM	intercontinental ballistic missile
IDO	International Disarmament Organization
IISS	International Institute for Strategic Studies
IKV	Interchurch Peace Council
INF	intermediate-range nuclear forces
IONDS	Integrated Operational Nuclear Detection System
IPPNW	International Physicians for the Prevention of Nuclear War
IRBM	intermediate-range ballistic missile
JEEP	Joint Emergency Evacuation Plan
JSS	Joint Surveillance System
JSTPS	Joint Strategic Target Planning Staff
KEW	kinetic energy weapon
KKV	kinetic kill vehicle
kt	kiloton
LANL	Los Alamos National Laboratory
LCC	launch control center
LLNL	Lawrence Livermore National Laboratory
LNO	limited nuclear option
LNW	limited nuclear war
LOADS	Low-Altitude Defense System
LOI	launch-on-impact
LOW	launch-on-warning
LRTNF	longer-range theater nuclear forces
LTA	launch-through-attack
LTB	limited test ban
LTBT	Limited Test Ban Treaty
LUA	launch-under-attack
MAD	mutual assured destruction
MADM	medium atomic demolition munition
MAGCOM	Magnetic Contour Matching
MAPS	Multiple Aim Point System
MARV	maneuverable reentry vehicle
MEECN	Minimum Essential Emergency Communications Network
MHV	miniature homing vehicle
MIRV	multiple independently targetable reentry vehicle
MLBM	modern large ballistic missile

MPS	multiple protective shelter
MRBM	medium-range ballistic missile
mrem	millirem
MRV	multiple reentry vehicle
MSBS	mer-sol ballistique stratégique
mt	megaton
MX	Missile Experimental
NAC	nuclear arms control
NATO	North Atlantic Treaty Organization
NCO	Nuclear Control Order
NDDS	Nuclear Detonation Detection System
NFZ	nuclear-free zone
NOP	Nuclear Operations Plan
NORAD	North American Aerospace Defense Command
NPG	Nuclear Planning Group
NTM	national technical means of verification
NUDETS	Nuclear Detection System
NUT	Nuclear Utilization Theory
NUWEP	Nuclear Weapons Employment Plan
OBS	Orbital Bombardment System
OD	observable difference
OPANAL	Agency for the Prohibition of Nuclear Arms in Latin America
OSI	on-site inspection
OTH	over-the-horizon radar
PACCS	Post-Attack Command and Control System
PAL	Permissive Action Link
PARCS	Perimeter Acquisition Radar Attack Characterization System
PAS	Primary Alerting System
PBV	post-boost vehicle
Pen-Aid	penetration aid
PGM	precision guided munition
PNE	peaceful nuclear explosion
PNET	Peaceful Nuclear Explosion Treaty
PRP	Personnel Reliability Program
psi	pounds per square inch
PSR	Physicians for Social Responsibility
PTB	partial test ban
PTBT	Partial Test Ban Treaty
Pu	plutonium

QRA	Quick Reaction Alert
rad	radiation absorbed dose
rem	roentgen equivalent man
RERF	Radiation Effects Research Foundation
RISOP	Russian Integrated Single Operational Plan
RV	reentry vehicle
SAC	Strategic Air Command
SADM	special atomic demolition munition
SALT	Strategic Arms Limitation Talks
SALT I	Strategic Arms Limitation Treaty I
SALT II	Strategic Arms Limitation Treaty II
SAM	surface-to-air missile
SATKA	surveillance, acquisition, tracking, kill assessment
SCC	Standing Consultative Commission
SDI	Strategic Defense Initiative
SDIO	Strategic Defense Initiative Organization
SEWS	Satellite Early-Warning System
SICBM	small intercontinental ballistic missile
SIOP	Single Integrated Operational Plan
SIPRI	Stockholm International Peace Research Institute
SLBM	submarine-launched ballistic missile
SLCM	sea-launched cruise missile
SLFCS	Survivable Low-Frequency Communications System
SOSUS	Sound Surveillance System
SRAM	short-range attack missile
SRBM	short-range ballistic missile
SSB	ballistic missile submarine
SSBN	nuclear-powered ballistic missile submarine
SSBS	sol-sol ballistique stratégique
SSD	United Nations Special Session on Disarmament
SSG	cruise missile submarine
SSGN	nuclear-powered cruise missile submarine
START	Strategic Arms Reduction Talks
SUBROC	submarine rocket
TACAMO	take charge and move out
TEL	transporter-erector launcher
TERCOM	Terrain Contour Matching
TNF	theater nuclear forces
TNW	theater nuclear weapons
TTB	threshold test ban
U	uranium

UCS	Union of Concerned Scientists
UNDC	United Nations Disarmament Commission
WIMEX	Worldwide Military Command and Control System
WTO	Warsaw Treaty Organization
WWMCCS	Worldwide Military Command and Control System

Bibliography

Aldridge, Robert C. *First Strike: The Pentagon's Strategy for Nuclear War.* Boston: South End Press, 1983.

Allison, Graham T., Albert Carnesdale, and Joseph S. Nye, Jr. *Hawks, Doves and Owls.* New York and London: W.W. Norton and Company, 1985.

Arkin, William M., and Richard W. Fieldhouse. *Nuclear Battlefields: Global Links in the Arms Race.* Cambridge: Ballinger Publishing Company, 1985.

Bechhoefer, Bernhard G. *Postwar Negotiations for Arms Control.* Washington, D.C.: The Brookings Institution, 1961.

Beckett, Brian. *Weapons of Tomorrow.* New York and London: Plenum Press, 1983.

Beres, Louis René. *Mimicking Sisyphus: America's Countervailing Nuclear Strategy.* Lexington: Lexington Books, 1983.

Bethe, Hans A., et al. "Space-Based Ballistic Missile Defense." *Scientific American* 251:4, Oct. 1984.

Biddle, Wayne. "New Trident Missile Bears a Payload of Apprehension." *New York Times,* 9 Sept. 1984.

Blackett, P.M.S. *Fear, War, and the Bomb.* New York: Whittsley House, 1948.

Boffey, Philip M. "Dark Side of 'Star Wars': System Could Also Attack." *New York Times,* 5 Mar. 1985.

———. " 'Star Wars' and Mankind: Consequences for Future." *New York Times,* 8 Mar. 1985.

Boutwell, Jeffrey, and Richard A. Scribner. *The Strategic Defense Initiative: Some Arms Control Implications.* Washington, D.C.: The American Association for the Advancement of Science, 1985.

Boyer, P. "Physicians Confront the Apocalypse." *Journal of the American Medical Association* 254(5), 2 Aug. 1985.

Bracken, Paul. *The Command and Control of Nuclear Forces.* New Haven: Yale University Press, 1983.

Bradley, David. *No Place To Hide, 1946/1984.* 2nd ed. Hanover: University Press of New England, 1983.

Broad, William J. "Reagan's 'Star Wars' Bid: Many Ideas Converging." *New York Times,* 4 Mar. 1985.

————. *Star Warriors.* New York: Simon and Schuster, 1985.

Browne, Malcolm W. "High Over New Mexico's Desert, A Giant Nonnuclear Cloud." *New York Times,* 24 Sept. 1985.

Bureau of Public Affairs. "SALT II: Senate Testimony." Washington, D.C.: U.S. Department of State, 1979.

————. "SALT II Agreement." Washington, D.C.: U.S. Department of State, 1979.

Caldicott, Helen. *Missile Envy: The Arms Race and Nuclear War.* New York: William Morrow and Company, 1984.

Carter, Ashton B., and David N. Schwartz. *Ballistic Missile Defense.* Washington, D.C.: The Brookings Institution, 1984.

Cassel, C.K., Jameton, et al. "The Physician's Oath and the Prevention of Nuclear War." *Journal of the American Medical Association* 254(5), 2 Aug. 1985.

Chant, C., and Ian Mogg. *Nuclear War in the 1980s?* New York: Harper & Row, 1983.

Church, George B. "The Superpowers Get Set for a Star Wars Showdown." *Time,* 11 Mar. 1985.

Cochran, Thomas B., et al. *Nuclear Weapons Databook.* Vol. 1. Cambridge: Ballinger Publishing Co., 1984.

Cockburn, Andrew. *The Threat: Inside the Soviet Military Machine.* New York: Vintage Books, 1984.

Committee on Banking, Housing, and Urban Affairs, United States Senate. "Economic and Social Consequences of Nuclear Attacks on the United States." Washington, D.C.: Congressional Research Service, Library of Congress, 1981.

Congressional Reference Division. "Civil Defense and the Effects of Nuclear War." Washington, D.C.: Congressional Research Service, Library of Congress, 1982.

————. "Nuclear Arms Control: START (Strategic Arms Reduction Talks)." Washington, D.C.: Congressional Research Service, Library of Congress, 1981.

Dahlitz, Julie. *Nuclear Arms Control with Effective International Agreements.* Melbourne: McPhee Gribble Publishers, 1983.

Day, B., and H. Waitzkin. "The Medical Profession and Nuclear War." *Journal of the American Medical Association* 254(5), 2 Aug. 1985.

Department of Defense. "Defense Against Ballistic Missiles: An Assessment of Technologies and Policy Implications." Washington, D.C.: U.S. Government Printing Office, 1984.

Department of Political and Security Council Affairs. *The United Nations and Disarmament: 1945–70.* New York: United Nations, 1970.

Disarmament: Who's Against? Moscow: Military Publishing House, 1983.

Drell, Sidney D., and Wolfgang K.H. Panofsky. "The Case Against Strategic Defense: Technical and Strategic Realities." *Issues in Science and Technology,* 1984.

Durch, William J. *National Interests and the Military Use of Space.* Cambridge: Ballinger Publishing Company, 1984.

Dyson, Freeman. *Weapons and Hope.* New York: Harper & Row, 1984.

Federal Emergency Management Agency. "U.S. Crisis Relocation Planning." Washington, D.C.: U.S. Government Printing Office, 1981.

Fine, Melinda, and Peter M. Steven. *American Peace Directory 1984.* Cambridge: Ballinger Publishing Company, 1984.

Fletcher, James C. "The Technologies for Ballistic Missile Defense." *Issues in Science and Technology,* 1984.

Ford, Daniel. *The Button.* New York: Simon and Schuster, 1985.

Fossedal, Gregory A. "Star Wars and the Scientists." *Wall Street Journal,* 14 June 1985.

Freedman, Lawrence. *The Evolution of Nuclear Strategy.* London: Macmillan, 1983.

Frei, Daniel. *Risks of Unintentional Nuclear War.* Geneva: United Nations, 1982.

Gelb, Leslie A. "Vision of Space Defense Posing New Challenges." *New York Times,* 3 Mar. 1985.

―――. "Moscow Proposes to End a Dispute on Siberia Radar." *New York Times,* 29 Oct. 1985.

Gilks, C.F., et al. "The Nuclear Arms Race and the Third World." *Journal of the American Medical Association* 254(5), 2 Aug. 1985.

Golden, Frederic. "Star Wars: The Research Heats Up." *Discover,* Sept. 1985.

Graham, Daniel O., and Gregory A. Fossedal. *A Defense That Defends.* Old Greenwich: Devin-Adair Publishers, 1983.

Groueff, Stephane. *Manhattan Project: The Untold Story of the Making of the Atomic Bomb.* Boston, 1967.

Gwertzman, Bernard. "U.S. Says Soviets Violate ABM Treaty." *New York Times,* 2 Feb. 1985.

Hafemeister, David. "Advances in Verification Technology." *Bulletin of the Atomic Scientists* 41(1), Jan. 1985.

Halloran, Richard. "The Arms Buildup: First Signs Visible." *New York Times,* 27 Oct. 1985.

Hamilton, Meredith, and Michael Kilian. "Battleground in the Heavens." *Discover,* Sept. 1985.

Hanrieder, Wolfram F., and Larry V. Buel. *Words and Arms: A Dictionary of Security and Defense Terms.* Boulder: Westview Press, 1979.

Hecht, Eugene. *Physics in Perspective.* Reading: Addison-Wesley, 1980.

Herken, Gregg. *Counsels of War.* New York: Knopf, 1985.

Holloway, David. *The Soviet Union and the Arms Race.* New Haven: Yale University Press, 1983.

Jasani, Bhupendra. *Outer Space: A New Dimension of the Arms Race.* Cambridge: Oegeschlager, Gunn & Hain, 1982.

Jastrow, Robert. *How To Make Nuclear Weapons Obsolete.* Boston: Little, Brown and Company, 1983.

Joint Chiefs of Staff. *Department of Defense: Dictionary of Military and Associated Terms.* Washington, D.C.: U.S. Government Printing Office, 1984.

Jones, Rodney W. *Small Nuclear Forces and U.S. Security Policy.* Lexington: Lexington Books, 1984.

Kahn, Herman. *On Thermonuclear War.* Princeton: Princeton University Press, 1960.

————. *Thinking About the Unthinkable.* New York: Horizon Press, 1962.

————. *Thinking About the Unthinkable in the 1980s.* New York: Simon and Schuster, 1984.

Kaldor, Mary. *The Baroque Arsenal.* New York: Hill and Wang, 1981.

Kaplan, Fred. *The Wizards of Armageddon.* New York: Simon and Schuster, 1983.

Karas, Thomas. *The New High Ground.* New York: Simon and Schuster, 1983.

Kegley, Charles W., Jr., and Eugene R. Wittkopf. *The Nuclear Reader: Strategy, Weapons, War.* New York: St. Martin's Press, 1985.

Keller, Bill. "Air Force Missile Strikes Satellite in First U.S. Test." *New York Times,* 14 Sept. 1985.

Kennan, George F. *The Nuclear Delusion.* New York: Pantheon Books, 1976.

Kennedy, Edward M., and Mark O. Hatfield. *Freeze! How You Can Help Prevent Nuclear War.* New York: Bantam Books, 1982.

Kennedy, Robert F. *Thirteen Days: A Memoir of the Cuban Missile Crisis.* New York: W.W. Norton and Company, 1969.

Keyes, Ken, Jr. *The Hundredth Monkey.* Coos Bay: Vision Books, 1982.

Keyworth, George A. "The Case for Strategic Defense: An Option for a World Disarmed." *Issues in Science and Technology,* 1984.

Kissinger, Henry A. *Nuclear Weapons and Foreign Policy.* New York: Harper & Brothers, 1957.

Labrie, Roger P. *SALT Handbook: Key Documents and Issues, 1972–1979.*

Washington, D.C.: American Enterprise Institute for Public Policy Research, 1979.

Lodgaard, Sverre, and Mark Thee. *Nuclear Disengagement in Europe*. London: Taylor & Francis, 1983.

Longstreth, Thomas K. "A View of Reagan's Report on Soviet Compliance." *Arms Control Today*, Mar./Apr. 1984.

———. "Soviet Countercharges." *Arms Control Today*, Mar./Apr. 1984.

Macy, Joanna Rogers. *Despair and Personal Power in the Nuclear Age*. Philadelphia: New Society Publishers, 1983.

Mandelbaum, Michael. *The Nuclear Revolution: International Politics Before and After Hiroshima*. Cambridge: Cambridge University Press, 1981.

———. *The Nuclear Future*. Ithaca: Cornell University Press, 1983.

Marbach, William D. "The Star Warriors." *Newsweek*, 17 June 1985.

Meyer, Michael R. "A Marketing Blitz in Western Europe." *Newsweek*, 17 June 1985.

Miller, Steven E. *Strategy and Nuclear Deterrence*. Princeton: Princeton University Press, 1984.

Mohr, Charles. "What Moscow Might Do in Replying to 'Star Wars.'" *New York Times*, 6 Mar. 1985.

Mydans, Seth. "Arms Issue Imperils U.S.-New Zealand Pact." *New York Times*, 29 Sept. 1985.

Myrdal, Alva. *The Game of Disarmament*. New York: Pantheon Books, 1976.

Nacht, Michael. *The Age of Vulnerability*. Washington, D.C.: The Brookings Institution, 1985.

Nitze, Paul H. "SDI: The Soviet Program." Washington, D.C.: U.S. Department of State, 1985.

Nye, Joseph S., Jr. *The Making of America's Soviet Policy*. New Haven: Yale University Press, 1984.

Ostling, Richard N. "Bishops and the Bomb." *Time*, 29 Nov. 1982.

Paterson, Thomas G. *Major Problems in American Foreign Policy, Volume II: Since 1914*. 2nd ed. Lexington: D.C. Heath and Company, 1983.

Peierls, Rudolf. "Reflections of a British Participant." *Bulletin of the Atomic Scientists* 41(7), Aug. 1985.

Peterson, Iver. "U.S. Activates Unit for Space Defense." *New York Times*, 24 Sept. 1985.

Pitman, George R., Jr. *Arms Races and Stable Deterrence*. Los Angeles: University of California, 1969.

Plano, Jack C., and Roy Olton. *The International Relations Dictionary*. New York: Holt, Rinehart and Winston, 1969.

Polner, Murray. *The Disarmament Catalogue.* New York: The Pilgrim Press, 1982.

Powers, Thomas. *Thinking About the Next War.* New York: Mentor, 1976.

"The President's Strategic Defense Initiative." Washington, D.C.: U.S. Government Printing Office, Jan. 1985.

Pringle, Peter, and William Arkin. *SIOP: The Secret U.S. Plan for Nuclear War.* New York: W.W. Norton and Company, 1983.

Pringle, Peter, and James Spiegelman. *The Nuclear Barons.* New York: Holt, Rinehart and Winston, 1981.

Richardson, James L. *Germany and the Atlantic Alliance.* Cambridge: Harvard University Press, 1966.

Rosenblatt, Roger. "The Atomic Age." *Time,* 29 July 1985.

Rotblat, J. *Science and World Affairs: History of the Pugwash Conferences.* London: Dawsons of Pall Mall, 1962.

Rotblat, Joseph. "Leaving the Bomb Project." *Bulletin of the Atomic Scientists* 41(7), Aug. 1985.

Schell, Jonathan. *The Abolition.* New York: Knopf, 1984.

——. *The Fate of the Earth.* New York: Avon Books, 1982.

Schlesinger, Arthur, et al. "U.S. Policy on the Use of Nuclear Weapons: 1945–1975." Washington, D.C.: Congressional Research Service, Library of Congress, 1981.

Scribner, Richard A., and Kenneth N. Luongo. *Strategic Nuclear Arms Control Verification: Terms and Concepts.* Washington, D.C.: The American Association for the Advancement of Science, 1985.

Sherwin, Martin J. "How Well They Meant." *Bulletin of the Atomic Scientists* 41(7), Aug. 1985.

Smith, Gerard. *Doubletalk: The Story of the First Strategic Arms Limitation Talks.* New York: Doubleday and Company, 1980.

Smith, Marcia S. " 'Star Wars': Anti-Satellites and Space-Based BMD." Washington, D.C.: Congressional Research Service, Library of Congress, 18 July 1984.

Snyder, Glenn H. *Deterrence and Defense.* Princeton: Princeton University Press, 1961.

——. *Deterrence by Denial and Punishment.* Princeton: Woodrow Wilson School of Public and International Affairs, 1959.

"Soviet Women's Group Arrives for U.S. Visits." *New York Times,* 16 Oct. 1985.

"Special Issue: World War II." *Life* 8(6), Spring, Summer 1985.

Stephenson, Michael, and Roger Hearn. *The Nuclear Casebook.* London: Frederick Muller Ltd., 1983.

Stephenson, Michael, and John Weal. *Nuclear Dictionary.* Essex: Longman Group Ltd., 1985.

Stine, William R. *Applied Chemistry.* 2nd ed. Boston: Allyn and Bacon, 1981.

Stockholm International Peace Research Institute. *World Armaments and Disarmaments: SIPRI Yearbook 68.* London: Taylor and Francis, 1968.

————. *World Armaments and Disarmaments: SIPRI Yearbook 72.* London: Taylor and Francis, 1972.

————. *World Armaments and Disarmaments: SIPRI Yearbook 79.* London: Taylor and Francis, 1979.

————. *World Armaments and Disarmaments: SIPRI Yearbook 84.* London: Taylor and Francis, 1984.

————. *World Armaments and Disarmaments: SIPRI Yearbook 85.* London: Taylor and Francis, 1985.

Sweeney, Duane. *The Peace Catalog.* Seattle: Press for Peace, 1984.

Talbott, Strobe. *Deadly Gambits.* New York: Vintage, 1985.

————. *Endgame.* New York: Harper & Row, 1979.

Thomas, Lewis. *Late Night Thoughts on Listening to Mahler's Ninth Symphony.* New York: Viking Press, 1980.

Tobias, Shiela, et al. *The People's Guide to National Defense.* New York: William Morrow and Company, 1982.

Tsipis, Kosta. *Arsenal: Understanding Weapons in the Nuclear Age.* New York: Simon and Schuster, 1983.